T0329738

UNMANAGEABLE CARE

Unmanageable Care

An Ethnography of Health Care Privatization in Puerto Rico

Jessica M. Mulligan

NEW YORK UNIVERSITY PRESS

New York and London

NEW YORK UNIVERSITY PRESS
New York and London
www.nyupress.org

References to Internet websites (URLs) were accurate at the time of writing.
Neither the author nor New York University Press is responsible for URLs that
may have expired or changed since the manuscript was prepared.

Library of Congress Cataloging-in-Publication Data
Mulligan, Jessica M.
Unmanageable care : an ethnography of health care privatization
in Puerto Rico / Jessica M. Mulligan.
pages cm   Includes bibliographical references and index.
ISBN 978-0-8147-2491-0 (hardback) — ISBN 978-0-8147-7031-3 (paper)
1. Medical care—Puerto Rico. 2. Medical policy—Puerto Rico.
3. Health care reform—Puerto Rico. 4. Privatization—Puerto Rico. I. Title.
RA395.P7M85   2014
362.1097295—dc 3   2014002840

New York University Press books are printed on acid-free paper,
and their binding materials are chosen for strength and durability.
We strive to use environmentally responsible suppliers and materials
to the greatest extent possible in publishing our books.

Manufactured in the United States of America

10 9 8 7 6 5 4 3 2 1

Also available as an ebook

I dedicate this book to my parents—I am lucky that a large number of people play that role. To Gerry Mulligan, Janet Mulligan, Sarah Baker Sultenfuss, and Tom Dooley. Thank you.

CONTENTS

ACKNOWLEDGMENTS

Ten years is a long time, a decade during which I have benefited from many acts of generosity, care, and support.

The time has also been marked by loss. To my stepfather, Tom Dooley, I am so sorry that I cannot share this book with you. I wish you could have seen how much of you is in it.

This book began at Harvard University where the Department of Anthropology, the Hemenway Fellowship of American Ethnology, the David Rockefeller Center for Latin American Studies, and the Salton-stall Population Studies Center provided generous financial support. The Department of Anthropology and the Watson Institute for International Studies at Brown University provided write-up funding and new intellectual connections.

Without my advisors and mentors—Arthur Kleinman, Joanne Rappaport, and Kay Warren—this project never would have materialized. Thank you for the years of continued support; I never realized that advising was such a long-term commitment. I am grateful to Arthur Kleinman for taking me on as an advisee post-fieldwork and then turning me into a medical anthropologist. His engagement with my work and sharp critical reading have made this book possible. Joanne Rappaport started me on this path. Being a student in her classes made me want to be an anthropologist. Kay Warren provided crucial support at key moments in this project and was always convinced that there was an interesting project here, even when I wasn't.

Charles Rosenberg and Mary Steedly provided valuable support and intellectual guidance at early points in the project. Michael Herzfeld helped me muddle through that excruciatingly difficult learning process that is figuring out how to write an academic article. Margarita Alegría was extraordinarily generous with her time and expertise.

Teaching in the Departamento de Sociología y Antropología at the University of Puerto Rico at Río Piedras provided a much-needed connection to anthropology while I was conducting research. Thank you to David Hernández and Jorge Duany who chaired the department in the years I was there.

Thank you to the Andrew W. Mellon Foundation, which sponsored a fellowship at Connecticut College where I received the precious gift of time to revise and rethink this book as well as funding that allowed me to return to Puerto Rico to conduct additional research. My thanks go to the Holleran Center for Public Policy and Community Action where Sunil Bhatia, Keisha Henry, Rebecca McCue, and Tracee Reiser were wonderful colleagues. I continue to admire the work they do in New London. Thanks also to members of the interdisciplinary faculty writing group (Cherise Harris, Shanshan Lan, and James Dale Wilson) and my fellow postdocs Allison De Fren and Wei Ying Wong.

At Providence College, my understanding of health systems has expanded as a result of working in an interdisciplinary setting with historians, sociologists, and political scientists. Many colleagues at Providence College have supported this research and have read multiple drafts of works in progress: thank you to Tuba Agartan, Robert Hackey, Deborah Levine, and Todd Olszewski. Bob generously helped steer me through the process of seeking out a publisher and preparing the manuscript. Debby's sharp wit and keen editorial eye strengthened the manuscript. In addition to her astute comments on the manuscript, Tuba and the entire Agartan family hosted me and my family on countless occasions. Michael Walker expertly assisted with various tasks like readying the manuscript for submission and formatting the citations.

In Puerto Rico, I learned from many people, some of whom I can explicitly acknowledge here and others who remain anonymous in order to protect their identities. The public health researchers and providers whom I interviewed and met with informally were invaluable in helping me to develop my analysis and understanding, however partial, of the incredibly complicated health care system in Puerto Rico. Special thanks to Glorisa Canino, Sarah Huertas Goldman, Luis Izquierdo Mora, Wendy Matos Negrón, Enrique Rivera Mass, Orlando Torres Pérez, and Marissel Velázquez Vicente.

I learned so much from my coworkers at Acme. I struggle in this book to understand their lives and their jobs even if I am critical of the structure in which we worked. It is my hope that the system changes in a way that allows their labor to be more about care and less about management. They also deserve better than a flexible system where getting fired is a constant fear.

I thank the Medicare beneficiaries who received me into their homes and spoke with me about their illnesses and experiences with the health system. I am dumbfounded that this happens: that someone would permit a stranger to hear, record, and walk away with his or her story. I feel obligated to everyone who spoke with me in a way that I will never be able to reciprocate. I have tried here to honor their stories.

To Tere, Maríta, María, Licette, Lázaro, Marisabel, and all the other women (and men) whom I played soccer with in Puerto Rico and now in Rhode Island, thank you for taking me in and keeping me (mostly) sane. Thank you also to my friends and former in-laws in Puerto Rico. Even though our relationships have languished, I would like to thank Aixa Mariani, Angie de la Torre, and Dana Montenegro.

Patricia Alvarez provided insightful research assistance and is now completing a doctorate in anthropology at UC Santa Cruz. I am grateful to Yara Alma Bonilla for the excellent job she did with the transcriptions.

P. V. August at the University of Rhode Island was an expeditious mapmaker who generously gave of his time and expertise.

Thank you to NYU Press and my editor, Jennifer Hammer, for believing in this project and helping me to hone the argument. Constance Grady provided much-needed technical assistance and expert advice.

Among the debts I have accumulated, I must count the critical readings from friends and colleagues that have sent me again and again to the editing room to clarify an idea, flesh out a description, or contextualize a claim. This book is much better as a result. Diana Allen, Eric Beverley, Clara Han, Katrina Moore, Wanda Rivera, Miriam Shakow, Harris Solomon, and Winifred Tate deserve special mention. Coffee, drinks, and writing dates with Andrea Mazzarino made the experience not just bearable, but fun. Maple Razsa read pieces of this work at almost every stage and pushed me to make it better. My friendship with Aimee Van Wagenen has challenged me intellectually and sustained me emotionally for the past 20 years. Of course, any remaining errors, unsubstantiated claims, or lack of context are my fault alone.

My anthropologist colleagues who study Puerto Rico have been a source of moral support and intellectual engagement. I have benefited immensely from the work and comments of Jimmy Seale-Collazo, Alexa Dietrich, Adriana Garriga-López, Patricia Silver, and Victor Torres-Vélez. Ida Susser and Mark Padilla served as discussants on panels and their comments helped me to revise the conclusion.

My big, complicated family has been a source of inspiration and perseverance, even if no one quite gets why this has taken so damn long. Thank you, Jeremiah, for the free legal advice and comic relief. For perspective, the right priorities, and much-needed time away from this manuscript, I thank the Mulligans X5, the Largos, and the Largo Wights. My father, the newspaper man, helped foster a love of words. From Peg, Paul, and my father, I hope I have learned something of the Mulligan penchant for storytelling. Thank you, Janet, for being generous and wise right when I needed it most. Vincent Sultenfuss is a free spirit who makes my mother very happy and that is a wonderful gift. Even if I didn't inherit her unflagging positivity, I am grateful that my mother taught me the importance of rebelliousness and fighting for social justice.

As an intellectual companion, Kyle Kusz read multiple drafts and countenanced my not-always-diplomatic reaction to criticism. I oversimplify sentences and cut out words. He urged me to add clauses, complexity, and context throughout. His additions make the book—and our life—much better. As a partner, we have built a life together that makes it all worthwhile. Kyle, I love you and thank you. Our daughter, Norah, provided the ultimate deadline for finishing the manuscript as she was making her way into the world. You have both taught me far more about care than I could ever have learned at an HMO.

Introduction

Learning to Manage

The tick-tack of high heels echoed on the polished tile floor. The health plan's employees had straightened up their desks, turned off their computers, and clocked out. They joked and gossiped as they hurried toward the lobby. It was 4:30 and the elevators descended through the modern glass office building packed with customer service representatives, authorization nurses, and claims processors who filed out to the parking lot. Cars already clogged the side streets; they lunged forward and stopped in the irregular rhythm of San Juan's rush-hour traffic. Many employees would drive for more than an hour before reaching homes in the more affordable municipalities of Bayamón and Carolina.

Inside, the steamy late afternoon heat was neutralized by central air conditioning set just above arctic. I longed to leave, too, but instead hunched over a management training book. The pod of cubicles that made up the Compliance Department sat outside my doorway. Six months ago, I worked in one of those cubicles. Now my name was etched on the plastic plate beside my office door.

I was a fledgling manager, behind on several projects and cramming before a meeting. On that day, as so many others, learning to manage overshadowed my other reason for being at this health maintenance organization (HMO): I was also an anthropologist studying daily life at the company, observing how the health plan managed patient care, and interviewing health plan members in their homes. To my knowledge, I was the first anthropologist to carry out fieldwork inside an HMO.

I reluctantly opened the thin, hardcover book entitled *Fish!* and skimmed the large type. The book's jacket described it as "a remarkable way to boost morale and improve results" (Lundin, Paul, and Christensen 2000). The reading was part of a new company initiative designed to coach managers—to provide the skills and tools necessary to supervise employees and meet production goals. Managers were required to complete online coursework in English on topics such as how to create objectives, evaluate employees, and motivate staff. For a previous session, we had filled out psychological profiles that revealed if our management styles were "intuitive, rational, sensitive, or active." Though I hated reading primers on being a better manager, I also craved some advice. Just the day before, the president of the company had brought up my management style. He was delicate about it, but the bottom line was that I needed to be more diplomatic. I should go for an educational, not punishing approach. Employees should feel as though they were part of a family, and family members do not always agree with one another. The company president assured me that one's management style was something that required constant self-reflection and could always be improved. I left his office with the acute sense that I had been managed.

The reading assignment was another in a long series of opportunities to learn how to manage others and, in so doing, to be managed oneself. *Fish!* tells the story of Mary Jane Ramirez, who stumbles upon the Pike Place fish market in Seattle and learns from a fishmonger named Lonnie how to energize her staff. She is beset by doubts about her own job security and that of her staff. She muses, "Does my staff know that the security they cherish might be just an illusion? Do they realize the extent to which market forces are reshaping this industry?" (Lundin, Paul, and Christensen 2000, 23). The central message of the book is that every employee should adopt a positive attitude in order to ease the fear, lack of morale, and insecurity generated in a flexible economy.

As an anthropologist, I bristled at how the focus on a positive individual attitude obscured larger social forces like uneven access to quality education and widening rates of income inequality that limit economic possibilities for most people, no matter how positive their dispositions.[1] But after reading these texts and discussing them at companywide management meetings, I saw that the other supervisors and managers took the advice on what I have come to think of as "learning to manage" quite seriously. In these books they found a road map (endorsed by their bosses) for navigating the day-to-day challenges of working at a rapidly changing company. During the meeting at which we discussed *Fish!*, managers formulated plans for how they intended to use the book's ideas to develop incentive programs and revitalize the work in their departments. Shortly after the group discussion, posters appeared throughout the office building with short motivational quotes from the book: *Make their day! Be present. This is an adult playground. Watch out for adult children.*

The positive-thinking message conveyed in management primers like *Fish!* shared much in common with the optimistic rhetoric of the health policies that created and funded this health plan—policies that trumpeted privatized managed care as the market-based cure for an ailing health care system. In retrospect, these trainings were new and exciting to my fellow managers at a particular moment when the company was growing precipitously, offering the possibility of steady employment, the acquisition of business know-how, and the potential to attain the lifestyle of a professional. The management training initiatives tapped into the personal aspirations of newly minted managers and created a sense of future possibility, a future that for most never arrived.

Eighteen months later, the company I worked for was sold in a transaction that resulted in tens of millions of dollars in profit for the founders. By that time, many of these same managers either had been fired or had quit. The lucky ones who were still around signed contracts promising that they would not work for a competitor. In return for their loyalty pledge, they received a bonus but no such promise that their own jobs would be secure.

Managing Care, Managing People: Market Reforms to the Health System

This company, which I hereafter call "Acme," rode a wave of anticipation, exuberant expansion, and then turbulent and stressful transformation in the wake of new legislation that extended the role of private contractors in the federal Medicare program. The legislation, popularly known as the Medicare Modernization Act, was signed into law by President Bush in December 2003. It vastly expanded the managed care program in Medicare by changing its funding structure, adding additional managed care plan types, and creating prescription-drug coverage that would be administered by private companies. I worked and researched at Acme at the peak of excitement, as managed care in Medicare first came to Puerto Rico, enrolling record numbers of beneficiaries and making profits that far surpassed what was possible on the mainland.

The Commonwealth of Puerto Rico (known as the Estado Libre Aso-ciado in Spanish, literally, the Free Associated State) is a territory of the United States and, as such, is unevenly incorporated into the U.S. health care system. Since the 1950s, health care had been available to all, regardless of the ability to pay in Puerto Rico (Arbona and Ramírez de Arellano 1978). But following a pattern that was already well established in international development circles (Harvey 2005; Pfeiffer and Chap-man 2010), in the 1990s, the health system in Puerto Rico underwent a series of market-based—or neoliberal—reforms.[2] First, the publicly funded regional health system was privatized by closing public health facilities and by enrolling eligible beneficiaries in private managed care health plans. During the next decade, privatization intensified due to market-based reforms in the Medicare program.[3]

Together these two waves of privatization radically remade the health system on the island. Puerto Rican citizens became consumers of private insurance coverage. The federal and Puerto Rican governments contracted with private corporations like Acme to deliver public ser-vices. Regulators employed new oversight strategies such as compliance auditing, performance monitoring, and quality measurement. Private health plans launched new technologies such as customer service and enrollment databases, electronic claims systems, and risk-management software to track how much consumers spent on medical care and to shape utilization patterns. These new technologies and oversight strate-gies sought to increase efficiency, improve the standard of care, allow data to be exchanged more quickly, and, importantly, generate profit. These technological transformations in how health care is organized and distributed represent novel attempts to mold and manage people according to market imperatives.[4]

Under a market-based health system, patients are increasingly called upon by public health officials and insurance companies to make healthy choices, become more knowledgeable about their own health care, and apply cost-benefit criteria to treatment and insurance coverage decisions (Lemke 2001; Rose 2007). For patients in Puerto Rico, this often entails following middle-class or American cultural norms like avoiding rice and beans or fried foods; conducting health research on the Internet; and putting more "skin in the game" (paying out of pocket for some care). Likewise, providers are urged by the managed care organizations with whom they contract to become more entrepreneurial and businesslike in how they administer their practices and treat patients. Providers are encouraged to switch to computerized payment systems, implement appointment schedules, and monitor their quality ratings. Health plan workers, in turn, not only must manage the care of plan members, but also must conduct themselves in a manner that is professional, efficient, and informed by management principles like those described in *Fish!* Though others have observed that managed care and health insurance seek to transform people into more responsible self-regulating subjects (Rose 2007), scholars know relatively little about how people actually respond to these efforts to mold them into subjects who value health, self-care, and economic forms of decision making.[5] Through the process of implementing health reform in Puerto Rico, did poor, elderly, and disabled patients grow into responsible, calculating consumers? Did physicians become cooperative contracted providers? Did employees learn how to manage? In short, did Puerto Rico realize the market promise of a more-efficient, higher-quality, and less-costly health system? On all accounts, the answer is "not quite."

This book is at heart an ethnographic work that asks how people made sense of market-based health reform, and it explores the daily practices through which reforms were implemented, including Acme's attempts to cultivate responsible health care consumers, alter the behavior of contracted providers, and train its managers. I begin by analyzing the reform projects, legislation, and policy documents that sought to transform the health system into a managed care model. But then the story turns to the everyday contexts in which market reforms were actually enacted—to the compliance department of a managed care organization, to the visits of federal auditors to a health plan, and to the homes of health plan members who recount their experiences trying to navigate the new managed care system.

This book analyzes market-based health reform projects in a bifocal perspective: the near lens is for reading up close the elaborate plans of market reformers while the distance lens focuses on the complex social transformations that took place when reform projects actually "touched down" in Puerto Rico (Kingfisher and Maskovsky 2008). Viewed in this way, health reform policies may be seen as messy, complex, and contradictory. As the inclusion of the word "unmanageable" in this book's title suggests, neoliberal health policies never quite remade the world in their image. Essentially, I argue that market-based health reforms failed to reorganize the health system in a way that promoted efficiency, cost-effectiveness, and high-quality care. The system became more expensive (not more efficient); patients rarely behaved as health-maximizing, information-processing consumers; care was more chaotic and difficult to access; and citizens continued to look to the state to provide health services for the poor, disabled, and elderly. The health system *was* dramatically transformed, just not according to plan.

The Managed Care Model

Managing was both a central feature of the daily work I carried out at Acme and the term given to what the company did at large. Acme was a managed care organization, commonly referred to as an HMO.[6] In order to understand how the health system was remade in Puerto Rico, it is crucial to examine the project of managing health care in its broader historical and political context, particularly the adoption of a for-profit business model focused on controlling costs.

When I refer to managed care, I mean a model for prepaying for health and medical services in which individuals access care through a network of contracted providers, according to certain predetermined rules. "Managing" occurs through activities like utilization review, which can include requiring preauthorization for some services, denying payment for services not deemed to be medically necessary, tracking the services that members are accessing, and monitoring the length of members' hospital stays. Managing health care also takes place by employing certain standardized treatment protocols, providing health education, and enrolling health plan members in care and disease-management programs. The premise and promise of managed care is that through the rational application of management principles to the organization and distribution of medical services, health care can be coordinated, more efficient, focused on prevention, less costly, and more profitable.

The rise of HMOs and managed care in the United States in the 1970s signaled a shift in U.S. health care policy objectives away from the goal of extending coverage to more people and toward the goal of making medical care more efficient and cost-effective (Katz 2008, 263; Starr 1982, 379–380). Factors such as rising costs (especially in Medicare and Medicaid), the perception of a crisis in health care financing, and the eclipsing prestige of the medical profession challenged the premise that more care was needed and that customary delivery arrangements were the best method for distributing it. HMOs provided prepaid (as opposed to fee-for-service) care to enrolled members and focused on prevention—for these reasons, HMOs were thought to create incentives to keep patients healthy and costs low.

The number of HMOs in the United States did not grow significantly until the 1980s. At that time, a combination of factors made HMOs more attractive to health care buyers, including "an economic recession [that] forced employers, who pay for most of the private health care in the United States, to reduce the cost of their workers' health care and other benefits" (Coombs 2005, xi–xii). The rapid expansion of HMOs in the 1980s was also accompanied by a trend toward for-profit, rather than nonprofit, status (Gray 2006, 326–327). For-profit plans tended to be organized differently from their nonprofit counterparts.[7] Rather than an integrated, local model where physicians and other providers were salaried employees of a particular HMO, many of the new for-profit plans served more members, covered a larger service area, offered multiple plan types, and contracted with a network of physicians who accepted patients from multiple HMOs and health insurance plans (Gabel 1997). These for-profit plans began "thinking in terms of the health of populations (rather than solely of individuals)" and in turn developed "methods to measure the performance of individuals and organizations in the health-care system" (Gray 2006, 332). This time period also saw increases in patient cost sharing through premiums and copays (Gabel 1997, 139).

By the late 1990s, HMOs began to provoke consumer criticism as they implemented more drastic cost-control mechanisms, including extremely brief maternity stays, denials of care often for technical reasons like not following plan rules, the shortening of doctor visit times, and confusing or nonexistent appeal procedures. In the mainland U.S. market, there was a "virulent and effective anti-managed-care backlash" that "led organizations that used utilization management methods to abandon them and to increase the size of their provider networks" (Gray 2006, 331). In 1996, 35 states passed laws to regulate HMOs, increase consumer protections, and weaken managed care (Bodenheimer 1996, 1601). The era of aggressive managed care did coincide with declines in health care inflation; however, analysts dispute whether HMOs caused this decline.[8]

Despite the backlash, perhaps the true mark of the success of HMOs is that managed care principles have been absorbed into almost all forms of health insurance in the United States through practices like (a slightly less aggressive version of) utilization review, care management, and trying to reduce the length of hospital stays.[9] In 2010, about half of the U.S. population received health care through an employer-sponsored plan where some form of managed care is the norm. In the public sector, which covers 29% of the U.S. population, a growing number of beneficiaries also belong to private managed care plans (KFF 2011a).[10] In 2011, U.S. managed care penetration (excluding Puerto Rico) was 71% in Medicaid (MACPAC 2011) and 25.6% in Medicare (KFF 2011b). As Puerto Rico and the states implement the Affordable Care Act and expand Medicaid, it is crucial that we better understand the financial and health-related implications of relying on privatized managed care for service delivery.[11]

Managed Care in Puerto Rico: Privatizing the Public Health System

The history of managed care in Puerto Rico is distinct from but related to the development of managed care in the mainland United States. The next chapter describes the introduction of managed care in Puerto Rico in detail, illuminating how a century's worth of reforms have produced the contemporary health system. Here, a brief overview situates the arguments of this book.

Since the late 1950s, medical care had been available in Puerto Rico through a regional system of government-run facilities and clinics that were once held up as a model to be emulated in the developing world (Arbona and Ramírez de Arellano 1978). In the public system, care was provided largely free of charge with no enrollment restrictions. In many community clinics, mental and physical health care were available at the same facility together with a dispensary for pharmaceuticals. There was also a parallel private system of care for those who had employer-based insurance benefits or were wealthy enough to pay for care out-of-pocket.

In 1993, the pro-statehood governor who was also a physician, Pedro Rosselló, spearheaded a campaign to modernize the health system and bring it in line with the managed care model then current on the mainland. The new program, which was based on President Clinton's health reform agenda, came to be known simply as La Reforma (Alegría, McGuire, Vera, Canino, Freeman et al. 2001, 383). Funding for La Reforma derives in part from Medicaid and other federal monies, but the majority of the financing comes from local taxes.[12] Significant differences exist between mainland Medicaid programs and La Reforma. For example, Puerto Rico's health programs serve a population with much higher poverty rates than the mainland (around 50%) and colonial relations of rule often limit the autonomy of local health policy makers. La Reforma transformed the government from a direct health care provider to a regulator of private insurance companies contracted to deliver covered services to eligible beneficiaries in exchange for a monthly insurance premium.[13] Eligibility was restricted to those living at or below 200% of the federal poverty line, which created a class of uninsured people in Puerto Rico for the first time. The published goals of the program were to eliminate the unequal, two-tiered system already in place, control costs, downsize the health care bureaucracy, and deliver high-quality care to the medically indigent (Commonwealth of Puerto Rico 1993, 1–2).

Because of its small size and colonial status, the island of Puerto Rico has repeatedly been treated as a laboratory by mainland investigators

and insular policy makers alike for projects that have included providing an alternative to Communist development models during the
Cold War (Grosfoguel 2003; Lapp 1995), implementing population-
control measures, and experimenting on Puerto Rican bodies during
the development of the oral contraception pill (Briggs 2003; I. Lopez
2008). More recently, the transformation of the island into a hub for
the biotech and pharmaceutical industries has revived the laboratory
metaphor (Dietrich 2013; Duprey 2010). Though La Reforma can be
interpreted as another iteration of this laboratory—in that it was a staging ground for the implementation of President Clinton's health reform
agenda—I do not want to push the metaphor too far. The implementation of La Reforma was made possible by the shifting political landscape on the island, with the statehood party growing in importance,
and it addressed a set of uniquely Puerto Rican concerns even as it bor-
rowed from neoliberal health reform models that were in vogue inter-
nationally. This book offers a complex and grounded understanding of
La Reforma that acknowledges, but goes beyond, the laboratory metaphor that is employed in so much of the scholarship on Puerto Rico.

The other major government-funded health program available on
the island is Medicare, which is health insurance for people over 65 or
with certain disabilities under 65. There are two ways to receive Medicare benefits. The first is fee-for-service, or "Original Medicare," in
which a beneficiary can visit any provider who accepts Medicare. In
Original Medicare, beneficiaries have few restrictions in provider selection, but they often face high out-of-pocket costs in the form of copayments and an annual deductible. The second way to receive Medicare is
through a managed care organization, currently known as the Medicare
Advantage program.[14] Payment to managed care organizations under
Medicare has existed in the mainland in one form or another since 1972
(Zarabozo 2000, 62), but the first Medicare managed care plan operating in Puerto Rico opened in 2000. Enrollment in Medicare managed
care grew very quickly on the island; 68% of the Medicare-eligible population was enrolled in a private for-profit Medicare Advantage plan in
2011, which is much higher than the 25.6% enrolled in Medicare Advantage in the United States (KFF 2011b). The higher rates of Medicare
Advantage penetration (to use the industry's language) in Puerto Rico
are due to a variety of reasons, one of the most important being that

Medicare Advantage plans offer enrollees more generous benefits with lower out-of-pocket costs than Original Medicare.

Medicare managed care organizations like Acme receive a capitation (payment) per member per month (PMPM) from the federal government to offer Medicare services through a network of contracted providers. By assuming the financial risk for a large-enough group of beneficiaries, the premise is that managed care organizations can provide benefits in addition to what is covered by Medicare, focus medical management efforts on prevention, control fraud by reviewing claims, and administer health care in a more efficient and businesslike manner, which will result in cost savings for the government and profits for the managed care organization.[15] The reality, however, has been that Medicare Advantage costs more, not less, than Original Medicare. Medicare Advantage plans on the island receive much higher payments relative to Original (fee-for-service) Medicare; in 2009, the Medicare Advantage rates were close to 180% of fee-for-service Medicare (MedPac 2009, 179). Many Medicare Advantage plans have flocked to the island to profit from these high premiums.

In a relatively short period of time, the health system in Puerto Rico underwent radical restructuring through two waves of privatization—the first to the public health system and the second in the Medicare program. I hoped that working at Acme would help me to understand how these two waves of privatization transformed the experience of accessing and providing care on the island.

Working and Researching at Acme

In researching this book, I employed a variety of qualitative, anthropological methods that enabled me to explore the complex social, political, and economic phenomenon that is privatization. Participant observation was key. I worked at Acme—a private insurance company under contract with the federal government to provide Medicare services—as a paid employee (initially as an editor of policies and procedures and eventually as a compliance manager) for an average of 35 hours a week for 31 months in the mid-2000s. At Acme, I was first and foremost an employee in the compliance department, not a researcher. During the workday, being a participant trumped being an observer. So I recorded my observations in fieldnotes at night, on the weekend, and often while I took my lunch breaks. As part of the research agreement that I negotiated with the company, I was permitted to gather company documents like meeting minutes, emails, and the manuals, policies, and procedures created within the HMO for complying with federal regulations. These documents—often scribbled with my to-do lists and impromptu observations—form a kind of bureaucratic archive that records the language, reporting structures, and regulatory changes that were prominent at the company during this time period. I returned again and again to these bureaucratic documents while writing this book. On subsequent research trips to the island in 2007 and 2009, I added to this archive by conducting open-ended interviews with some of my former coworkers at Acme.

Though I was primarily known as an employee at Acme, my research was not undercover or secret. I obtained permission from Acme's CEO to research at the company, and I submitted my project for human subjects review at Harvard University, where I was a graduate student. I disclosed my research activities to my immediate colleagues, who were aware that I was an anthropologist and taught at the local university. I told my colleagues and the CEO that I was researching quality of care on the island and wanted to understand how managed care in Medicare and La Reforma impacted quality (which was how I understood my research at the time). In order to protect the privacy of research subjects, the name of the company as well as the names of health plan members, individual doctors, and health care workers have all been changed. Public figures such as government representatives are presented with their own names unless otherwise indicated. For interested readers, I describe how I gained access to Acme and some of the ethical issues raised by this research in greater detail later in this chapter and also in appendix 1.

This book is about more than what it was like to work at Acme. I wanted to understand the interrelationships among regulators, the corporation, and plan members as part of a larger effort to transform the experience and organization of health care on the island. Privatization involved multiple actors and played out across spatially and temporally dispersed sites. So I used a multimethod and multisited approach that others have termed "studying through."[16] "Studying through" is an adaptation of the anthropologist Laura Nader's (1972) term "studying up," which refers to anthropological accounts that investigate institutions or individuals who marshal considerable financial resources, political influence, or symbolic importance. Whereas anthropological methods like participant observation were initially developed for the study of small-scale societies or villages, Nader argued that we should use the same tools to study actors like chemical companies, government institutions, and economic elites. What makes studying through different from studying up is that it also involves studying down and sideways (Nader 1972, 292). Instead of just looking at well-paid health care executives, I also examine midlevel managers and bureaucrats as well as health plan members. In other words, studying through is a methodological approach for examining systemwide change that takes place at multiple levels and among multiple differentially situated actors (Shore and Wright 1997, 14; see also Reinhold 1994).

An essential part of my research was to interview health plan members about how their experiences with the health system had transformed as a result of the two waves of privatization that hit the island during the 1990s and the first decade of the 2000s. To this end, I conducted 35 semistructured, open-ended life history interviews with Medicare beneficiaries. Appendix 2 contains a brief description of each of the interviewees.[17] While living in San Juan, I also interviewed physicians and government officials, analyzed press coverage of health care reform, and performed archival research on the formation of Puerto Rico's health care system.

This combination of participant observation, discourse analysis, and qualitative interviewing allowed me to understand privatization from multiple perspectives. Over and over again, I saw how the goal of managing care (a goal that many Acme employees genuinely believed in and thought would improve members' health) was never completely achieved. The following story, of the first two members whom I interviewed, illustrates some of the most significant gaps between the project of rational care management as imagined at Acme and the often disjointed, not quite rational, care experienced by Acme's plan members.

Unmanageable: Life Histories and Corporate (In)efficiencies

Driving back into Hato Rey, I was struck by the trees lining the streets, well-lit white leather sofas in the windows of furniture stores, and a dozen restaurants filling up on a Friday evening. I never realized how opulent the banking district of San Juan could look.

I always thought of it as dusty, baking in the sun, somehow unfinished. Construction of the Tren Urbano, a commuter train system, had splintered open the city streets, leaving the district with constant detours and aggravating the already-clogged traffic. Car pollution and mildew stained the paint on the middle-class apartment buildings, but the balconies teemed with plants and the views extended over the city with distant glimpses of the bay or even the ocean. The street vendors, who at noon sold lunch outside the government buildings, now peddled snacks or canned beers to the office workers enjoying the *viernes social* (social Friday).

I was returning to San Juan from Río Grande, a small town on the northeast coast of the island located close to *el Yunque*, the rain forest and tourist attraction. I had just interviewed two brothers—Don Enrique and Don Ignacio—about their experiences with the health care system. It was jarring to see Hato Rey after having sat on the brothers' porch watching a very different viernes social unfold. In their neighborhood, the concrete houses were tightly packed on small lots. The original two-room, barracks-style home provided by the government had been modified by some with a second floor, a new shade of paint, or religious ornaments. Other houses were not aging so well and showed cracks in the cement walls or appeared to be abandoned. The brothers lived behind a cemetery.

The small porch where we sat wrapped around the house and led to the backyard. Don Ignacio said his son came out once to help them take care of the yard, but it would be better if he did not come back. Don Enrique liked to fix things so the yard was littered with extra parts and half-repaired fans. His son worked an office job and lived in a gated neighborhood in San Juan. He said that all of the plastic and metal pieces were garbage and threw them away. But Don Enrique would rather have the fan parts back so he could work on them. We talked over the hum of Mexican ballads interrupted by *reggaetón* from passing cars. The brothers called out to neighbors, joked about lost loves, and showed me pictures of their children on the mainland and on the island.

Don Ignacio was far more jovial than his brother, Don Enrique, who sat in a wheelchair, shirtless in a pair of shorts with a bandage on his left foot. The white gauze covered the toes up to his ankle. He explained that he was to have his foot amputated on Monday.

A small cut had developed into gangrene. In the house, they showed me several blood glucose monitors that Acme had sent. They were frustrated with the company and could not understand why it kept sending the wrong machine. They wanted the old one with the large-print display, but that machine had stopped working. The brothers both had Type 2 diabetes and neither was able to monitor his glucose levels regularly.

The brothers did not know it, but Acme had contracted with a new durable medical equipment provider as a cost-saving strategy and the transition to the new provider was fraught with complications: orders were botched or never delivered and customer complaints were flowing into the Acme offices.

Don Enrique said he was thinking about the impending operation. His pensiveness contrasted markedly with Don Ignacio, who fried up seafood-stuffed empanadas and insisted that I sample his homemade hot sauce. He showed me big cans of processed bulk food purchased at the new Sam's Club. He said the small amount of money he received from Social Security goes much farther at Sam's.

Don Enrique said he had known something was not right with his foot, but he let it go. He put off seeing the doctor for too long. He winced occasionally and mentioned the pain. He blamed himself.

As this fragment of the brothers' story illustrates, management— whether of one's diabetes, a patient's care, or the delivery of medical equipment—can go wrong. When Acme sent Don Ignacio and Don Enrique multiple glucose monitors that they could not read, the unused machines gathered dust in their living room. Acme's attempts to streamline its order and delivery process did not materialize into an effective and efficient system. Instead, the new durable medical equipment company substituted a less expensive, but harder-to-read model for the machine that the brothers had become accustomed to, and their care, in turn, suffered.

Clearly, the brothers were not efficiently managed by the health plan, and neither were they effectively remade into self-regulating, health care consumers. The brothers expressed interest in managing their diabetes but ate a diet full of starchy foods, enjoyed a few beers now and again, and were less than vigilant in attending to minor ailments. They visited their physicians regularly, but still their diabetes was uncontrolled and leading to serious complications like gangrene and amputation. The self-management model trumpeted by market-based reformers failed to improve their health; in its implementation, the model confronted both material and cultural barriers. The brothers' story reveals some of the fissures between what market-based reforms set out to accomplish and what actually transpires in the complicated contexts of people's lives.

Government Goes Entrepreneurial: From the Great Society to Privatizing Medicare

By the time that I showed up for my first day of work at Acme, more than 30 years of market-based public-policy programs had considerably changed the Medicare program since its inception under the auspices of President Johnson's Great Society and the War on Poverty. The Medicare and Medicaid programs were intended to fill gaps in the existing medical system by providing health insurance for the elderly, the poor, and disabled. At the time, government was seen by the Johnson administration as the solution to social problems like poverty, inequality, and racial discrimination in the nation's health facilities (Engel 2006). When Medicare was initially implemented, it was framed as a right and as an alternative to charity. President Johnson called on all Americans to participate in making the public program successful:

> Medicare begins tomorrow. Tomorrow, for the first time, nearly every older American will receive hospital care—not as an act of charity, but as the insured right of a senior citizen. Since I signed the historic Medicare Act last summer, we have made more extensive preparation to launch this program than for any other peaceful undertaking in our Nation's history. Now we need your help to make Medicare succeed. . . . This program is not just a blessing for older Americans. It is a test for all Americans—a test of our willingness to work together. In the past, we have always passed that test. I have no doubt about the future. I believe that July 1, 1966, marks a new day of freedom for our people. (Johnson 1966)

Johnson described Medicare as the result of a massive collective undertaking led by government that would enhance "freedom for our people." In contrast, the Bush administration framed the role of government quite differently at the signing of the Medicare Prescription Drug Improvement and Modernization Act of 2003 (commonly called the Medicare Modernization Act, or MMA):

> These reforms are the act of a vibrant and compassionate government. We show are [sic] concern for the dignity of our seniors by giving them quality health care. We show our respect for seniors by giving them more choices and more control over their decision-making. We're putting individuals in charge of their health care decisions. And as we move to modernize and reform other programs of this government, we will always trust individuals and their decisions, and put personal choice at the heart of our efforts. (Bush 2003)

Whereas Johnson presented Medicare as a right, Bush emphasized "compassion" on the part of the government and framed the new legislation as a "gift." Further, Johnson referred to collective responsibility and spoke of Medicare as a national project. Bush emphasized individual choice and decision making. "Personal choice," not collective responsibility, was placed "at the heart of our efforts."

This distinction between Medicare as implemented in 1965 and as reformed in 2003 illustrates a crucial shift in the objectives of public policy over the same period, from a policy that promoted collective responsibility for social welfare to one that valorized personal responsibility and consumer choice. Though the Bush reforms of 2003 did not completely privatize Medicare (beneficiaries can still opt to receive their Medicare services through the original program), the reform represents a significant move to structure Medicare according to business models based on consumer choice. For example, the new prescription-drug benefit must be administered by private companies called pharmacy benefit managers, the government is prohibited from negotiating prescription-drug prices, and the types of managed care plans that beneficiaries can choose to join under the Medicare program are significantly expanded.

Public-policy shifts toward making the delivery and administration of public services conform to business models did not just occur in health care. The Clinton welfare reforms and the Bush administration's No Child Left Behind Act in education are two additional examples of public-policy reforms that attempt to downsize and privatize public service provision, make government more efficient, and transform recipients of public services as well as public employees into more responsible, accountable individuals. These policies have been widely discussed as "neoliberal reforms" (Giroux 2008; Harvey 2005); however, I find the more narrow term "entrepreneurial governance" (Holland et al. 2007) useful for articulating what was unique about how neoliberal policies developed in the United States and Puerto Rico during the 1990s and the first decade of the 21st century.

"Entrepreneurial governance" seeks to transform government into an efficient and streamlined enterprise in partnership with the private sector (Holland et al. 2007). On the whole, the United States has not advocated the same kind of radical dismantling of public institutions at home that USAID and other development institutions have proscribed abroad.[18] The focus domestically has been on the more politically palatable projects of cultivating partnerships with the private sector, lowering taxes, contracting out public services, minimizing regulation, and creating a more business-friendly and businesslike environment in public administration. When public services have been significantly cut or restructured according to entrepreneurial principles (as with welfare), these reforms have been disproportionately targeted at the poor, women, immigrants, and racial minorities (Katz 2008).

It is important to note that privatization does not eliminate government, but rather it changes its form (Barry et al. 1996, 14; Ferguson and Gupta 2002; Shore and Wright 1997, 28). When health programs were privatized in Puerto Rico and the United States, the government was still concerned with how patients were cared for and how public money was spent. So regulatory agencies employed techniques for "governing from afar" like audits and performance measurement (Clarke 2004; Rose 1996, 43) that allowed oversight to continue in an altered form. A social policy researcher, John Clarke (2004), has termed this the "performance-evaluation nexus," and others refer to it as "audit culture" (Shore and Wright 2000; Strathern 2000) or "audit society" (Power

1997). As a result of contracting out a wide swath of public programs and services (education, health care, war, etc.), the government increasingly functions as a contract administrator while corporations deliver public services and open themselves to government scrutiny and regulation. In the process, citizens become hybridized citizen consumers who receive public services from and whose rights are ostensibly protected by corporations.

In health care, entrepreneurial governance is supposed to work when regulators hold insurance companies to a minimum level of accountability, companies optimize the efficiency of health care delivery in a competitive marketplace, and informed consumers engage in rational decision making about their health options. But this *model* for how relationships among the state, corporations, and citizen consumers are redrawn by entrepreneurial governance is far more tidy on paper than in the complex social contexts where policies are actually enacted. Drawing this distinction between a model and its enactment makes it possible to understand how and why policy justifications for managed care are often incongruous with how privatization unfolds in the world. For example, proponents of market-based economic policies oppose state involvement in the provision of many kinds of basic services (trash collection, water treatment, road construction, education, health care, etc.), but contracting out these same services to private corporations can actually expand government expenditures (Holland et al. 2007, 124). The 2003 Medicare legislation discussed above that extended the use of managed care plans and added a prescription-drug benefit vastly increased the cost of the Medicare program and in turn resulted in a larger federal bureaucracy to oversee the new plans. Furthermore, managed care in Medicare costs 13% more to provide than traditional fee-for-service Medicare (Zarabozo and Harrison 2009, W55). The irony is that programs that were aimed at streamlining and downsizing government involvement in the provision of health care had the opposite effect.

As various anthropological studies have shown (see, for example, Horton et al. 2001; Lamphere 2005; Stan 2007; Waitzkin et al. 2002), the process of privatizing health care is often fraught with contradiction and unintended consequences. For example, when the Medicaid system in New Mexico was subjected to a privatized managed care model, access to care through the use of primary care physicians initially improved.

However, privatization also resulted in enrollment difficulties, more bureaucracy and rules for providers, an added burden on safety-net providers, access barriers for rural clients, and decreased access to mental health care (Lamphere 2005, 13). Across the globe, market-based reforms to health systems have created access difficulties for the poor, even when these reforms were designed to extend coverage (Abadía and Oviedo 2009; Armada and Muntaner 2004; Foley 2010; Horton et al. 2012 and 2014; Kim 2000; Pfeiffer and Chapman 2010). In Senegal, for example, one anthropologist found that "recent health reforms fail to accomplish their stated objectives, and they aggravate social inequalities in ways that have important implications for vulnerability to disease" (Foley 2010, 3). When it comes to market-based reforms to health systems, failure may be the rule, not the exception.[19]

Understanding public policy *anthropologically* necessarily entails putting the contradictions and messiness of policy creation and implementation at the center of analysis (Li 2007). Therefore, I engage here in close readings of policy documents and programs, but I also explore the complex social processes through which policies were implemented and, in their implementation, transformed. Market-based policy programs set out to redraw relationships between government, private enterprise, and citizen consumers, but, in their implementation, policy programs are themselves transformed by prior practices, social relations, power dynamics, institutional constraints, and unpredictable subjects. In this book, I contend that market reforms to the health system became "unmanageable" in Puerto Rico because of colonial relations of rule and a political culture that continued to see a strong role for government in the provision of health services. Privatized for-profit managed care is also far better at making and managing money than managing health (or people), especially in the context of high poverty rates that leave many "consumers" outside of the market. Most important, market-based public policies vastly overestimated their own ability both to remake the world and to understand the people in it.

Up to this point, I have treated managing (be it care or people) as an organizational principle, a rationalizing and economizing method for conducting oneself and directing the conduct of others. By participating in and observing daily life at Acme, it became clear to me that managing was also a moral and ethical project.

The Moral Project of Market-Based Care

Critics of privatized managed care have tended to cast it as immoral or opposed to the common good:

> Health care as a right is not compatible with health care as commodity; the former is grounded in principles of justice and social good, whereas the latter is rooted in profit motives that pay lip service to the "laws" of supply and demand. Continuing to allow market forces to unilaterally dictate the policy agenda and shape of health care delivery in this country ensures that profound inequalities will continue to grow. By default, modern medicine will have to become increasingly adept at managing inequality rather than managing (providing) care. (Rylko-Bauer and Farmer 2002, 477)

While this critique usefully points to the role privatization can play in exacerbating inequality and placing cutting costs above patient care, it ignores how market-based reforms like the one implemented in Puerto Rico are themselves moral projects. "Moral" here is taken in its sociological sense to mean "what a society, or a group, defines as good or bad, legitimate or inappropriate" (Fourcade and Healy 2007, 301). Market reforms in health care are moral in the sense that they are invested in naturalizing market solutions to social problems, promoting competition, creating more consumer choice, and fostering calculative, economic forms of decision making on the part of consumers.

The managers with whom I worked at Acme did not see a stark opposition between the market on the one hand and social good on the other. They, too, were worried about inequality. In fact, they felt that they were alleviating some of the inequalities in the Puerto Rican health system by providing managed care to the Medicare population. They pushed physicians to improve their documentation, conducted quality inspections of offices, and enrolled beneficiaries in disease-management programs. They ran Acme to make money, certainly, but also gained moral satisfaction from the work. Managed care in Medicare was not just another business: for them it was the right thing to do. Through working in managed care, my coworkers understood that they were modernizing the health system in Puerto Rico.

Privatization and managed care cannot be fully understood as a bureaucratic or technical enterprise aimed at reorganizing how health care is delivered. This book argues that managed care is also a moral project—one in which new notions of responsible patients are developed and one in which efficiency and economization become not just economically expedient but also morally imperative. This project is communicated in policy statements and politicians' speeches, but it is also transmitted in the everyday practices through which privatized managed care is organized and administered.

The moral aspects of managed care became clear to me through the process of working at Acme. When I first began my job editing policies and procedures, I had no intention of writing a book about it; I planned to work part time for a few months while I got established in Puerto Rico and started a research project on reproductive health. But at Acme, I observed how my coworkers struggled to master the lingo of managed care, support their families, and please their bosses. Managers, in turn, distilled lessons about how to dress, show up on time, comply with regulations, and exhibit the right attitude. I saw elderly and disabled beneficiaries patiently waiting in the Customer Service department to speak with someone face-to-face, often flanked by several family members. And I wondered what the "managed" in managed care meant. As time went on, I found the rows of cubicles and reams of insurance regulations increasingly compelling so I began to concoct a new research project. I approached my direct boss, who already knew I was in the middle of a doctoral program, and pitched a study on managed care and quality, which was how I saw my research taking shape at the time. She encouraged me to approach the CEO for permission. I was nervous to speak with him, because I thought he would balk at my request. Who would allow an anthropologist unfettered access to their company? Instead, he enthusiastically supported my idea. Shortly thereafter, I obtained human subject approval to work at the corporation, observe daily life, and interview Acme members. The CEO signed the research agreement without even asking me to change the language (language that stated that whatever information I collected would be my property).

Within 6 months, I was promoted to Compliance supervisor. Shortly thereafter, I became a manager in the department. After 9 months at

Acme, my fieldnotes showed I was trying to make sense of managed care and chart out some sort of ethical terrain from which to assess it. In short, I found the moral discourse of managed care both compelling and insidious—I spoke in its language. I wrote,

> FIELDWORK MONTH 10. What I'm doing now feels so compromised, so closely linked to the government, to a corporation, to the privatization of Medicare. But somehow it feels honest. There is no way to feign innocence as the compliance manager of a largely U.S.-run company. I'm entangled. But the access is an anthropologist's dream.
>
> FIELDWORK MONTH 11. When I first started at Acme, a coworker mentioned off-handedly, "We make money as long as the members are healthy." What a strange confluence of the public good and capitalism. There's almost something utopian to the notion that the application of sound scientific methods in medicine and managed care will produce a healthier population, create profits, and allow us to distribute a limited good more widely. Always lurking in the background of this discussion (at least here in Puerto Rico) is the possibility of universal health care. But then the profit motive brings us back to reality. For me, part of this is an ethical issue: is it moral to let private corporations profit off of Medicare and Medicaid? Are limits on their profits a sufficient controlling factor? (What the hell does "controlling factor" mean? I find myself more and more using this techno jargon, becoming what I describe.)
>
> FIELDWORK MONTH 12. I would rather get my care through an HMO. I want my care to be managed. I want someone auditing the provider and making sure that I can appeal. I want disease and diabetes management programs. I am buying into the life-and-death stakes. I want order—rational delivery of health care. But I still have a problem with profit. Medicare is going bankrupt and the CEO is buying a yacht. I'm not sure if he is what's wrong or the answer. How did my position get so muddled?

Muddled indeed. I was remade through working at Acme by participating in the daily routines of managing care and reading scores of management primers, regulatory manuals, and company policies and procedures. However, I was also already amenable to the language of neoliberalism from growing up in the United States, attending university, and having worked previously. There was a playfulness in my musings derived from knowing that this was fieldwork, in part a performance, and that it would at some point end. But there was also a real consternation when I realized that I knew how to do things like run a business meeting, describe how insurance worked, and monitor employees even though I could not pinpoint how I came to possess such knowledge. Part of the problem was that I needed to be able to work everyday and thereby had to learn to operate within this corporate world even as I tried to reflect on what it meant.

While working at Acme, I became caught up in competing moral discourses about managed care; I found some of its promises genuinely compelling. Recall Bush's framing of more managed care in Medicare as the act of "a vibrant and compassionate government" that was concerned with dignity and quality health care. He characterized the reform as part of efforts to "modernize" government that would "always trust individuals and their decisions, and put personal choice at the heart of our efforts" (Bush 2003). Who wouldn't want modern care, high quality, more choice, and dignity? From within, surrounded by its language, managed care seemed rational, beneficent, and modernizing. And yet I constantly saw the ways in which it went awry—initiatives designed to protect consumers' rights created layers of inscrutable bureaucracy; efficiency and cost-saving schemes produced new problems with the delivery of medical equipment; unmanageable employees were routinely fired. Managed care was itself a moral project invested in creating certain kinds of subjects (rational, calculating, health seeking) and instilling certain values (efficiency is good, efficiency coupled with cost-saving is better). But as a moral project, it was contested from within and without.

Acme as a Contact Zone

Over the course of my research, I began to think of Acme as a "contact zone" (Pratt 1992) where diverse organizational forms (corporate health care, federal bureaucracy, and a "Puerto Rican" workplace) rubbed up against one another in the process of creating a private health plan with a federal contract in a colonial context. Conceptualizing Acme as a contact zone foregrounds "copresence, interaction, interlocking understandings and practices, often within radically asymmetrical relations of power" (Pratt 1992, 7). The corporation itself, and especially the Compliance Department where I worked, formed a crossroads where a group of diverse actors—federal government regulators, mainland health care entrepreneurs, Puerto Rican workers (from highly experienced and educated health care professionals to entry-level office workers), and elderly and disabled plan members—all interacted with one another and in so doing actively shaped the course of health care privatization on the island.

When Acme is understood as a contact zone, rather than as a blank slate on which governmental or managerial rationalities can inscribe themselves unopposed, then one can begin to appreciate some of the moral complexities of life at this managed care organization. The moral project of managed care was just one project among others directed at shaping employees' actions and their ethical orientation toward their work.

Workers at Acme already had political and moral ideas about privatization before they became part of the organization. One important source of these ideas was electoral politics. The three main political parties in Puerto Rico are organized around political status, and elections are interpreted as referendums on the island's future relationship with the United States. The Popular Democratic Party advocates for maintaining the current relationship with the United States. The New Progressive Party is pro-statehood and favors ending Puerto Rico's colonial status by becoming the 51st state of the union. The Independence Party supports complete political separation from the United States. *Independentistas* and *populares* tend to oppose privatization; they see privatization as a loss of political and cultural patrimony, and managed care in particular has come under criticism for being corrupt and too invested in profit making. Statehooders have led most privatization campaigns and support downsizing the Puerto Rican government in order to make it more modern, efficient, and more likely to become a state (Colón Reyes 2005, 301). For the purposes of understanding privatization as a contested moral domain, it is important to point out that employees came from all of the parties—an *independentista* led at least one department while many employees openly supported statehood.

Many employees were highly religious (both Catholic and various Protestant denominations) and hence understood "care" in a broader moral sense having to do with one's obligations to others and a duty to behave piously rather than the purely medical-technical and bureaucratic notion of care implied in "managed care" (I was once asked incredulously if the CEO was really an atheist). Employees often greeted one another and plan members with "*Dios te bendinga*" or "*bendición*" (God bless you, or blessing) indicating an ethical-religious orientation toward one another that exceeded their roles as rationalized health care workers.

Cultural expectations about how one should behave were also a frequent topic of conversation at the company with multiple opinions about "American" and "Puerto Rican" management styles. Almost all of the Puerto Rican–born employees at least partially spoke English, though most preferred to communicate in Spanish. Some managers were ridiculed behind their backs for being "too Puerto Rican" and not American enough in their management style (for example, if they were late to meetings or permissive with employees they were friendly with). Some American managers were derided for being too cold and businesslike (occasionally that person was me). The American executives took Spanish classes and tried to learn about the island (albeit returning to homes and apartments in exclusive, gated neighborhoods in the evenings). Finally, health care practitioners like the registered nurses (RNs) who worked in utilization review or case management came to Acme with competing ethical notions from the Hippocratic oath and their professional training in which letting financial considerations enter into medical decision making was seen as ethically wrong. These are the employees who probably struggled the most with their new work-selves at a managed care organization. In short, thinking about Acme as a contact zone allows one to contextualize the moral project of managed care as it unfolded in an intercultural milieu that was already saturated with moral practices.

Organization of the Book

Even if management did not always work as planned, new market-based public-policy programs *did* reshape the health system on the island and *did* draw citizens, corporations, and government into new kinds of relationships. Market-based public-policy programs radically reconfigured the provision of care when private managed care organizations contracted with the federal and Puerto Rican governments to provide publicly financed health services to poor, elderly, and disabled beneficiaries on the island. Privatization was also a moral project that cast market intervention as good, right, and natural while it set about trying to remake patients into responsible consumers, health care workers into managers of themselves and others, and health care providers into medical entrepreneurs. Each of the chapters that follow explores both the managerial and moral projects of implementing market reforms to health care.

In part 1, "Elements of a System," I examine the constituent parts that make up the health system in Puerto Rico. Chapter 1 retraces a 100-year history of reforms to the health system on the island beginning with the U.S. occupation in 1898. The shifting organizing principles of health planners and regulators are highlighted in this chapter and include sanitation and controlling communicable diseases during the first half of the 20th century, public health goals and ensuring universal access to care at midcentury, and efficiency and the free market beginning in the 1990s. Chapter 2 depicts the everyday nature of regulation through audit, performance management, and corrective action plans. It also shows the unstable side of private enterprise by retelling the stories of Acme employees who were fired, quit, or downsized. Chapter 3 tells the life histories of particular citizen consumers who struggled to obtain care in the privatized health system. This chapter also argues that the subject-making aspirations of neoliberal health policies never quite managed to remake patients into calculating, health-seeking consumers.

Part 2, "The Business of Care: Market Values and Management Strategies," consists of shorter chapters focused on specific technologies for managing care. In a sense, it shows the system in motion—it relates how the actors (health planners and regulators, HMO administrators, citizen consumers, and health care providers) come into contact with one another through the contradictory project of managing care. Chapters 4, 5, and 6 explore specific technologies and practices that are essential to managed care: quality measurement, complaints processing, the role of choice, and partnering efforts between the federal government and managed care organizations. In each chapter, management sets out on an ambitious project of remaking the organization of care and the behavior of individuals who work in and are served by the health care system. Yet, in each chapter, management never quite achieves its aims. In the conclusion, I argue that failure and the unmanageable are central components of market reform. The conclusion revisits the moral implications of market reform, the legacy of U.S. colonialism in Puerto Rico, and the future of health reform on the island and the U.S. mainland.

Following research on the anthropology of policy (Shore and Wright 1997) and answering calls to study managed care and market medicine ethnographically (Horton and Lamphere 2006; Rylko-Bauer and Farmer 2002), this book explores "the growing influence of market ideology and corporate structures that are shaping medicine and health care delivery" (Rylko-Bauer and Farmer 2002, 476). I combine this critical approach to the privatization of health care with a set of concerns that are influenced by the work of Michel Foucault and others on governmentality and practices of self-regulation that are characteristic of neoliberal society (Foucault 1991; Lemke 2001; Rose 2007). But though I find these ideas compelling, they tend to cast the neoliberal person as a fait accompli. In my search for neoliberal consumers, few people responded as the system predicted. Instead, I saw Acme as a contact zone where managed care and market-based public-policy programs were one moral project among others that were invested in shaping how people behaved. Likewise, many of the patients who were enrolled in neoliberal self-management projects (like the brothers mentioned earlier) did not behave first and foremost as cost-benefit-calculating health care consumers. And so the workings of managed care, the moral project of market reform programs, and the promotion of self-care became ethnographic problems.

PART I

Elements of a System

1

A History of Reform

Colonialism, Public Health, and Privatized Care

When neoliberal programs come to life, when they are transferred from the pages of policy tracts to historically constituted and dynamic social institutions, the programs are fundamentally altered. Policies are not implemented in a void—they are grafted onto a corpus of already existing cultural practices and legal traditions that in themselves ascribe to no internal logical consistency. In order to understand what privatization does, this chapter explores what came before. When privatization was sutured to the public health system in Puerto Rico, it was one more in a long history of reforms aimed at refashioning health and health care on the island. Instead of undoing the past, the new managed care system was incorporated into that history.

Since the United States annexed Puerto Rico in 1898, the health system has been the object of almost constant reform. A diverse cast of characters, including the U.S. colonial military government, American philanthropists, Puerto Rican technocrats, federal bureaucrats, and statehood advocates, has diagnosed what is wrong with the health system and has proposed reforms to cure it. In the early U.S. colonial period, military health officials battled communicable diseases such as hookworm, smallpox, tuberculosis, dysentery, and malaria by imposing compulsory sanitation measures. By midcentury, a more autonomous Puerto Rican government turned away from the overtly colonial and militaristic approach to controlling the spread of disease and created an innovative regional health system based on the goal of enhancing population health through the provision of publicly financed medical care. This regional health system, once lauded as a hallmark of progress and development, was eventually seen as outdated and inefficient; it was privatized by a pro-statehood governor and replaced by a managed care model in the early 1990s known as La Reforma.[1]

Though the public health system has largely been privatized, the past continues to matter to how island residents access care, experience illness, reckon the colonial relationship to the United States, and make claims about the appropriate role of government. As I discuss below, many patients and public health officials continue to see a strong role for government in the health system and to conceptualize health care as a right, not a commodity.

The "War Ward": Colonial Medicine and Municipal Health Services, 1898–1954

When the United States invaded Puerto Rico in 1898, health and sanitation were of immediate concern.[2] The military government sought to improve the water supply and curb the spread of infectious disease in order to keep U.S. military and colonial officials healthy. The first half of the 20th century was characterized by sporadic large-scale sanitation and disease campaigns, while the public health system remained organized largely around municipal governments that were responsible for basic health care through local clinics and hospitals.

The municipal health system had its origins under the Spanish colonial system in Puerto Rico. Though U.S. colonial writings paint the island's medical system as backward and primitive, the Spanish colonial regime actually maintained strict control over medical professionals through education and credentialing requirements (Arana-Soto 1974, xix–xx).[3] In fact, some *practicantes*[4] and dentists supported U.S. annexation—their anti-Spanish sentiment arose from the rigidity of Spanish regulations and the consequent lack of prestige afforded these professions (Arana-Soto 1974, 611–612). Under the Spanish, physicians were required to care for the poor free of charge and serve the needs of the Crown when called on by local officials such as at the scene of a crime, in prisons, or to control epidemics. Two legacies of the Spanish colonial system are the existence of municipally run health care with considerable local political influence in medical matters as well as the expectation that the government should provide for the sick and poor (Arana-Soto 1974, 635).

The U.S. invasion in 1898 militarized medicine on the island.[5] As several studies have pointed out, health was a military affair insofar as, through public sanitation and venereal disease campaigns, Puerto Rico was to be made safe for U.S. soldiers and the "civilizing" colonial project (Flores Ramos 1998; Santiago-Valles 1994; Suárez Findlay 1999; Trujillo-Pagán 2003). The union between health and military matters is perhaps best illustrated by the army medical officer, Bailey K. Ashford, who participated in the U.S. invasion and went on to identify the hookworm parasite that was responsible for widespread anemia on the island. He led hookworm eradication campaigns and was active in founding the Institute of Tropical Medicine (which later became the School of Medicine of the University of Puerto Rico). One of Ashford's initial assignments was to describe the countryside and people of the United States' new colonial possession, an experience that he recounts in his autobiography, *A Soldier in Science*:

> A few weeks after our military occupation of Mayagüez, the regimental Colonel sent for me and told me to ride northwest over the mountains to Aguadilla, where Columbus had landed four hundred years ago. I was to report the condition of the countryside, and also the physical state of the people en route. That official report, still grimy with the mud of rich tropical hills, bears my first impression of the Puerto Rican jíbaro—the picture that was to stare me accusingly in the face, until I had solved the scientific problem which it represented. I reported to the War Department that the country people were "a pale, dropsical, unhealthy-looking class, evidently suffering from lack of meat, although there must be something else, not yet understood." (Ashford 1934, 28)

Ashford depicts the people of these lush hills as ill; even the report was stained with mud, underscoring what he saw as the filthy, though beautiful, conditions of the countryside.[6] U.S. colonialists like Ashford framed their work as curing Puerto Rico from disease, backwardness, and misery. This time writing about himself in the third person, Ashford went on to claim that his discovery of the hookworm parasite was significant for all of the Americas:

> He began to think geographically. Of course he must be very prudent, but—the anemia pandemic in Puerto Rico could not be limited to this one little island. It was all through these latitudes. It must be. He had heard of the indolence of Mexicans, of Central Americans, of people everywhere in the old Spanish Main. He could not *say* that their indolence was caused by disease. Secretly, however, he knew now that it was, though he couldn't say so—yet. But he could say so for Puerto Rico, for our war ward, so newly under our Flag, and so sick. (1934, 4)

With phrases like "soldier in science" and "war ward," Ashford imagines the U.S. colonial project as a medical campaign. The United States is cast as the benevolent physician and Puerto Rico plays the role of the sick patient. As Ashford begins to think "geographically," he sees all of the Americas as a potential patient (i.e., potential colonial possession). Ashford speaks from a position of military authority and also in the voice of scientific authority derived from the emerging importance of laboratory medicine.

The work of medical officers like Ashford was set within an administrative framework established by the military and subsequently, civilian governments. The formal military rule of Puerto Rico ended in 1900 when President William McKinley signed the Foraker Act, which established a civilian government on the island. The civilian government was still largely appointed by the U.S. president with only the lower House of Delegates of the Legislative Assembly and the nonvoting representative in the U.S. Congress (called the Resident Commissioner) being popularly elected (Office of Puerto Rico 1948, 64–80).[7]

The U.S. colonial government created the Superior Board of Health, whose responsibilities included everything from preparing regulations concerning the practice of medicine to maintaining registers of vital statistics, street cleaning, vaccinating, imposing quarantines, supervising travel and traffic, and licensing plumbers (Pabón Batlle 2003, 86–91). The initial actions of the Superior Board of Health focused on smallpox vaccinations for more than 800,000 people, which were completed by 1904 (Arbona and Ramírez de Arellano 1978, 9; Trujillo-Pagán 2003, 66–68), and the work of the Anemia Commission that treated hookworm. The Superior Board of Health established health officers and sanitary inspectors at the municipal level who worked with municipal officials like the mayor to provide basic health services free of charge to the poor as well as to enforce modern standards of hygiene. These responsibilities included inspecting establishments that sold food or drinks, supervising the butchering of meat, and ensuring that waste was properly disposed of (Trujillo-Pagán 2003, 68–78). Criminal charges, resulting in fines, could be brought against the noncompliant. The sociologist Kelvin Santiago-Valles's study of colonial illegalities in this period shows that "violation of sanitary laws" was the seventh most common cause of arrest in 1902 (1994, 100–103). In early reports from the governor back to the U.S. Congress and the president, the difficulties encountered by U.S. sanitary officials on the Superior Board of Health are described:

> To the difficulties thus encountered are to be added bad conditions of sanitation, ignorance by the people of the simplest rules of health, strong prejudice against change, particularly if it involves present outlay, and a lack of intelligent medical assistance throughout the island. (Allen 1901, 318)

The report justifies the "benevolent" colonial enterprise by portraying island physicians and residents as unable to administer their own affairs.[8]

Recent scholarship on this period, however, has emphasized how in these early attempts at Americanizing the health system, U.S. administrators misunderstood local conditions while Puerto Rican patients and medical personnel resisted their colonial interventions.[9] The historian and legal scholar Blanca Silvestrini (1983), for example, illustrates how the U.S. administration encouraged hospital births at a moment when hospitals were sparse, unsanitary, and located far from many poor people's homes. A more appropriate public health measure, she argues, would have been an educational campaign regarding making home births safer. When Puerto Ricans did not flock to the hospitals to give birth, U.S. administrators attributed this to their "lack of intelligence."

There is also considerable evidence that the dire health condition of the Puerto Rican peasantry during this period was created—not remedied—by U.S. intervention on the island. Food shortages and economic privation were the product of abuses by the U.S. colonial government. Small producers were separated from their land, which turned the peasantry into wage laborers available for North American capital (Santiago-Valles 1994, 55–58). With the loss of subsistence agricultural practices, many peasants were on the verge of starvation throughout the early U.S. colonial period.

Over the next three decades, federal legislation modified the health system, but its basic contours remained intact. In 1911, the health system was reorganized with the creation of the Public Health Service (Arbona and Ramírez de Arellano 1978, 9) and in 1912 the Institute of Tropical Medicine was created (Izquierdo Mora 2005, 4). The next major alteration to Puerto Rico's political status occurred in 1917 with the Jones Act, which made Puerto Ricans U.S. citizens; citizenship was granted just in time for Puerto Ricans to be drafted into World War I. The Jones Act also created a Department of Health to be led by the Commissioner of Health who served on the Governor's Executive Council (Office of Puerto Rico 1948, 90).

Gradually, the administration of health matters took on more importance within the colonial bureaucracy as the provision of basic health services became further separated from the enforcement of sanitary laws. From 1933 to 1934, 19 Public Health Unit buildings were constructed with New Deal money from the Puerto Rico Emergency Relief Administration (PRERA) (Izquierdo Mora 2005, 6). These units were administered through the Department of Health and established in every municipality by 1938. The Rockefeller Foundation provided funding and technical support (Arbona and Ramírez de Arellano 1978, 10–11). The Health Department then slowly began to assume more responsibility for the creation of insular facilities that were financed and run by the central government (as opposed to the municipality). PRERA monies also funded campaigns to control malaria and establish birth control services (Arbona and Ramírez de Arellano 1978, 12).

A report published in 1937 by the physician and public health officer Joseph Mountin gives a sense of the state of the public health system at the time. *Illness and Medical Care in Puerto Rico* recommended that the insular government should assume more responsibility for the administration of health care services for the poor. The report surveyed families and found that "the great majority do not have sufficient income to provide food, shelter, and clothing in amounts necessary to afford health and a reasonable degree of comfort" (Mountin, Pennell, and Flook 1937, 29). The study showed that Puerto Rico had a higher birth rate, a higher death rate, and higher incidence rates of communicable diseases than the United States, coupled with lower per capita spending on health care and higher poverty levels. Mountin advocated removing some of the burden of providing health care from the municipal level and instead having the insular government assume more authority for service provision. In part due to the Mountin report recommendations, district hospitals were created that served the surrounding municipalities and these can be seen as the beginning of the regional system (Arbona and Ramírez de Arellano 1978, 12).

Between 1930 and 1940, priority was given to constructing facilities in isolated communities or in those that did not have a functioning municipal hospital (Nine Curt 1972, 58–59). Several decades after their construction, however, many of these outlying facilities had closed for lack of resources, especially human resources. At the same time, the tendency when seeking care had transformed: rural patients were increasingly willing and able to travel to the nearest town where the public health centers were better staffed and equipped (Nine Curt 1972, 59).

By the late 1940s, the political relationship between the United States and Puerto Rico was undergoing a major reconfiguration that created more political autonomy for the island. In 1947, the Elective Governor Act allowed for the popular election of the governor (Office of Puerto Rico 1948, 113). The following year, the charismatic Luis Muñoz Marín was elected governor. These political changes ushered in a new era for health care on the island.

From 1898 until the late 1940s, the "war ward" was characterized by concerns about sanitation, quarantine, and large-scale disease-eradication measures. These public health interventions were based in colonialist understandings of Puerto Ricans as inherently sick and in need of tutelage and were at times met by resistance from physicians and patients. Gradually, the colonial administration turned its attention

to creating public clinics for the poor, but this infrastructure was combined with a municipal system inherited from the Spanish colonial
regime. By the early 1950s, a more autonomous Puerto Rican administration had emerged and with it came a reconceptualization of how
the government should provide health care to the population. With
the consolidation of the capitalist order, rural-to-urban migration, and
the loss of most noncapitalist forms of subsistence, the health system
became more concerned with creating a healthy workforce, limiting
family sizes, and providing basic, primary care for the population. This
was accompanied by a Keynesian shift in the economy that opened up
a larger role for the insular government in regulating the economy and
how people lived (Santiago-Valles 1994, 197).

Epidemiological Principles, the Estado Libre Asociado, and Regionalized Health Care

By the 1950s, Puerto Rico could no longer be cast as a "war ward" by
U.S. colonial officials. Instead, the United States increasingly touted
Puerto Rico as a "'symbolic showcase' of U.S. Developmentalist policies"
(Grosfoguel 2003, 2). The regionalized health system in Puerto Rico
that was created in this period was held up as a model to be emulated
in the developing world by international bodies like the World
Health Organization (WHO) and the International Epidemiological
Association (IEA):

> There are few examples of a developing country deliberately setting out
> to create a balanced set of health services that embrace all levels of care
> from basic, primary, or general care, through secondary or hospital care
> and its supporting services, to university medical centre care, all related
> in accordance with the concepts and practices of regionalization. . . . This
> must certainly be one of the first reports of health care planning in which
> epidemiological principles not only permeated but dominated the think-
> ing of both the architects of the overall scheme and those responsible for
> its practical application. (Arbona and Ramírez de Arellano 1978, v)

The epidemiological principles celebrated in this statement entailed
collecting data about the population's health status, regularly evaluating

the health system itself, and developing programs and interventions based on the population's economic and disease profile. The shift from the "war ward" to a health system based on "epidemiological principles" represents a very different framework for thinking about the role of government; instead of a benevolent physician, the government is cast in the role of rational planner.

The regional health system was a flagship project of the new, more autonomous Puerto Rican government. In 1952, the Popular Democratic Party[10] (PPD, according to the Spanish acronym) celebrated the ratification of a new Constitution that formally changed the island's political status to the Estado Libre Asociado (literally, the Free Associated State, in English; this is translated as the Commonwealth).[11] Though it fell short of full decolonization, the Commonwealth status did formalize more autonomy for Puerto Rican policy makers who in turn implemented the PPD political agenda.[12] This agenda included projects for economic development, addressing poverty, and cultural nationalism. The PPD-led development model was oriented toward free trade, an export-based economy, low wages, and limited restrictions on foreign (especially U.S.) capital (Dietz and Pantojas-Garcia 1993; Grosfoguel 2003; Padín 1997; Silver 2007).[13] These policies were combined with an extensive welfare state (enabled in part by transfers from the U.S. federal government) that provided assistance for education, health care, housing, and nutrition.[14]

The regional health system began in earnest in 1958. By that time, a pilot project in the municipality of Bayamón had already been operating for several years. Based on the encouraging results from the pilot project, a regional office was created in the Department of Health to administer the rollout of the program on an islandwide basis. In the regional organization, primary and preventive care as well as public health functions were to be delivered at local health centers. There would be at least one local health center in each municipality where residents could access care free of charge. Secondary and tertiary care was to be provided at the regional level by the base hospital, which would also be available to back up the local health center for attending to primary-care cases. The central administration was to be responsible for oversight and creating and enforcing policies and procedures. The system was designed to "destroy the barriers which separated medical from social services, prevention from therapy, and personal from environmental services" (Arbona and Ramírez de Arellano 1978, 26). The designers focused on improving communication between and among the different levels of care, ensuring that clinics were appropriately equipped to handle more primary services, promoting continuity of care, and integrating medical records in a "family folder" that considered the patient within his or her "ecological setting." Emphasis was also placed on education, especially in training physicians and nurses to be generalists and focus on primary care in resource-poor settings (Arbona and Ramírez de Arellano 1978, 23–29).

The island was divided into five regions by 1960 (Arbona and Ramírez de Arellano 1978, 39–40). The Puerto Rico Medical Center was also designed to be part of the regional system. It consolidated the Medical, Nursing and Dental School of the University of Puerto Rico with specialized and general hospitals that would also serve as teaching, training, and research facilities. The buildings were physically integrated and the concept was that the center would serve the supra regional level because it could handle the most complex cases (Arbona and Ramírez de Arellano 1978, 47–49).

The regional system did meet with some initial opposition. For example, the Puerto Rican Medical Association called the regionalization program socialist (Arbona and Ramírez de Arellano 1978, 56–57). Another area of conflict arose regarding medical education. The university sought to stress new technologies and high-tech, modern medicine while the realities of the health system called for a focus on basic care in primary settings with few resources. This tension led to internal criticisms of the system where larger public health goals came into conflict with the demands of providing cutting-edge medical education (Arbona and Ramírez de Arellano 1978, 59).

Despite these criticisms, the regional system was celebrated as a model to be emulated because it boasted an integrated approach to health based on epidemiological principles and rooted in the larger development goals of the ruling PPD. The regional system is credited with achieving remarkable improvements in population health such as bringing about declines in birth rates, general mortality rates, infant mortality, maternal mortality, and stillbirths while also increasing life expectancy (Nine Curt 1972, 9).

The application of epidemiological principles, however, did not occur in a vacuum, nor even in a laboratory, no matter how often this metaphor is applied to the island.[15] The optimistic planners and administrators in the new Estado Libre Asociado butted against entrenched political interests at the municipal level, professional practices and hierarchies that ran contrary to their new holistic vision of primary health care, and a parallel private health infrastructure for the wealthy, middle class, and beginning in 1965, those with Medicare. During this period, a complex health delivery system emerged that was organized around regional principles, but it maintained some of the earlier municipal features while also being influenced by the emergence of new capital-intensive, technology-driven treatments and parallel private health markets.

The Regional System Strains and the Private Sector Grows

In the 1970s and 1980s, the regional health system went from being an innovative development model to a mature institution. This period was characterized by a number of tensions that strained the ability of the public system to continue fulfilling its mission, including the growth of a parallel private insurance market, rising medical costs, the role of Medicare and Medicaid in contributing to the chronic underfunding of the public system, and staffing shortages. The survival of municipal networks of patronage further points to the inability of the regional system to satisfy all of the demands put on it. This section examines the successes and failures of the regional system in the period leading up to its privatization.

In 1972, Dr. Nine Curt, the Dean of the School of Public Health at the University of Puerto Rico, authored a study on the state of the health system. Nine Curt's analysis seems far removed from the current neoliberal moment because he explicitly framed the provision of health care as an obligation of the government and argued for a universal health system that would address the disparities between the public and private sectors. His was an optimistic assessment of the successes of the regional system in shepherding Puerto Rico through the epidemiological and demographic transitions. Nine Curt advocated for reforming the existing regional system in order to maximize efficiency and

make the most of scarce resources, particularly because the public sector spent far less per person per year than the private sector did (Nine
Curt 1972, 81). He argued for integrating preventive medicine as well as
rehabilitation into the model. Finally, the changes he proposed would
better coordinate between the private and public systems in order to
keep from duplicating services and unnecessary costs (1972, 60). His
report was celebratory in tone and recognized the efforts of the medical community in dramatically improving the island's health status in a
relatively short period of time.[16]

Just one year after Nine Curt's report, the discourse began to change.
A new way of talking about health care emerged that involved managing risk and coordinating care. The epidemiological principles of the
regional model (rational evidence-based planning of a state-directed
system with constant improvements derived from measuring health
outcomes and effectiveness) were supplanted by pooling risk and
enrolling the population in private health plans. The beginnings of this
discursive shift can be found in a study that was commissioned by the
government in January 1973. The new study was sympathetic to the
regional system and argued for universal coverage, but it also called for
managing the population in new, more businesslike ways. The major
problems the report identified with the regional system were (1) a lack
of integration between the public and private systems, (2) few financial
resources, (3) no maintenance system for facilities and equipment, and
(4) inadequate distribution of the available human resources (Puerto
Rico Legislative Assembly 1974, 24). Health care costs were also increasing faster than general inflation, with the most drastic increases being
for hospital care. The proposed solution to escalating costs was to think
less like an epidemiologist and more like a business manager:

> To deal with the problem of rising costs in health care, it will be nec-
> essary to use in the health care sector, the economic and management
> techniques analogous to those used in any other activity that involves
> investment and operational costs. (Puerto Rico Legislative Assembly
> 1974, 47)

Though the commission's recommendations for a universal system
(with one scenario calling for enrolling the entire population in private

insurance plans) were not implemented, the report foreshadows the marketization of the health care system that did occur in the 1990s.

The creation of the federal Medicare and Medicaid programs in 1965 put additional strain on the regional health system in Puerto Rico. Medicaid, which is a needs-based program designed to provide care for poor children, pregnant mothers, the disabled, and the poor elderly, has long been a source of funding for Puerto Rico's public health programs. However, Medicaid moneys in Puerto Rico have been capped since 1968 and the proportion of federal dollars used to fund Puerto Rico's health programs for the medically indigent is much lower than it is stateside, which exacerbates the underfunding of the public system on the island (discussed further below).

Medicare provides medical coverage for the elderly and disabled. Medicare has done a great deal to protect the elderly from financial ruin for health-related causes and has improved health outcomes for this population. However, in Puerto Rico, Medicare undermined the effectiveness of the regional health system for two reasons. First, Medicare had the contradictory effect of pushing more physicians into the private sector where they could see Medicare patients on a fee-for-service basis. In other words, moneys for the outpatient care portion of Medicare (known as Part B) did not flow into the public regional system, but instead supported the growth of private practices throughout the island. Medicare, therefore, contributed to the widening gulf between the public and private sectors in Puerto Rico. Second, Medicare spending at hospitals in Puerto Rico (known as Part A) has been at rates that are significantly lower than on the mainland; initially these rates were set at 25% of federal levels, then raised to 50% in 1997 and 75% in 2004 (Collins 2003). Even though Puerto Rican residents pay Medicare taxes at the same rates as their counterparts on the mainland, the hospital reimbursement rates are much lower on the island (Friedman 2005). As many hospitals were public institutions in Puerto Rico, higher reimbursement rates would have flowed into and benefited the public health system. Instead, Medicare drained human resources from the public system and contributed to the chronic underfunding that characterized hospital-based care on the island. In one of the many ironies of Puerto Rico's colonial relationship to the United States, federal programs designed to aid the elderly, poor, and disabled had the contradictory effect of weakening the regional health system.

During the 1970s and 1980s, the regional system remained intact although modified slightly by each subsequent administration.[17] In practice, the regional model never quite achieved the integrated system so carefully planned by its architects. For example, the system maintained many of the earlier municipal features of political patronage by mayors. Rooted in the political system inherited from the Spanish, municipal residents could still expect to receive aid from the mayor's office to pay medical bills. Consider how Teresa Ramírez, a 43-year-old Medicare recipient in San Juan, described how the system worked on the eve of the implementation of La Reforma:

> Before La Reforma it was better. Before I started at the newspaper I worked for a [music] group, one of those like Menudo, and I fell on stage. I fell on some stairs and twisted my wrist and my ankle and they gave me a cast. It was in Caguas, not in my town. They took me to the regional hospital, which today is San Juan Bautista. And there they treated me free of charge. You know, before you would go and they would treat you. I also had the same experience in my town, as with all the small towns, if you could not pay for your prescriptions you would go to the mayor's office and there they would sign off. Because that's how it was here in Puerto Rico. I remember back when I was working—we were doing an interview one day with the mayor of Fajardo. And people came and he signed their prescriptions. That happened a lot. It still does. Many people who have a special need go to the mayor. It still happens because just last year I submitted a bill to the mayor's office in a small town where I had given some classes. And before me was a woman who they signed off to do some remodeling to her house and to buy medical equipment for her son. A lot of things get paid for like that. Paid for by the small towns and neighborhoods. It's still the custom.[18]

Though free care could certainly be obtained in the regional system, municipal officials maintained networks of patronage that made up for the inadequacies of care, especially for procuring prescription medication or medical devices. These networks existed before the regional system and they continue to operate today. This narrative also begins to show that the experience of accessing care was far different than the efficient vision put forth by the designers of the regionalization model. Care could not have been completely integrated at the local health center if the patient had to travel to the mayor's office to obtain approval for medication or medical supplies. The lack of prescription drugs at government dispensaries was a criticism lodged against the regional system and a rationale used to argue for the privatization of the system.

Another criticism that was cited as a rationale for privatization was that the licensing standards were lax and health matters were often handled by untrained personnel. Sarah Huertas Goldman, a psychiatrist and former administrator at the Mental Health and Substance Abuse Administration (ASSMCA, according to the Spanish acronym), recounted her training in the regional model:

> I remember when I was a resident, for example, that the person who ran the adolescent area during the day had only finished high school. That was her preparation. She was a great person. One of those people who is naturally talented, you know, who can handle kids and everything. But this was the person that ran the area. Today, we would never even dream, wouldn't even think, wouldn't dare to have someone like that be in charge of the services.

Though the regional system did set standards for professional qualifications, the system was often short of properly trained health workers. The bureaucracy allowed for a degree of informality and still placed a premium on personal relations (such as asking the mayor for help or having a good rapport with adolescents as opposed to formal training). Professional preparation and accreditation of facilities become increasingly important during the implementation of La Reforma as these areas are more closely identified with the provision of modern, managed care.

During the 1970s and 1980s, the regional system strained under the pressure of new medical technologies, chronic underfunding, a growing private sector, inflation, and staffing shortages. Nonetheless, it continued to provide publicly financed care free of charge to anyone who showed up at a public facility. By 1993, epidemiological principles were cast aside in favor of the rationality of the market.

Privatizing Public Health: La Reforma de Salud

Fundamental changes in politics and medicine propelled the next wave of health reform. In the decades leading up to the 1990s, electoral support grew for the statehood party and confidence waned in the ability of insular government bureaucracies to provide high-quality public services. Privatization became the rallying cry of statehood policy makers who initiated various attempts to privatize and downsize state-run services, including education, the telephone and water companies, and the public health system (Colón Reyes 2005; Silver 2004). Medical realities had also transformed; chronic conditions, pharmaceuticals, and technology increased in importance, while the growing private sector allowed health care to be seen increasingly as a business, rather than as a public patrimony.

As mentioned in the introduction, in Puerto Rico, neoliberal reforms must be understood in the context of struggles over the future political status of the Commonwealth. The Popular Democratic Party oversaw the creation of the Estado Libre Asociado in 1952 and advocates maintaining the current semiautonomous relationship with the United States. The Independence Party, which favors complete separation from the United States, is extremely important to cultural and intellectual life on the island, but it typically receives less than 2% of the popular vote. The New Progressive Party (PNP, according to the Spanish acronym) supports statehood and tends to be the party behind privatization initiatives. The last 30 years have seen an increase in electoral support for the statehood party so that the island is currently divided almost evenly between the PPD and PNP. The alignment of the statehood party with neoliberal reforms stems in part from the desire to have Puerto Rico be accepted by the United States and the identification of these reforms with modern political development:

> Welfare reforms and privatization are part of the current trend of conservative "neoliberal reforms" that are occurring globally and it is the vision of the statehood proponents that opposition to these changes could put the brakes on Puerto Rico's possibility of becoming the 51st state. (Colón Reyes 2005, 301)

When the public health system was privatized in 1993, it was done under the auspices of the newly elected statehood governor, Dr. Pedro Rosselló. As an example of how neoliberal ideologies are both universalizing and highly localized (Kingfisher and Maskovsky 2008), in Puerto Rico privatization is not just about spreading market rationalities or being more efficient, it is also tied to how one wishes to see the future political status of the island.

The policies that came to be known as La Reforma were based on President Clinton's reform model and were developed in Puerto Rico at a time when it still looked like the United States would undergo national health reform. I use the term "La Reforma" to describe a series of interrelated neoliberal changes in the health care system that were passed as a result of Law 72 in 1993. The most important change was the implementation of a managed care system for the medically indigent that was administered by private insurance companies. Other changes include the selling off of public health facilities, such as hospitals to private companies; the creation of a new government agency charged with negotiating and enforcing private insurance contracts; and the institution of eligibility requirements and procedures. The goals of La Reforma were to eliminate the unequal, two-tiered system already in place, control costs, downsize the health care bureaucracy, and deliver high-quality care to all island residents "regardless of the economic condition or ability to pay of those in need" (Commonwealth of Puerto Rico 1993). As such, La Reforma was based on key neoliberal principles that hold that (1) the private sector is more efficient than the public sector; (2) the role of government should be restricted to oversight, not service provision; and (3) market-based health reforms lead to innovation in health care provision and improvements in the population's health status.

La Reforma Falls Short of Its Promises

Despite the goal of making La Reforma universal, in practice, eligibility was restricted to those living at or below 200% of the poverty line. By 2000 when it finally covered the entire island, La Reforma beneficiaries numbered 1.8 million; this number later fell to around 1.54 million, or approximately 38% of the population when the government instituted

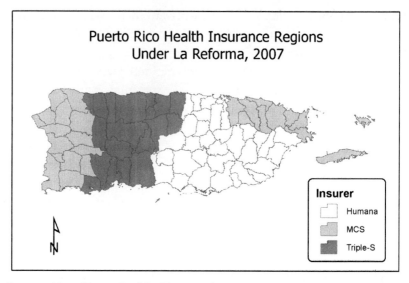

Figure 1.1. Map of Puerto Rico's health regions by insurance company, 2007. During the time period of this study, the newly created Health Insurance Administration contracted with three different insurance companies for physical health and two companies for mental health under La Reforma. Each managed care organization operated in different, mutually exclusive regions in Puerto Rico. MCS (Medical Card Systems) was founded in 1983 in Puerto Rico (though it is currently owned by a U.S.-based investment firm) and provides Medicaid, Medicare, and employer plans on the island. As of 2011, MCS is no longer a Medicaid provider due to breach of contract. Humana is based in Kentucky but has been operating in Puerto Rico since 1997 where it offers a variety of health insurance products. Triple-S is a publicly traded insurance company that was founded in Puerto Rico in 1959 by a group of physicians; it is the largest health insurance plan on the island and in 2009 it acquired Blue Cross Blue Shield. The original version of this map appeared on the ASES website (ASES 2007). The map was recreated by P. V. August for publication in this book by using data obtained from the Portal Datos Geograficos Gubernamentales (gis.pr.gov).

stricter eligibility criteria (Velázquez Vicente 2005). Importantly, the eligibility criteria created a population of uninsured individuals in Puerto Rico for the first time, numbering 330,299, or 8% of the total civilian noninstitutionalized population (U.S. Census Bureau 2009).

La Reforma also failed to reduce health costs. Although initially intended to save money and be more efficient, La Reforma is a much more expensive program than the regional health system that it replaced (Velázquez Vicente 2005). In 1990 health costs accounted for 3.6% of all government expenditures in Puerto Rico, but by 2004, this figure had climbed to 14.3% (Alm 2006, 342). A 2005 study by the

Colegio de Médicos Cirujanos (College of Physicians and Surgeons) showed that Puerto Rico spends 26% of its gross national product on health care compared with 13.3% in the United States, 11.4% in Canada, 10.4% in France, and 7% in the United Kingdom. The report went on to argue that spending more does not improve the care received by Puerto Ricans because of the costs incurred by the "administrative bureaucracy of medical plans" (C. López 2005). The financing for La Reforma combines Medicaid, other federal moneys, and funds from local taxes. The funding breakdown for 2004 according to the Secretary of Health was 12% federal, 3% SCHIP (State Children's Health Insurance Program), 10% municipalities, and 75% central administration (Rullán 2004). The federal proportion of overall spending is so low because, again, since 1968, Medicaid spending in Puerto Rico has been capped. The cap amount was originally set at $20 million, but through periodic increases, it is currently set at $219 million. For this reason, the major- ity of the funding for local health programs derives from local taxes (Delgado 2005a, 2005b). According to a former governor, "If the 1968 cap had been authorized to grow at the same rate as Medicaid grew nationally, Federal support for Medicaid in Puerto Rico would now approximate $1.7 billion, as opposed to the current Federal support of $219 million" (Acevedo-Vilá 2005). To give a sense of the magnitude of the imbalance here, in comparable states with a high proportion of residents on Medicaid, the federal share of spending is 78.6% in Mis- sissippi and 73.3% in West Virginia (University of Puerto Rico and the Vanderbilt Center for Better Health 2008, 5).[19] In sum, not only did La Reforma fail to reduce costs, but it also produced a growing bur- den on the insular government's budget (and part of the funding for La Reforma pays for administrative overhead and profits at private insur- ance companies).

One of the most controversial aspects of La Reforma has been its reliance on capitating primary-care physicians. In other words, every Reforma beneficiary had to sign up with a primary-care physician (PCP) who in turn received a monthly payment (capitation) for each patient that he or she managed. This transfers risk to the level of the physician. The idea is that physicians will spend more time managing their patient population and promoting preventive care if they have a financial stake in the outcome. Under this system, physicians have money deducted from their capitation for referring patients to specialists or prescribing medications. The predictable result is that the system incentivizes rationing care: the fewer referrals and prescriptions that a PCP provides, the higher his or her monthly payout from the Reforma program. Because of this conflict of interest, the College of Physicians and Surgeons on the island came out as adamantly against the capitation of PCPs (Velázquez Vicente 2005).

Though La Reforma expanded access to dentists and is associated with improvements in oral health, in many other domains, health outcomes have not improved as a result of health reform on the island.[20] In one of the few comprehensive reports that attempts to assess how La Reforma impacted health status, the Comisión Para Evaluar el Sistema de Salud del Estado Libre Asociado de Puerto Rico (the Commission to Evaluate the Health System of the Commonwealth of Puerto Rico) found that many health problems either stayed the same or got worse under La Reforma.[21] For example, the commission found no evidence that the quality of services improved for hypertensive, asthmatic, and diabetic patients (2005, 75). In comparison to the private sector, infant mortality rates are higher for beneficiaries of La Reforma (75). Cesarean section rates have increased dramatically and low birth weight and prematurity also increased in the period 1981–2003.[22] Cancer care is particularly problematic: "Patients continue being diagnosed in advanced stages of their cancer, they do not receive timely treatment following their diagnosis, and they do not accept or do not complete the proscribed treatment regimen" (75). Finally, access to mental health care is seriously inadequate: "Almost three quarters of adults and children who need mental health services do not receive them" (75). Mental health care on the island also suffers from a shortage of providers, access barriers in the form of denied services and medications, very limited services and facilities for the severely mentally ill, outdated medication practices, and unrealistically low reimbursement rates for mental health providers (88).

Patient and Provider Evaluations of La Reforma

Many health professionals, and especially physicians, describe La Reforma as an unmitigated disaster. Patients, however, have tended to evaluate the program in more positive terms. What for some was the selling off of a national achievement, for others represented an enfranchisement symbolized by the *tarjeta de salud* (health insurance card). The remainder of this chapter uses ethnographic interviews to illustrate some of the contradictory assessments of privatization that I heard from government officials, health workers, and beneficiaries.

For many people classified as medically indigent in Puerto Rico, the first time they received a health insurance card was when La Reforma was implemented. Previously, access to insurance was restricted to Medicare beneficiaries, government workers, and those in the private sector with relatively well-paying jobs or with union contracts. In interviews, Reforma insurance cards were often referred to as *la tarjeta del gobierno* or *la tarjeta de Rosselló* (the government card, or Rosselló's card). The card itself became an important symbol of economic and social enfranchisement; the poor no longer had to use a separate health system from the middle class and wealthy.

Don Ignacio, a working-class man from Río Grande in his late 60s whom we met in the introduction, when asked what had changed most in Puerto Rico during his life answered:

> Changes here have never benefited me at all. The only thing that actually benefited me was Rosselló's insurance card. It helped me because I could get an operation on my eyes . . . this was the only thing where I didn't have to pay a penny. With the card, they would give me medical exams and everything.

Don Ignacio was very critical of the uneven development that Puerto Rico had experienced in his lifetime. His household was relocated to an undesirable site by the government to allow for the construction of the highway that runs through Río Grande. His roof was also beginning to leak and he had been unable to obtain government assistance in repairing it. He said that poor people were often treated like dogs in Puerto Rican society. Though he was critical of the privatization of hospitals and local health centers that accompanied the introduction and initial financing of the program, Don Ignacio said that La Reforma had made a real difference in his life. The irony is that through the privatization of health care provision, Don Ignacio felt that the government was finally looking after his needs. His Reforma card featured the logo of a private insurance company and he received his Medicare benefits through a private company as well. Echoing a belief shared by many interviewees, Don Ignacio thought that the quality of care was better in the private market and that the poor received inadequate and inferior services at public clinics and hospitals.

Formerly, uninsured Puerto Ricans had access to basic health care services through the regional health centers and at public hospitals. Doña Marta, a 67-year-old, working-class woman from Coamo, described these services at length in comparison to the current system. I asked her what used to happen when someone got sick:

> Well, they would be taken to the public hospital. There they were treated. For that time, the service was good. Now, when you go, the hospital is private. Before it was public. They would give you your medicine there. The doctor would treat you. . . . It wasn't like it is now with the doctors in their offices, no, that system is no longer around. Now it's all the private doctor. . . . It's good [now] because you go and you have your doctor, even more, you can choose the doctor that you want. It's not like before when you would only have one doctor. Now you have one for your heart, for this and for that, for different reasons, now it's better. . . . I think this changed about 10 years ago. More. They started to make it private and then with the government card, everyone modernized.

Doña Marta associated managed care with privatization, specialization, and modernization. She was not overly critical of the regional model, but it was seen as something from the past. Clearly the state-led development project of regionalization has lost its symbolic monopoly on the "modern" and "progress." Choice was also extremely important for her (now you can choose your doctor; in fact you can have a different doctor for every body part). The narratives of Don Ignacio and Doña Marta both offered positive assessments of La Reforma: assessments that hinged on the very material government insurance card and a feeling of being incorporated into a private health system from which they were formerly excluded.

Nonetheless, the elimination of the two-tiered system that existed previously should not be overstated. There still exists prejudice against Reforma patients and increasingly physicians and facilities are understood to either accept Reforma or not. Take the following example of

Doña Bárbara, a 72-year-old woman living in her childhood hometown of Loiza Valley after spending most of her adult life working at a factory in New York City and raising her three children on her own. I asked Doña Bárbara if she had any complaints about the quality of care that she received from her PCP and she said no, except when he started to accept Reforma patients:

> At first it was fine because they were people who had Medicare and Social Security—you know, an insurance plan. But then, when La Reforma began it was a mess. A lot of people. A lot of problems with the people. Because it just filled up terribly. Sometimes there wasn't even a place to sit. And you had to wait many hours; you had to wait such a long time. Sometimes you would arrive in the morning, at seven, and sometimes at noon you would still be there, even later. That was, well, I didn't like it.

To escape these "problem" patients, Doña Bárbara switched to a new doctor who did not accept La Reforma. Though the insurance card ostensibly erases differences between private patients and beneficiaries of the government health plan, Reforma patients are still marked. This becomes one of the attributes through which social class positions are ascribed in the neoliberal consumer society that has taken hold in Puerto Rico. A coworker at Acme who used to work at a private hospital on the west coast of the island offered a telling description of the implementation of La Reforma. Once Reforma patients were admitted to the hospital, everything went missing from sheets to telephone cords—he insisted that everything had to be tied down. This anecdote gives a sense of the enormous class divisions in Puerto Rico, especially between the professional classes and the poor. I was often warned by friends and colleagues in the professional classes to beware of muggings and carjackings (even though most violent-crime victims are poor). Rather than mention missing telephone cords as evidence of what really happened, this detail speaks to how health reform was experienced as a traumatic transformation by those who understood their access to the private health care system as something they deserved and as a marker of class privilege. When Reforma beneficiaries began to use private facilities and providers, some health care workers and other patients reacted negatively to their presence.

Negative attitudes toward La Reforma beneficiaries did not go unnoticed by the beneficiaries themselves. Esteban, the oldest son of Doña Miranda, an 83-year-old widow from Cupey, explained that La Reforma worked through discrimination and by delivering substandard care to beneficiaries. Doña Miranda left La Reforma for a private Medicare plan because of difficulties in finding a participating physician close to home. Esteban's perspective was also informed by his work at a hospital in the metro San Juan area:

> What happened is she no longer receives La Reforma. That was before. But what one perceives in the hospitals is that, well, it's traumatic. There are patients who have to wake up at dawn, they spend the whole day there and then are told that they can't be operated on. There are many physicians that say they won't accept La Reforma because it doesn't pay. You know, they are discriminating against the patients in La Reforma. Before a patient would come into the office and they would say, "Hello, what is your name?" Not now, now there are no names, just "What is your insurance plan?"

Public health officials were also skeptical of the claim that the regional health system was inferior to La Reforma. A high-level government official in San Juan who opted to remain anonymous explained in an interview that

> when La Reforma was implemented, even though people received a card and could go to the private sector, this whole element was lost. The education component, the personal component the "*tú a tú*" [face-to-face interactions]. . . . [The system we have now] is very individualistic. It's a system that even though they say it works with the whole family, the reality is no. The reality is that no doctor in Puerto Rico can truly say that he uses a holistic approach with the family and with his patient. . . . As far as I'm concerned, they have distorted what the practice of medicine used to be.

Instead of enfranchisement, in this vision, the card represents a loss. As shown above, the regional system was organized around caring for a patient and seeing the patient within his or her social context. Where the regional model cared for the entire community, the neoliberal model operates under more individualistic principles. For this official, the fragmented, individual vision is a distortion of how medicine should be practiced.

But even those who are critical of La Reforma like former Secretary of Health (from 1985 to 1989) Luis Izquierdo Mora recognize that the insurance card is an extremely valuable political commodity. In an interview in Río Piedras, he explained:

> La Reforma is an irreversible phenomenon, it's irreversible, there is no going back, what has to be done is to modify it. . . . Because no one is going to say to the poor, I am going to take away your insurance card. No one. No one. No one would dare say that. Poor patients must be treated and they are the responsibility of the state.

This position signals how important the introduction of La Reforma has been to the medically indigent in Puerto Rico. Dismantling the system would be political suicide. Instead, Izquierdo Mora argues that the system should be altered. Ironically, he links the fundamental responsibility of the state to provide health care for the poor to the continued dominance of a market-based health-delivery model.

The epidemiological principles of the regional health system and the use of data by the state for effective planning have also largely been eliminated under La Reforma. Researchers and government officials described the lack of data that was part of the new system. Although insurers are contractually required to report on certain predefined indicators and quality measures, in practice, the availability, reliability, and validity of the data suffered under La Reforma. According to the same high-level government official quoted above,

> Here no one knows what people get sick from. There are no studies about this—about why people visit medical offices. Here no one knows what the impact of La Reforma has been. Before, before we at least had data that we could use to make public policy decisions, in population statistics. But the registers have fallen, there are no registers.

Health data in Puerto Rico are no longer public; the data were privatized and used to calculate bids for future premiums during contract negotiations rather than feeding into a national strategy for creating a healthier Puerto Rico.[23]

A closely related problem is the lack of consistent and transparent auditing and government oversight of private contractors. The contract between insurance companies and the government clearly establishes quality control and utilization standards as well as auditing authority and procedures. However, in practice, these contract provisions are not enforced (Comisión Para Evaluar el Sistema de Salud 2005, 80, 244). A government official in the health sector explained how the contracts work in practice:

> The contract provides many spaces so that things are done correctly, but there is no auditing, the will is not there to enforce it like it should be. And everyone does as they please. And then they catch one person and draw and quarter him. . . . They kill him, they haul him in. And the rest watch and that's where it stays. But all of the ones who were committing atrocities, they keep committing atrocities. There is no system. That is the problem. There is no system for oversight. There is no system of control.

In the rare instance when violators are punished, they are made into extreme examples. This overreaction makes the system appear arbitrary rather than governed by predictable practices of oversight and auditing.

Finally, the elimination of many training opportunities was an unintended consequence of privatizing public hospitals and other facilities. According to reports in the major daily newspaper *El Nuevo Día*, the number of interns and residents has decreased by 68% since the implementation of La Reforma (Sosa Pascual 2005g). Jorge Sánchez, the head of a governor-appointed commission to evaluate the health system, is quoted in the same article as saying "this is a disaster." The press as well as the physicians I spoke to described the changing medical education system as a crisis. In Boston, I interviewed a young physician named Mariana Ortiz who had trained in Puerto Rico but moved off the island soon thereafter. Her experiences speak to how medical education was transformed after the health system was privatized. Her medical degree was from San Juan Bautista in Caguas and she had completed her internship at a hospital on the outskirts of the metropolitan San

Juan area. Many of her friends had left the island to finish their medical training. Some left in order to find residency programs because many had been closed since the implementation of La Reforma. She said that on the island there are a number of *residencias criollas* (creole residency programs), but fewer and fewer accredited residency programs. Physicians also leave in search of a higher quality of living. To make a decent living on the island, she explained, doctors open weight-loss clinics, pick up hours at the emergency room, become holistic practitioners, and take private patients on the side.

Mariana Ortiz trained at a smaller medical school outside of San Juan, but similar processes were occurring at the island's largest medical school. Training programs were becoming more scarce and physicians were increasingly faced with the ethical and financial dilemmas of care rationing. Whereas the regional system sought to integrate training into Puerto Rico's public health system, privatization disarticulated the connection between training, treatment, and research. Luis Izquierdo Mora, the former Secretary of Health and a practicing primary care physician, emphasized in an interview the connection between privatization and shrinking opportunities for medical education:

> They sold the hospital in Arecibo. They sold the hospital in Ponce. They sold it in Guayama. They almost, almost sold it in Mayagüez. They sold it in Aguadilla. . . . Obviously the Reform had a huge impact, because many of the privatizers, well, their priority was not, let's piously say: their priority was not education, it was service delivery. Nor did they prioritize research. And medicine is made up of three things: service, education, and clinical and scientific research.
>
> Right now we are in a huge fight with the Hospital in Carolina, which we are trying to defend for the Medical School of Puerto Rico. Because the University of Puerto Rico would like to hand the hospital in Carolina over to privatizers. We are against it. It's that the experience we've had with the privatizers, I'll say it again, they are not very interested in education. And they are not as interested in clinical and scientific research as they are in services as such, you see? They provide the services, but they're not interested in the other part. But we have to maintain a balance between service, maintain a balance with education so that there will be residency programs. The Hospital in Carolina, right now, if they

eliminate the question of teaching there, we would lose 11 residency programs. Eleven programs. And we've already lost so many. Emergency medicine, anesthesiology . . . a ton of things have already been lost. That is why we are against turning that hospital over to the privatizers, because the impact this has had on medical education has just been devastating.

Dr. Izquierdo Mora struggled to maintain residency programs, but he was not optimistic about the future prospects for medical education on the island.

Listening to provider and patient evaluations reveals the many unintended consequences wrought by La Reforma. Clearly, evaluations of the program are mixed and depend greatly on who is being asked. Some beneficiaries celebrated gaining access to care in private physicians' offices through their government insurance cards. Others were more skeptical of the program, citing care rationing and discrimination against Reforma patients. A number of middle-class interviewees thought that Reforma beneficiaries overcrowded and contaminated the private system. Health professionals, in contrast, were likely to be critical of La Reforma and lament the many positive aspects of the regional system that have been lost. The major problems that health professionals emphasized were the lack of data for planning and decision making, the absence of auditing and government oversight, ethical dilemmas imposed by capitation, the loss of the social focus of the regional system, the selling off of public facilities, and the disappearance of medical residency programs.

Conclusions

This chapter charted the transforming health system in Puerto Rico from the "war ward" to "epidemiological principles" and finally to neoliberalism. By describing the layers of policies and practices on which the current "unmanageable" system stands, I hope to counter the ahistorical and acultural perspective of neoliberal reformers who imagine that all that came before can and should be wiped away and replaced by the market. From the practice of seeking medical aid from a town's mayor to many medical professionals' continued insistence that the health system should be a public patrimony, past practices color how people use the health system and think about the appropriate role of government in Puerto Rico.

Colonialism has consistently shaped the structure and goals of the health system in Puerto Rico. The role of colonialism was quite obvious at the beginning of the 20th century when military officers implemented compulsory sanitation and disease-control measures. Though the contemporary impact of colonialism on the health system is more subtle, it is nonetheless still determinative at the beginning of the 21st century. The unequal levels of funding in Medicare and Medicaid and the turn to a market model are both artifacts of the colonial relationship. Unfortunately for Puerto Rico, it is tied to the country in the developed world that spends the most on health care in return for mediocre health outcomes (OECD 2008; WHO 2008). As a new round of health reform is implemented, this colonial relationship is likely to further lock Puerto Rico into a market model replete with many of the same problems as in the United States: growing inequality, stark health disparities, rising costs, and struggling safety-net institutions. These problems are further compounded in Puerto Rico by higher poverty rates, chronic underfunding, and a crisis in medical education.

2

Regulating a Runaway Train

Everyone Is Replaceable

Two executives—one Puerto Rican, the other a gringo from the Midwest—stood before a group of 50 middle managers. The restaurant banquet room on the first floor of Acme's modern office building used to easily hold the company's management, but now the long tables were crammed with chairs. Some attendees had difficulty finding a spot on which to rest their plates. In the past, meetings provided easygoing opportunities to gossip and catch up with friends. Today, however, there were far fewer kisses on the cheek and calls of *Dios te bendiga* (God bless you).

The purpose of the meeting was to tell the managers that the company's CEO had just been fired. The two executives called the group to order and began to click through their PowerPoint presentation emblazoned with Acme's logo. Very little was revealed about why the CEO was sacked. Instead, the two executives turned the somber occasion into an opportunity to educate the managers about the company's culture; the talk was titled "Acme: A different type of company." As was common at Acme, the Puerto Rican executive moved easily between English and Spanish. He described the dizzying rate of growth that the company was experiencing and the need to be flexible when faced with constant change.

The two executives wore khakis with dress shirts and no jackets. Acme was more informal than other insurance companies on the island, where a dark suit was the standard garb for a male executive. The American founders promoted a style that was more like an Internet startup than a stuffy insurance company.

The core of the presentation was a list of the company's "basic principles." The first item on the list was "Gringos + Boricuas = Results" followed by "Acme = the land of opportunity."[1] Many of the aphorisms had been plucked from popular management how-to guides like *Fish!* and *Who Moved My Cheese?* The gist of the talk was that managers should be team players who aren't afraid to make decisions; they should take the initiative and do the right thing. Acme's final two basic principles were:

> Don't attempt to stop the train, it will run over you . . . and nobody will even notice. Everyone, even me, is replaceable.

> Have fun!!!! *Pero no confundas el pasarla bien con el "vacilón"* [But don't confuse having fun with goofing off.]

The runaway train principle was accompanied by a slide stating that cemeteries are full of irreplaceable people; an image of a gravestone directly preceded the call to have fun. Like a newly diagnosed cancer patient, managers were warned that a positive attitude was a prerequisite for survival at the company. Though the fired CEO hadn't made it at Acme, new candidates would be hired and the company would keep growing. This company is not for everyone, they said. Some good people who are successful in other places just cannot adapt to Acme's culture. The Puerto Rican executive once again invoked the metaphor of the runaway train: workers could climb on board or risk being run down. Everyone is replaceable.

During the question and answer segment, no one spoke.

Regulating for Creative Destruction

The executives in the story above repeatedly drew on the metaphor of a runaway train to explain the volatility created by the rapid growth of the Medicare Advantage market. In a remarkably honest, if stark, presentation, they told Acme employees not to expect stability and security. The company had seemed even more unpredictable than usual after a buyout, the installation of new management, and the firing of several of the new leaders. Instead of promising that the turmoil would pass, the surviving executives focused their presentation on the unstoppable, careening forward motion of growth, as if Acme were a force beyond all human control.

The executives lectured the management about Acme's culture, but also, and perhaps unintentionally, about the cultural dynamics of capitalism itself. Similar symbolism can be found in the works of some of the first critics to describe how capitalism remakes the world and transforms social relations. The literary critic Marshall Berman argues that this conflict between capitalism's dual propensity to create and destroy is perhaps best captured in Karl Marx's *Communist Manifesto* by the phrase "all that is solid melts into air":

> "All that is solid"—from the clothes on our backs to the looms and mills that weave them, to the men and women who work the machines, to the houses and neighborhoods the workers live in, to the firms and corporations that exploit the workers, to the towns and cities and whole regions and even nations that embrace them all—all these are made to be broken tomorrow, smashed or shredded or pulverized or dissolved, so they can be recycled or replaced next week, and the whole process can go on again and again, hopefully forever, in ever more profitable forms. (1999, 111)

Capitalist economic relations unleash unprecedented creative forces, quickly followed by destruction on a massive scale, only to then create again.[2] In Puerto Rico, colonial relations of rule fuel the creation/ destruction process with tax breaks for foreign firms, generous incentives to locate on the island (particularly for biotech firms), and weak enforcement of environmental standards (Dietrich 2013; Duprey 2010).

During my research, Acme was in the throes of creative destruction. Acme destroyed previous care-giving networks, built a new claims payment and provider infrastructure, and created a corporate culture only to sell itself to the highest bidder who in turn created a newer, bigger company through mergers. Within 2 years of leading this meeting and explaining the runaway train to the management, the two executives (along with many other employees) no longer worked at Acme.

The image of the runaway train captures the momentum and sheer force of Acme's growth and constant transformation. The image is convincing in a visceral way; it is overpowering and incapacitating (the only option is to get on board or be run down), but it is also misleading. The train image—as a careening out-of-control machine—detracts attention from the human decisions, social relations, and public-policy priorities that make Acme possible. By accentuating growth and constant change, the executive's story deemphasizes the organization's status as a highly regulated health plan operating in a colonial context in which almost all revenue was received from the federal government. Ironically, this runaway train was fueled by tax dollars, and its flexible culture flourished within boundaries that were monitored by a federal agency. Likewise, the departing executives were not simply casualties of a rail accident; a fellow executive decided to fire them and did so personally after receiving a barrage of complaints about their leadership style. They were deemed expendable in what was euphemistically referred to as a "business decision."

In both popular imagery and even much academic writing, the market is seen as out of human control, as operating according to its own internal rules like supply and demand or the "invisible hand." It is depicted as a force with its own dynamics and self-correcting mechanisms. But a basic insight of economic anthropology is that confusing market abstractions and models with how markets actually work on a day-to-day basis is a mistake because "economic practices are embedded in social networks, relations, and institutions" (Ho 2009, 32).

Subjecting any realm of human activity and interchange to the rules of the market proceeds through policy, deliberation, calculation, and very human forms of political struggle and coercion. Placing publicly financed health care within a market framework is a clear example. Marketizing care pulls some services and activities into the market (in other words, makes these services and activities reimbursable and potentially profitable) such as 15-minute medication checks with a psychiatrist, new pharmaceuticals, and administrative work directed at coordinating care. At the same time, other services and activities may be excluded or severely restricted from repayment like nonpharmaceutical forms of psychiatric care that take more time such as therapy (Donald 2001; Willging 2005), caregiving by relatives or safety-net providers (Boehm 2005; Horton 2006; Horton et al. 2001; Lamphere 2005; Nelson 2005; Waitzkin et al. 2002), administrative work at physicians' offices to deal with billing and insurance eligibility issues, and services that were not properly preauthorized or did not meet other administrative requirements (L. López 2005; Maskovsky 2000; Wagner 2005). While some activities become marketized, others are excluded from reimbursement. This work is produced not by an abstract, invisible hand but rather by human decisions and calculations.

Industry Turned Government Turned Industry

The Medicare Modernization Act (MMA) was crafted with little thought as to how it would impact Puerto Rico; the only explicit mention of the island in the legislation referred to changes in hospital reimbursement rates.[3] Nonetheless, the MMA had a major impact on the entire health care system in Puerto Rico by creating a lucrative market in Medicare plans and funneling new federal funds to the island. A closer look at the MMA reveals how market-based government policies created organizations like Acme and fueled the volatility in the Medicare market that characterized the first decade of the 2000s.

The MMA was signed into law in December 2003 by George W. Bush and tied the distribution of Medicare benefits more closely to market forces. The legislation created the Medicare Advantage program, which expanded the types of managed care health plans that could contract with the Centers for Medicare and Medicaid Services (CMS) and established funding levels that were extremely attractive for insurance companies. The MMA also added a prescription-drug benefit to the Medicare program; it was known as Part D and was to be administered by private plans.

The MMA was the largest expansion of a federal entitlement program in 40 years. Though it was supported by the Republican Bush administration, some fiscally conservative Republicans were critical of the bill because of its price tag and because it created a new entitlement program. But since the bill relied on using private corporations to expand the Medicare program (rather than allowing the government to directly provide services or negotiate prescription-drug prices), most Republicans eventually signed on and showed support. The final bill passed largely along party lines with Republicans supporting it and Democrats opposing it.

The estimated cost of the MMA was the subject of considerable controversy: "Weeks after it was passed, the White House cost estimate shot up by one-third, to $534 billion over 10 years. Compounding the problem, a government investigation later found that the top Medicare official, Thomas A. Scully, had intentionally withheld data from Congress indicating the higher costs" (Pear and Toner 2004). Soon after the passage of the legislation, this same "top Medicare official," Scully (together with many other CMS employees and congressional staffers), left CMS and became a lobbyist for several pharmaceutical companies and medical associations that were "affected by the new Medicare law, which Mr. Scully helped write" (Pear 2004; see also Kroft 2007).[4] As evidenced by the deliberate withholding of cost estimates and the exodus of government officials into private industry immediately following passage of the law, the line between industry and government was quite permeable during the writing and passage of the MMA. This interpenetration of business and government continued to characterize the program during its implementation as regulators adopted a cooperative and business-friendly approach to assisting plans in meeting the new compliance requirements.

The MMA spurred the rapid growth of managed care and prescription-drug plans throughout the United States as it signaled an intensified commitment on the part of the Bush administration to delivering Medicare via private plans. In Puerto Rico, Medicare Advantage plans increased their share of the Medicare market from around 3% in 2003 to 68% in 2011 (compared with 25.6% in 2011 in the United States as a whole).[5] In the wake of the passage of the MMA, new Medicare insurance plans flocked to the island; these private plans were created by already existing insular firms, entrepreneurial startups, and by U.S.-based health conglomerates.[6]

The Medicare Advantage market share is higher in Puerto Rico for several reasons, the most important being the unusually high premiums. Whereas in the United States, Medicare reimbursement rates are considered low, in Puerto Rico, they are high relative to other payers, and Medicare Advantage rates are higher still. In 2009, the Medicare Advantage premiums paid to private health plans were close to 180% of

Table 2.1. Growth in Medicare Advantage Enrollment in Puerto Rico, 2003–2011

	2003	2004	2005	2006	2007	2008	2009	2010	2011
Medicare Advantage Enrollees	19,535	44,292	102,580	306,313	336,487	337,757	321,291	429,941	453,808
Total Medicare Population	588,869	601,773	611,993	620,287	618,433	620,497	638,600	654,709	670,555

Source: KFF (2011a).

Original Medicare reimbursement rates in Puerto Rico (MedPac 2009, 179). From the beneficiary's perspective, Medicare Advantage plans are attractive in Puerto Rico because they offer additional benefits beyond Original Medicare, including buying down the beneficiary's monthly Part B premium.[7]

Though Republican rhetoric extolled the virtues of limited, small government, the MMA enlarged government agencies, increased the cost of Medicare, and extended the government regulatory apparatus into new domains. The MMA was also the product of a fluid boundary between government and industry where consultants, the authors of legislation, congressional staffers, and lobbyists all regularly interchanged positions.

The Compliance Department

Acme depended on being found substantially in compliance with federal regulations. All communication from the regulatory agency (CMS) was supposed to pass through the Compliance Department, which served as the conduit for information about audits, changing rules, and upcoming regulatory deadlines. Part of the reason that I was hired and then promoted at Acme was because I was a bilingual North American who could navigate through the bureaucratic documents and regulations. This research location at the interface between the corporation and a federal regulatory agency allowed me, as an anthropologist and employee, to observe the daily processes through which state regulation shaped the conduct of business at the corporation. In turn, I documented how interactions with the government regulator limited what the health plan was allowed to do and contributed to an environment within Acme that emphasized compliance and following the rules. From this position, I also observed how Acme attempted to shape relations with the regulator to its advantage and the many moments in which the process of oversight—especially through audit—slipped into excess and absurdity.

Members of the Compliance Department tended to be more highly educated than most company employees. Almost everyone had attended some college, and several people had bachelor's or were working on master's degrees. In other departments, it was common to wear matching polo T-shirts, but in Compliance, employees preferred a business casual dress code and opted not to wear a uniform, signifying that they saw themselves more as professionals than as workers.[8] When at their desks, the staff researched complaints, reviewed marketing materials, and wrote audit reports. Apart from the member complaints that lit up the phones, Compliance was one of the quieter departments in the company, partly due to the confidentiality of the issues it documented, partly because this island of taupe cubicles bordered the CEO's corner office on one side and the Chief Financial Officer (CFO) on the other.

The department head inculcated the belief that Compliance would only be effective if members of the department set an example. Members of the Compliance Department were often held up as experts. Female department members were sometimes called *las chicas de Compliance* (the Compliance girls) when they entered the lunchroom on break together. They seemed to enjoy it when colleagues from other departments asked if a certain answer was right or if CMS permitted them to do certain things. This request for help acknowledged their expertise and familiarity with complicated and difficult-to-understand government regulations. Compliance employees were also privy to the goings on in other departments through audits and complaints investigations.

Every Monday morning at 7:30, a member of the Compliance Department led a training session for new hires. On orders from the compliance officer, latecomers were refused entry to the training room and had to inform their supervisors that they would need to attend again the following week. The new employees who arrived on time looked bewildered as the presenter launched into her scripted, PowerPoint presentation in the freezing conference room. New employees were thrown into a sea of English-language health care acronyms and were directed to protect members' private information. Most new hires had no prior exposure to Medicare or working at a health plan; they filled entry-level vacancies for customer service representatives or claims clerks. A concern with obeying rules was often described as culturally American by Acme executives. And so, to emphasize the importance of complying, members of the Compliance Department warned that compliance violations would be dealt with seriously by the federal government, unlike the Puerto Rican government, which was perceived as much more lax in its enforcement and oversight of rules.[9] The presentation emphasized that everyone was responsible for knowing and following federal regulations; one of the final slides claimed "we are all Compliance."

Another attempt to mold employee behavior and incentivize a compliant attitude toward work involved creating a "culture of service" at the organization. In one of his many discussions of culture and culture differences at Acme, the president of the company who was Puerto Rican once explained to me that there was a culture of absenteeism at Acme that was part of the larger Puerto Rican culture. To address this problem, the management embarked on several efforts to create a "culture of service" that promoted politeness, helping customers, and being punctual through activities like attendance rewards, a contest for a customer service slogan, and companywide events like a family day and a talent show. An alternate explanation for at least some of the lateness was that the company offered no childcare and company hours were 7:30–4:30, which was very difficult for parents of young children in daycare (many daycares were not open at 6:30 or earlier, which is the time that employees who lived in the more inexpensive surrounding suburbs would have to leave in order to get to the office on time).

Forging Compliant Dispositions: Demonstrating the Willingness to Comply

The day-to-day work of the Compliance Department was aimed at ensuring that Acme employees understood and followed the federal regulations that affected their work. To achieve this end, my colleagues and I advised other departments, trained personnel, conducted audits of each department in the corporation, studied the federal rules and regulations available on the CMS website, and investigated complaints. More rarely, we attended government conferences or rewrote company policies and procedures to comply with a change in the regulatory environment or internal reorganizations. The following example illustrates both the kind of inquiries that the Compliance Department fielded on a daily basis and the disposition that Compliance tried to inculcate in Acme employees.

Maria, a customer service supervisor, hesitantly knocked on my open door. She wore khakis with a short-sleeved, button-down shirt embroidered with the company's logo. Maria was accompanied by Bibiana, an appeals and grievance coordinator who used to work downstairs with Maria before Bibiana was promoted.

Bibiana ushered her into my office and announced that Maria had an important question. The supervisor quickly explained that her representatives in Customer Service were having a hard time with the new information-release rules. Acme had just implemented new privacy rules as a result of HIPAA (the Health Insurance Portability and Accountability Act). The privacy rules were supposed to protect patients by only releasing their protected health information (PHI) for treatment and payment purposes or when written authorization was granted. Maria said that she understood the purpose of the rules, but it was very difficult to enforce and members were upset. Many elderly and disabled callers wanted the customer service representatives to speak with their family members over the phone—they were not accustomed to and did not like having to send in authorization letters. They relied on children or spouses to handle their health-related affairs. It was very strange, she added, to hear the member talking in the background but then not be able to discuss an issue with a spouse, son, or daughter.[10]

We looked at the written policy and the procedure and found some exceptions to the rules—release without authorization was permitted to the Veterans' Administration or for some public health purposes. But for the most part, I advised that members would have to keep sending in letters. I acknowledged that we were asking them for letters that they did not want to send so that we could protect their rights. I sighed and apologized.

Maria nodded and said she thought this would be my answer, but she had to check. She assured me that she would keep requiring the customer service representatives to ask for written authorization. The Compliance Department wanted employees to question themselves about whether their activities and decisions were permitted. If in doubt, like Maria, they should seek out consultation. As such, Compliance was quite explicitly engaged in shaping the conduct of employees and calling on individuals to regulate themselves. This attempt to guide the "conduct of conduct" is an example of what Foucault terms government: "any more or less calculated means of the direction of how we behave and act" (Dean 1999, 2). And yet it was clear to everyone in my office that day that compliance could be futile; the signed authorization did not protect members; if anything, it protected the organization. Maria knew that she had to demonstrate a willingness to comply with the privacy rules even though this would not help members get answers to their questions about coverage, a denied service, or how to find a doctor. Months later, when I listened in on customer service calls, I noticed that written authorizations were not being uniformly requested.

Just as Acme employees demonstrated a willingness to comply by attending trainings, seeking guidance, and participating in audits, Acme had to demonstrate to federal regulators that it, too, was concerned with compliance. Audits were an integral part of corporate compliance, and demonstrating a willingness to comply is crucial to successfully passing an audit.

The Social Life of Audits

Auditing has its origins in finance and accounting. As a practice, it was initially confined to the independent review and verification of financial balance sheets, but since the late 1980s auditing has migrated into new domains (Power 1997, 5). Anthropologists and other observers of culture have become increasingly interested in auditing as a social practice and form of government. Part of this interest stems from the ways in which academic labor itself has been transformed by auditing; accountability, accreditation, and ever more administrative oversight are remaking academic workplaces and now affect everything from tenure standards, publishing expectations, and curriculum development to service work (Shore and Wright 2000; Strathern 2000). Beyond their own work lives, anthropologists have also noted that auditing is a common practice outside of the academy, including in health care (Mulligan 2010), international development (Harper 2000; Vannier 2010), environmental inspections (Brown 2010), and social welfare programs (Clarke 2004; Scherz 2011). "Audits," therefore, as a form of verification and oversight, both impinge on the professional lives of anthropologists and are ubiquitous in the contexts in which we conduct research.

One important contribution of the literature on accountability is that it has examined how auditing is linked to transformations in government. Auditing becomes necessary as a verification and oversight tool when government services are contracted out to nongovernmental entities like corporations and nonprofits. In one of the first major works on auditing, Power (1997) linked the importance of auditing to transformations in government that "dismantle the public-private divide" (10); in other words, an "audit is not simply a solution to a technical problem; it also makes possible ways of redesigning the practice of government" (11).

There is less agreement, however, on what the uptick in auditing means as a social practice. Some see auditing as a coercive practice that is rooted in neoliberal modes of thought with politically dangerous implications such as making market logics like efficiency and cost-effectiveness the central organizing features of education, government, and even individual behavior (Shore and Wright 2000, 61). Others depict auditing as a more benign, if flawed, technology for creating oversight in complex societies where trust cannot be taken for granted (Brown 2010). Though I tend to agree with the "coercive" perspective that holds that the explosion of auditing is inextricably linked to neoliberal ideas about government and the market, the descriptions here of auditing at Acme focus more on the contradictions and unexpected consequences of auditing in practice. This is because the practice of auditing tends to diverge from both its explicit policy goals (regarding accountability and democratic oversight) and its more implicit neoliberal political agenda.

This chapter comes at the problem of auditing from an ethnographic perspective by asking how auditing was conducted at Acme. What relationships did auditing establish between the federal government and the private corporation? What did accountability mean in the everyday interactions through which audits were actually conducted? An ethnographic perspective necessarily draws attention to the disjuncture between the aspirations of auditing as a policy of accountability and what it actually achieves in practice through the concrete application of auditing operations by social actors.[11] What emerges is a portrait of auditing where maintaining good social relations between governmental auditors and health plan personnel and the performance of a willingness to comply become paramount and are too often the primary focus of auditing. Meanwhile, the health policy goals of creating public accountability for private plans, ensuring that Medicare beneficiaries receive the services to which they are entitled, and holding health plans to account become secondary concerns.

The Self-Regulating Corporation

"Compliance" names a contemporary form of government oversight in which the company (or an individual) must submit to the requirements of regulators *and* continuously document its own attempts to comply. This form of government partially privatizes the work of oversight by requiring companies to monitor themselves. As I will discuss below, the role of compliance is not to guarantee that every process in the company is being carried out correctly (which is impossible). Instead, it is to compel departments to enact and document a willingness to improve and the intention to comply. This process occurs at individual and organizational levels. The Compliance Department attempted to instill in individual Acme employees the disposition to do the right thing. In so doing, Compliance promoted and extended practices of self-regulation. For example, employees were surrounded by signs of the company's contractual obligations to CMS, from the compliance training they received on the first day of work to daily reminders in posters, emails, and written policies. One target of these trainings and reminders was to shape individual behavior so that a concern with compliance came from each employee, ideally transforming compliance into one's inner voice.[12]

However, the Compliance Department did not rely solely on the personal transformation of each employee into an agent of compliance;

it also tried to shape the organization. In order to promote self-regulation at an organizational level, Compliance employees imitated the very same oversight techniques that were used by government regulators; they reproduced the practices of audit, documentation, and creating corrective action plans within Acme. Perhaps the most important piece of the process whereby a concern with compliance was internalized by the organization was through the corrective action plan (rather than the audit itself, which has received the bulk of scholarly attention, particularly regarding its use in education). Following audits by CMS and the internal audits that the Compliance Department conducted at Acme, each department was required to develop a corrective action plan that addressed the findings and that described how the health plan or the department intended to bring itself into compliance. The plan or department then implemented the corrective action plan and reported on its progress until the next audit. The concept behind this practice was that no plan or department would be perfect, but what mattered was that deficiencies had been identified and were actively being addressed. The emphasis was on documenting the process of improvement. The corrective action plan also extended the temporal frame of the audit; instead of an event, it became a never-ending process.

Consider the following example of how self-regulation and a concern with compliance shaped daily work practices at Acme. Late one afternoon when I was still new to the Compliance Department, the supervisor of Provider Credentialing stopped by my office and hesitantly asked what order CMS required the documents to be assembled within each provider's file. Before a provider can contract with the health plan, he or she must submit an application and provide evidence of an appropriate license, current malpractice insurance, and good standing with Puerto Rico's Board of Medical Examiners. The supervisor showed me a blue file bursting with copies of diplomas, licenses, evidence of malpractice insurance, attendance certificates for continuing education classes, printouts from websites, the contract, a CV, and the application. How exactly did CMS want her to organize the file? At first, I thought the question concerned insignificant minutiae. The federal government did not issue instructions on how to arrange the individual sheets of paper in a file. But the supervisor was adamant—she needed further guidance. She produced the negative findings from the last CMS audit and pointed me to the reviewer's comments that the files were messy. In an effort to satisfy the auditors, we took this review instrument and created a checklist to go in the front of each file that the supervisor would fill out and initial. We then wrote the solution into a policy and procedure. From that point on, the staff would organize the files so that they would come across each item in the order it appeared on the audit worksheet. After this conversation, the supervisor hired additional staff and trained them on how to assemble the files correctly. She told the credentialing coordinators that the files must always be assembled in this particular way because of CMS mandates.

In this example of corporate bureaucracy making, regulations filtered through the organization and informed daily work practices. The translation of regulations into standardized processes at the company often entailed a considerable movement away from the purpose or intent of the law. CMS required that managed care organizations establish credentialing procedures in order to monitor the provider network and to protect Medicare beneficiaries from unqualified health care providers. Organizing the papers in the file probably did not advance that goal. Nonetheless, considerable resources within the organization were dedicated to cleaning up the files and during the next CMS site visit, the department received accolades for having some of the most well-organized files that the auditors had ever seen.

The key to arriving at this particular solution was that the actual audit tool was incorporated into departmental policy as part of the corrective action plan. Recent work on the technology of auditing in higher education has shown that "audit thus becomes a political technology of the self: a means through which individuals actively and freely regulate their own conduct and thereby contribute to the government's model of social order" (Shore and Wright 2000, 62). Individuals surely self-regulated in my example. Exhibiting compliant behavior was important for anyone interested in remaining employed at Acme. The supervisor in particular was keen to demonstrate her total commitment to addressing the initial negative findings. In the process, she convinced me that the issue was important enough to merit the development of a new policy and procedure. However, the audit was also a political technology for making the self-regulating *corporation*. Most of the work processes at

Acme were shaped in this ongoing translation of regulations into practices; the law became practice through the intervention of the audit.

In general, the concern with compliance at Acme created an intense focus on issues of process and developing standardized, documentable procedures. The intent of the law on provider credentialing was to keep unqualified and sanctioned providers out of the health plan's network. In its implementation, however, the law's purpose was overshadowed by a concern with demonstrating and performing compliance. The organizational resources and time that staff focused on creating documentation, responding to audits, and developing policies and procedures largely replaced discussions about the content or intent of the rules.[13]

Regulating through Audit

Throughout this book, I argue that privatization must be understood as the reformulation, not retraction, of government. Though Medicare Advantage organizations enter into contracts with CMS to offer coordinated care plans under Medicare, it would be a mistake to see this as the selling off of Medicare to private companies who can then do as they like. CMS regulations touch on almost all aspects of the plan. The law mandates how plans must manage certain key areas: enrollment and disenrollment, marketing and sales, required benefits, financing, cost sharing, and claims processing. For Medicare Advantage organizations, manuals and rules issued by CMS have the same weight as the law. Plans must ensure that they are familiar with government regulations and design processes that comply with the requirements. Every 2 years, government auditors conduct site visits to verify compliance. In between visits, the plan is expected to self-regulate through its own auditing and internal oversight.

During my fieldwork, I participated in two CMS audits, also referred to as site visits. The CMS site visit was a major event for the organization, and planning for it began at least a year in advance. The second site visit that I participated in occurred shortly after the executives mentioned earlier were fired. It was a hectic time for the organization; we had new ownership, new laws, a new prescription-drug benefit to implement, and constant turmoil surrounding the activities of the competition (the new owners were alarmed about competitors' sales agents spreading rumors that Acme beneficiaries would lose their coverage or that the company was going bankrupt). My fieldnotes capture some of the stress of that time:

> I worked all day Sunday and Saturday so this is my ninth work day in a row. Nine more to go until the site visit is over. With all of this, my boss wants letters to go out complaining about marketing violations by the other plans. He's trying to get a Senate investigation. We have a ton of marketing materials to submit to CMS for approval for Part D. And then there are the usual 20 issues a day that someone asks Compliance about. That muscle from the shoulder blade to the collar bone is tensing up again—it feels almost prickly. I hope that I don't get another tension headache.

The tension was often palpable at Acme, and I was not the only one who felt the stress of the impending site visit. Managers, supervisors, and front-line employees throughout the organization worried about how their departments would perform. One way that the Compliance Department prepared individuals at Acme for the CMS site visit was by performing mock audits that followed CMS procedures as closely as possible. We interviewed people whom CMS representatives were likely to interview and this made employees *very* nervous, especially because the interviews were in English. Sometimes in the mock interview, respondents would switch into Spanish, fidget, blank on answers (even with questions that asked them to describe how they carried out a certain process—one that the respondent did every day). One particularly nervous individual described feeling lightheaded and eventually blacking out during the mock interview.

The stress was amplified by the unpredictability of the auditors. Although auditing is ostensibly an objective process, everyone involved was acutely aware of the degree to which it relied on subjective perception in determining if the organization was compliant enough to pass the inspection. All kinds of factors can influence the success of a visit. At Acme, the weather was almost a determining factor. For example, though we were planning for the auditors who were based at the regional office in New York to come in September, they expressed an interest in coming to the island in June (citing the nice weather as an explanation). When I received the email from our plan manager stating the desire to come in June, I panicked. I asked the president of the company to intervene—CMS had to reconsider because we had been planning on September. I felt that we couldn't possibly be ready by June. The president persuaded the plan manager that the weather would be fine in September (the concern being the hurricane season) and argued that we had scheduled all of our internal efforts around a September date. These interpersonal details about performing mock interviews and communicating with the regulators capture some of the ways in which Acme navigated the regulatory relationship in order to get what it wanted. Ultimately, the visit did take place in September. Though the regulators were clearly the authority in the relationship, they could be persuaded, convinced, and swayed to behave in ways and make decisions that were favorable to Acme. The other reason I include these details is to give a sense of the momentousness of going through an audit. Many accounts of auditing that focus on higher education critique the technology itself, the way it impinges on professional autonomy, and the imposition of business logics and values on education (Shore and Wright 2000). Unlike Acme employees, academics tend to be very comfortable assuming a critical stance and many are protected by mechanisms like tenure and the expectation of academic freedom. Employees at Acme, in contrast, had much more at stake in doing well on an audit and far less critical space within which to maneuver. Poor audit findings could result in being fired, having one's department restructured, or the shame of other people knowing that one was not doing a good job. While it is crucial to critically assess how the audit worked and what it accomplished at the organization, one must also account for employees' emotional and material investment in performing well.

CMS conducts its review with audit tools that are posted on the Internet and available to the organization. The tools measure certain processes for compliance with regulatory mandates. The tools focus on items that are easily measurable and can be marked as "met" or "not met." For example, audits check time frames for completing processes (14 days to process an authorization request, 30 days to resolve a grievance) or verify that a required piece of information is included on communications with members (privacy disclosures, a description of the right to appeal if a service is denied). After tallying the results on the audit tools and reviewing all documentation, the auditors prepare a report; any item that is "not met" requires a corrective action plan. Because our internal auditing had already turned up a number of noncompliant areas (including the areas that I was responsible for managing), we were pretty worried about the upcoming visit. Executives were also concerned that Acme might be scrutinized especially rigorously because of ongoing conflicts with the CMS regional office regarding its unwillingness to investigate allegations of wrongdoing by Acme's competitors.

The auditors shared their itinerary with Acme ahead of time so that interviews could be scheduled and conference rooms reserved. The audit visit consisted of an entrance interview, review of files, interviews with key staff, and an exit interview. While auditors are on site, they may request to see whatever they like and speak with anyone. In practice, they tend to stick to a standard schedule and request additional interviews through the Compliance liaison due to time constraints and the audits that are in turn performed on the auditors. Although the audits are standardized to a certain extent, as reflected in the audit tools, in practice the experience of an audit is nerve-wracking for the organization because of the unexpected. As alluded to above, how an audit is conducted also largely depends on the auditors' personalities. In Compliance, we were concerned about who precisely would be assigned from the CMS regional office. We all had our favorites, and of course, the people whom we considered difficult and hoped would not be assigned. In the end, the team consisted of three monolingual English speakers from the New York CMS regional office and one person from the Puerto Rico office who spoke English and Spanish (the Puerto Rican office did not have any authority over the Medicare Advantage plans on the island). They were all women and we only knew one of the New York–based auditors because she was Acme's plan manager.

When the auditors arrived, we showed them to the conference room that had been set aside for their use. The room had already been outfitted with office supplies, restaurant menus, and paper files for review. It was also wired to the company's intranet where the bulk of the documentation had been uploaded for the reviewers. My role was to provide the auditors with whatever they requested—including additional documentation, workers to interview, and directions to lunch spots. I recorded in my fieldnotes that the visit was utterly exhausting and felt like a final exam. The auditors began on friendly, cordial terms, but soon each time I entered the room, I was asked to fetch additional documentation. They expressed disappointment in one of the medical management programs by describing it as superficial (in turn, the manager of this area was deeply offended). One of the auditors left the room and sought out people directly, asking for more documentation. The Compliance Department was made uneasy, because the department preferred to manage the auditors' conversations by coaching interviewees. The visit itself was hectic to monitor because there were four reviewers and sometimes two interviews occurring simultaneously. My office was set up like a war room. When someone left an interview, they were expected to come immediately to Compliance in order to debrief. The Compliance Department kept a list of all the additional documentation requested, when it was requested, by whom, and when it was delivered. A list of the auditors' hot topics was compiled and used to coach the next interviewees on what to expect and how best to respond.

The Compliance Department attempted to shape every answer and every document that the auditors encountered. The audit was not just a technology for surveillance and verification; it was also a communicative act shaped by the participants involved. Being polite and providing reviewers with whatever they requested immediately was part of the performance that Acme enacted to convince the reviewers of the organization's willingness to comply. This is an instance of what John Clarke describes as "performing performance." In his work on how privatization has transformed the welfare state in Great Britain and the United States, he argues that evaluation involves a process of co-construction and collusion between the auditors and the audited where both parties are invested in making the process appear objective (Clarke 2004, 140). Despite the pretense of going through an objective process (which was important to Acme executives as they tried to attract investors by showing positive audit results), the work of the Compliance Department was clearly premised on being able to shape, influence, and manage the audit process: "Compliance necessitates calculation—how to present the organization, how to make the fit between the organization and the evaluative categories, and how to manage the 'face-to-face' encounters of inspections, audits and site visits where they are part of the evaluative regime" (138). The Compliance Department attempted to present the organization as highly knowledgeable of the regulations, professional and polite in interpersonal interactions, and innovative in its use of technology (such as assembling most of the required documentation for the audit in electronic, rather than paper form). One error in calculation on the part of the Compliance Department was not realizing how invested the auditors were in documenting internal audits.

The Compliance Department did not initially volunteer internal audit reports as they felt this would reveal all of the organization's weaknesses to the auditors. One senior compliance staffer asked, "Why do their work for them?" However, the auditors were insistent about understanding the processes that Acme had put in place for identifying and correcting problems. Once the auditors were given a binder containing the internal audits and corrective action plans from the preceding 2 years, they were very pleased. One of the auditors mentioned that they passed the binder around at the hotel in the evening as it had something to do with each of the areas that they were responsible for. The auditors admitted that interviewees consistently spoke of how they had identified various problems (such as grievances that were not resolved within the mandated time frame), but it was only when they were able to review the audit binder that they could truly see what Acme had done to address the deficiencies.

Most of the week was spent scurrying after documents and many interviewees agreed that the reviewers had sour attitudes. They felt that some of the reviewers were sarcastic or accusatory. As the week progressed, the feeling in the Compliance Department was that the visit was a catastrophe. We felt as if a disaster was unfolding. To channel these concerns productively, we immediately began working on a corrective action plan for one of the areas where we knew there would be "not met" findings. We came to the exit interview with copies of the draft corrective action plan to present to the auditors, which showed a willingness to comply even before receiving any actual findings. Whereas I had been one of the primary people interacting with the auditors all week, this meeting included the CEO of the company, the president, and the chief medical director. To my surprise, the auditors (who were all women and the executives were all men) were suddenly charming and complimentary. They began the meeting by thanking everyone for their hospitality and spoke very favorably of the health plan. They mentioned in broad brushstrokes what their findings were but indicated that overall they were pleased with what they found. They hoped to have the audit report to us in a few weeks. They explained that they needed so many copies of things, because their work was also audited.

In this spiral of verification and oversight, the audit as a tool for documenting deficiencies was more important than the content of what was deficient. The site visit focused far more on spreading the audit as a mode of (self) regulation than evaluating the quality of medical care that was being delivered to Medicare beneficiaries through managed care arrangements. The organization responded by managing the relationship and exhibiting a willingness to comply through being polite and producing copious amounts of documentation.

Replaceable

It is difficult to reconcile the image of the runaway train that began this chapter with the systematic, bureaucratic practices of audit and oversight. And yet both aspects of Acme's dynamics coexisted—that of rapid growth and destruction as well as auditing and compliance. In some ways this juxtaposition appears contradictory. One might expect that the bureaucratic rationality created by auditing and regulation would lead to an ordered, predictable workplace. But this was not the case. Instead, auditing was concerned with process (not health outcomes), invested in maintaining good social relations, experienced as arbitrary, and the source of considerable insecurity and anxiety. In their exploration of auditing in academic settings, the anthropologists Shore and Wright (2000) explicitly link auditing to the creation of insecurity in the workplace: "the substitution of trust by measurement, the replacement of academic autonomy by management control, the deliberate attempt to engineer competition and a climate of insecurity are all features of . . . [the] disciplinary grid of audit" (78). The reliance on an audit is indicative of a lack of trust between the audited and the auditor, hence the need for oversight and verification. This lack of trust and reliance on performance monitoring likewise characterizes the relationship between employers and employees. The nervousness with which employees approached internal audits and their eagerness to demonstrate a willingness to comply demonstrated their heightened job insecurity brought about by constantly being subject to oversight and verification.

Just as the turn to more entrepreneurial forms of government has prompted a concern with auditing and governing from afar, it has also contributed to the increasing "flexibility" of privatized workplaces. Flexibility is often heralded for allowing companies to be nimble, to adapt quickly to change, and to shed dead weight. The flexible corporation is celebrated by the same people who condemn such relics as traditional government bureaucrats, union workers, or tenured teachers for expecting good benefits and secure employment. As publicly financed services are increasingly delivered by private corporations, the move is toward more job insecurity in the form of flexible and non-unionized workplaces. The effects of this transition are worth examining.

In her ethnography of Wall Street, the anthropologist Karen Ho (2009) argues that traders experience and also perpetuate a culture of volatility in which compensation is the reigning value and employees expect to be downsized or to change jobs very frequently. This Wall Street model of hyperinsecure employment has in turn become the prototype for much of corporate America. The types of workers described by Ho, however, are quite different from Acme employees on a number of levels. Personal networks become an important tool used by Wall Street traders for navigating job insecurity. Most had Ivy League educations and cultivated extensive professional networks that allowed them to effectively couple insecurity with mobility and opportunity in a way that was not available for most of the downsized or fired employees from Acme whom I spoke with. On Wall Street, insecurity is high, but so is compensation. The majority of employees at Acme, however, made wages that did not afford a financial buffer for surviving periods of unemployment. Further, in Puerto Rico, steady, middle-class employment is hard to come by (roughly half of the population lives below the poverty line) and the headhunters and placement services that Ho encountered were far more rare. Working at Acme afforded many employees a middle-class existence that included health insurance and a 401k retirement savings account (though very few employees opted to pay into the 401k plan). Within months of beginning their jobs, several Compliance employees bought their first homes or new cars—obviously not imagining that their continued ability to make the mortgage or car payment was so precarious. Being fired was a personally and financially devastating event for most Acme employees and was not an accepted part of the work culture as it has become on Wall Street.

The casualness with which the management shed jobs at Acme became a frequent, if hushed, topic of conversation around the office. I was told in interviews in 2009 that after a merger, whole departments were just let go only to be re-created months later. A high-level employee revealed that she was constantly worried that she would be fired next; she planned to eat bread and water until she was eligible for Social Security because she was not willing to leave the island and viewed her prospects of being hired anywhere else as slim, given her age and high rank. Whereas Ho's informants referenced the ups and downs of the market to make sense of the insecurity of their own jobs, Acme employees did not use such abstract analytic explanations. Instead, I was told that the company was completely crazy, the most recent CEO was simply mean and would fire people if he was in a bad mood, and that the American-based owners were too rough and did not understand people. As evidence of this "roughness" one worker added that the American owners even scheduled meetings on Good Friday. This act was understood as the height of cultural insensitivity and met with disbelief by some employees.

In 2009, I interviewed Irene, an Acme executive, who explained how the firings affected the climate at the office. She said that there was no tolerance any longer for mistakes and that she felt very insecure in her job: "I have expressed it to the human resources vice president. A lot of people feel that way, but they will not talk. People are afraid to talk." One of the most difficult aspects of the firings was that they were often done for no apparent reason:

> Some people were terminated and they were just told "you are terminated." They were not even given a reason. Do you know how sad that is? Because if I have a reason, tell me why, then I'm OK with it. If you have

identified that I'm not doing something correct, then tell me how to do it correct. That's what I do with employees when I terminate them. I have terminated employees. But you try for them to modify, to improve. . . . I know a person that was very sick for several months. I mean, this person needed health care. This person had to go to a psychologist and needed care because this person was so committed to that company. Came in early. Worked long hours. Even Saturdays. And she was not given a reason. She was just terminated.

Irene explained that the terminated employee, who was also an executive, was probably given 6 months' pay when she was fired: "But even that money doesn't make up for the suffering. There is no money that makes up for that. There just isn't."

Employees expected that hard work and loyalty would be recognized and protected at the organization. Irene and others I spoke with had trouble making sense of the meaninglessness and randomness of being fired "without cause"; they found the indiscriminate firings unconscionable, not the inevitable result of market forces like a downturn. Many fired employees struggled with depression and found it very difficult to move on. Some took years to find new jobs.

The examples above involve people who were fired "without cause," but it was also common to be fired with cause. As a manager, I felt pressure to fire people who did not produce at a high level (i.e., did not close enough appeals cases) or who behaved in ways that did not fit the company (sometimes with the vague condemnation that they just didn't get it). Paloma was an example of the latter. A sensitive, unusually quiet young woman, she worked as an appeals and grievance coordinator. Paloma lived with and cared for her own disabled mother and tended to empathize with members' complaints. Unlike her more fashion-conscious colleagues, Paloma wore loose, boxy shirts and skirts. Her cubicle was decorated with pictures of animals. She often daydreamed, failing to find expeditious ways to close grievance cases. After she accumulated several warnings (and hence suspected that a termination was imminent), Paloma left Acme of her own volition. Her inability to fit in and to treat members as cases to be resolved made her particularly vulnerable to being fired "with cause."

One Saturday, the Human Resources department hired consultants to give a required workshop to middle managers on how to discipline, document, and fire employees. The consultants were labor lawyers and delivered their training session dressed in formal suits. Their slides and handouts quoted employment laws and gave the impression that firing is an action of last resort and must be justified. Conversations during the training, however, emphasized that documentation—not having a just cause—was the most important component of the termination process. Anyone could be fired, we were assured, as long as there was documentation and no evidence of discrimination. When I returned from this training, I soon learned that I had interpreted it too literally. My boss warned me not to document so much. If you look hard enough, you can always find something, she said. And if you document it all, then you may quickly find that you have to take some kind of disciplinary action, even if it's not really merited. One should exercise discretion when documenting, she warned.

Managers and workers struggled to navigate this flexible space. Much office talk was dedicated to trying to figure out whether terminations were made with or without cause. Was there justification? Was it arbitrary? The commonplaceness of firings created an insecure environment and eroded trust and social cohesion. To counteract this, the management made claims that the corporation was like a family, clearly forgetting that it is very difficult to fire one's family.

The upper management was able to create a flexible, unstable work environment because Acme was a private HMO, workers were not organized, and they believed that people were replaceable. The bigger picture was one of mergers and acquisitions in which the primary importance was to increase revenue by acquiring more "covered lives," which is insurance-speak for a subscriber or health plan member. The objective was to collect as much in monthly premiums as possible from the federal government. A fast way to do this was to purchase a competitor and thereby acquire all of their covered lives. What happened to the workers who were also acquired in these buyouts was of secondary importance.

Derailing the Train

This chapter began with a warning from an Acme executive: do not let yourself be struck down by a runaway train. I have tried to show that this careening, out-of-control machine was made through deliberate policy choices and government regulation.

In the most direct sense, Acme was legislated into being. It was made possible by legislation that authorizes payment to private managed care organizations in exchange for providing Medicare services to beneficiaries. Regulation was also an ongoing activity—CMS, the federal agency that oversees the Medicare program, was charged with ensuring that managed care organizations under contract with it complied with the law and delivered Medicare services according to established rules. CMS regulated through audits and the electronic exchange of data with the plan. The plan in turn self-regulated by training employees to be agents of compliance and by mimicking the same oversight practices of audit, constant documentation, and corrective action plans used by CMS. Finally, regulation was also an imminently social process in which rules were selectively followed, the performance of the audit was more important than actual audit findings, and the difference between being in or out of compliance often hinged on maintaining good social relations.

This ethnographic encounter with auditing and oversight provokes a number of policy questions. Is the system of auditing that structures daily life at Medicare Advantage organizations a good use of regulators' and HMO administrators' time? Is this costly system of arm's length-control the best way to administer Medicare funds (recall that Medicare Advantage is 13% more expensive on the mainland and 180% more expensive in Puerto Rico than Original Medicare, which operates with no HMO intermediary)? Are other methods of accountability possible that focus more on content and care rather than on process and data elements that are easily quantifiable? And, finally, particularly in a time of high unemployment and the transformation of the job market toward lower-paid, less-secure positions, should government programs be contributing to the kind of job creation described here that is incredibly insecure and volatile? In other words, can we imagine other options beyond getting on the train or being run down?

By focusing on how Acme was made, rather than solely on its out-of-control growth and constant transformation, one realizes that this system was crafted through policy and ongoing regulation, and as such it can be unmade or reformed. The executive who spoke to the Acme managers did not last much longer at the company, nor did I. In a sense, we were both run down. But that destruction can spur new beginnings.

3

New Consumer Citizens

Life Histories

In addition to the time I spent working at Acme—avoiding getting fired, preparing for audits, and creating policies for putting papers in a file—I also wrote to Acme members and asked if I could interview them. I was received into homes all over the island where Acme members answered intimate questions about illness, disability, how they were brought up, and their economic struggles. This chapter recounts some of what I learned from listening to their stories.

In life history interviews, I asked Acme members how they made sense of the changing health system and how they understood their own roles as consumers, patients, and citizens. Though market reformers imagine Medicare recipients as calculating, decision-making health care consumers, this vision of the health care consumer is not a reflection of the world as it is; instead it is a projection of how neoliberal policy makers would like it to be. In practice, market-based health policy failed to transform patients, family members, workers, and citizens seamlessly into neoliberal health care consumers in Puerto Rico. This chapter offers a number of explanations why. First, compared to the mainland, market reforms came relatively late to Puerto Rico and the government had a larger symbolic and functional role in caring for the sick and poor. Second, the model of the decision-making consumer does not account for the moral and social criteria that people actually employ when making decisions about their health care. Third, the able-bodied, individualistic assumptions underwriting the notion of the health care consumer are out of place in describing how people react to and experience illness, disability, and dependency. Fourth, the "choices" that consumers can actually make regarding their care are quite limited.

Becoming Private Consumers of Publicly Financed Care

Users of health care services are increasingly called upon to act more like consumers: they are expected to make informed choices, seek out quality services, demand competition, and employ marketplace criteria like efficiency and cost-effectiveness to evaluate services (Tomes and Hoffman 2011).[1] The contemporary emphasis on being a health care consumer must be understood within the context of market-based reform projects aimed at downsizing the role of the state, creating more choice for recipients of public programs, and redesigning public service provision according to private enterprise models.

As discussed in previous chapters, the 2003 Medicare Moderniza-tion Act (MMA) shaped the care available to Medicare beneficiaries in Puerto Rico by extending the role of private managed care organi-zations and private prescription-drug plans within the Medicare pro-gram. In the speech he gave while signing the MMA into law, former President George W. Bush ascribed to Medicare beneficiaries wants, desires, and habits characteristic of consumers:

> We're giving our seniors more health care choices so they can get the coverage and care that meets their needs. Every senior needs to know, if you don't want to change your current coverage, you don't have to change. You're the one in charge. If you want to keep your Medicare the way it is, along with the new prescription benefit that is your right. If you want improved benefits, maybe dental coverage, eyeglass coverage, man-aged care plans that reduce out of pocket costs, you'll be free to make those choices as well. And when seniors have the ability to make choices, health care plans within Medicare will have to compete for their busi-ness by offering higher quality service. For the seniors of America, more choices and more control will mean better health care. (Bush 2003)

This brief quote contains the central assumptions of neoliberal health policies: consumers want choices and when they can make choices in a competitive marketplace, the health system improves. The decision-making consumer is the linchpin that holds the system together. "You're the one in charge," Bush says. In a telling oversight, Bush referred to Medicare recipients exclusively as "seniors" and did not mention the disabled.[2] This is an example of how neoliberal policy makers tend to ignore disability and dependency in favor of able-bodied conceptions of calculating consumers.

The neoliberal view that consumer choice is the foundation on which the health system is built is echoed in statements from insurance industry leaders. In a piece in the *New York Times* discussing the new Medicare legislation, Karen Ignagni, the president and chief executive of America's Health Insurance Plans (AHIP), stated:

> During the 1990's, Americans decisively rejected a single-payer system. They were concerned about the rationing of care, endless delays and lack of access to state-of-the-art procedures experienced in countries with government-run systems. . . . Americans deserve a real health care debate and real solutions, starting with evidence-based medicine, medical liability reform and the information they need to make better decisions. (2005)

In his speech, Bush asserts that seniors want more choices. Ignagni claims that a collective decision was made in the United States and that Americans chose the current market system. Both Bush and Ignagni place freely choosing consumers at the center of their vision of the health system. But who are these consumers? How and under what conditions do they make choices? Do they feel "in charge" when they interact with insurance companies and medical practitioners? What are the differences between how policy makers understand consumers and how recipients of publicly financed health services experience and understand themselves?

In practice, both consumers and citizens are "more contingent, contested and contradictory figures than their conventional depiction might allow" (Clarke et al. 2007, 6; see also Gabriel and Lang 2006). In order to understand how people actually make sense of the roles they are called on to perform and the choices they are compelled to make in the wake of market-based health care reforms, it is important to analyze speeches and policy documents, as well as the practices through which policies are implemented and experienced.[3] This chapter explores how the elderly and disabled Medicare beneficiaries whom I interviewed relate to new discourses on being a consumer of medical care and a client of insurance companies within the larger context of their life trajectories. I focus here on "choices" that Acme beneficiaries made regarding how they cared for themselves, the doctors they consulted, and the treatments that they followed (in chapter 6, I explore the "choice" of joining a private health plan). For the individuals I interviewed, more choice and more information were not their priorities. They coped with losing their sense of purpose as they aged and became less mobile, expressed disappointment in the substandard care they received from public and private facilities alike, and strived to get by on very little. They may have acted as consumers when they chose to enroll in a private Medicare health plan, but the term "consumer" does not come close to exhausting the roles they played and the ways they talked about their own relationships to their health and the health care system.

Interviewing "Consumers"

Over a period of 18 months in the mid-2000s, I conducted 35 life history interviews with 44 individuals who were enrolled in Acme, a private managed care plan contracted to provide Medicare services to eligible beneficiaries (at some of the interviews, more than one individual participated). In order to recruit study participants, I asked the IT department at Acme to generate a random sample of members from the membership database. I sent each member on the list a letter that explained my project, and I followed up with a phone call asking if they would like to be interviewed. I disclosed in the letter, on the phone, and before the interview that I was an employee at Acme and an anthropologist. I explained that the interview would not affect the care that the members were receiving and that they could refuse to participate at any time. All but two interviews took place in the interviewees' homes. The interviews were transcribed by a professional transcriber and translator in Puerto Rico and then translated and edited by me. Pseudonyms are used for interviewees. (For a fuller description of the interview methodology, the human subjects review process, and ethical considerations, see appendix 1.)

About half of the 35 semistructured interviews took place in the San Juan metropolitan area and half took place in other areas of the island. (Appendix 2 contains a complete list of each interview location and demographic details about each interviewee.) Interviewees met Medicare enrollment criteria: they qualified by disability or age (65 and older). I interviewed 22 men and 22 women. Of the interviewees, 68% were over 65 and 32% were younger than 65; 36% were currently on La Reforma, 18% had previously been on La Reforma, and 43% had never been on La Reforma (2% had unknown Reforma status). Though the sample was generated randomly, this is by no means a representative sample of Medicare beneficiaries in Puerto Rico. My intention was not to account for every municipality or every possible variation in income level, religious background, occupation, health status, and so on. Instead, my purpose was to understand the diverse ways in which particular elderly and disabled Puerto Ricans had created meaning from their experiences with the health care system.

Like all formal interviews, these conversations occurred in unusual situations. By "unusual," I mean that I, as a stranger, asked participants to reflect on their lives in terms they were probably not accustomed to and by using categories that did not always resonate. For example, questions about "quality of care" were usually met with some confusion (see chapter 5 for a discussion about how interviewees discussed "quality"). One of the most revealing interviews took place with Teresa Ramírez, whose story I recount later in this chapter. She formerly worked middle-class jobs and was university educated. Through years of psychotherapy and her more recent work as an activist for the mentally ill, she had crafted a nuanced way to talk about her experiences and had developed her own analysis of the health care system. For most of the respondents, however, our conversation probably resembled a social service interview. As many were beneficiaries of means-tested programs like La Reforma, they were accustomed to answering questions about their income, health status, and personal affairs.

Interviews are always both constrained and enabled by the subject positions of the interviewer and the interviewee. Things we feel comfortable revealing to some people, we may conceal from others. In her interviews with working-class residents of the Puerto Rican municipality of San Sebastián, the anthropologist Gina Pérez (2004) found that her family ties to the area both opened research avenues and imposed constraints on who and how she could talk to residents. Working at her aunt's store, for example, gave her access to masculine domains that otherwise might not have been available to her as a woman who was born *afuera* (off the island). As such, she occupied a hybrid insider/outsider position that was accentuated by her unmarried status and educational background (26–28). Conversely, Puerto Rican informants whom Pérez interviewed in Chicago were sometimes hesitant to invite her into their homes given their class differences and worries they might be judged or considered less than respectable if she saw their modest living situations.

I cannot know for sure how my subject position influenced the way that interviewees responded to me. Surely they omitted details and wove their narratives in response to my subject position. When I first arrived in people's houses, before the formal interview began, we invariably discussed my background and where I was from. In these conversations, I tried to convey my interest in how the health care system had changed since privatization, and I revealed my own personal connections to the island. All told, I lived and worked in Puerto Rico for more than 3 years. At the time, I was married to a Puerto Rican man and interviewees were always interested in my marriage and my relationship with his family. Though I expected respondents to be concerned that I was an Acme employee, they seemed more interested in my family situation; they wanted to know where I met my husband and what my mother thought of the fact that I was still in school and did not have children even though I was almost 30. As an outsider, I missed some cultural references and did not know all the names of local herbal remedies for illnesses. This was problematic, but my outsider status also conferred certain privileges. People were probably not as concerned about demonstrating standards of respectability around sensitive issues like divorce, extramarital affairs, and disability. Nor were they worried that what they told me would find its way into local gossip circuits.

For the purpose of this chapter, I retell the stories of three people. They are not the most typical or representative stories. As with many life history interviews (Behar 1993; Crapanzano 1980; Mintz 1974), I have focused on some of the most eloquent respondents because they articulated their stories in a way that was compelling and revealed something important about what happens when one gets sick before and after market-based health reforms. The three stories I retell here emphasize some of the problems experienced by low-income beneficiaries in accessing adequate care in a privatized delivery system.

For interviewees who retired after working in the formal sector or who had a spouse who did, paid into Social Security, belonged to a union, and/or received a pension, the health system worked pretty well. These interviewees were the most satisfied with their care—they included Doña Fátima (interview 10, discussed in chapter 6), Don Octavio (interview 14), Don Julián and his wife, Doña Adoración (interview 26), Doña Eduarda (interview 29), Doña Bárbara (interview 30, discussed in chapter 1), and Don Felix (interview 32). These beneficiaries were also the best off economically and had few, if any, mental health needs. They maintained a higher standard of living and had enough disposable income to make their medication copays. They also had access to transportation for their medical appointments and prior experience with private insurance. Don Octavio, for example, was both a veteran and a retiree of the telephone company, which in Puerto Rico is considered a well-paid job with generous benefits. His employment history meant that he was eligible for a variety of supports in retirement including veterans' health benefits, a pension, Medicare, and Social Security. He owned his modest home and a car. He also described himself as healthy and liked his private Medicare plan. In sum, those with the fewest problems using the privatized system also tended to be better off economically, more educated, and had family supports to assist them in getting to appointments, navigating the health bureaucracy, and obtaining their prescription medications.

But for those who were disabled, had mental health needs, did not work in the formal sector, or did not pay into Social Security (because they were homemakers, owned their own businesses, or worked in agriculture) they struggled to make ends meet and to obtain adequate care. I focus on the latter stories here. If market-based programs work less well for people who are more vulnerable, it is important to understand how and why.

In retelling these "illness narratives," I have tried as much as possible to leave the stories in the words of the interviewees. However, I also frequently interject in order to clarify the interviewee's "model for arranging experiences in meaningful ways" (Kleinman 1988, 49) and to link the stories to the sociopolitical changes that reshaped health and health care in Puerto Rico over the course of the interviewees' lives.

In several cases, the interviewee called on me not to forget their stories, not to go back to the university and forget what was happening to them. Though this chapter is inadequate to that call, it is written in that spirit.[4]

Don Anastasio: Work as Health

Don Anastasio and his wife of 46 years lived in a two-story white house that had formerly belonged to his in-laws. The cement house clung to a green hill in a rural sector of Trujillo Alto where rocky, uneven terrain kept the upscale housing developments at bay. Inside, the floors were brown painted cement and the ornate furniture was covered in plastic. The house was clean and spare, though the white paint on the walls and ceiling swelled with moisture. We talked over the whirr from the standing fan and occasional downpours of rain.

At the time of the interview, Don Anastasio was 64. He portrayed his youth as a time of vigor, good health, and a close relationship with the natural world. He described an idyllic rural upbringing where money was scarce but food was abundant—he assured me that wounds healed more quickly in the past. As an adult, he boasted about his strength and tenacity as a worker. He lamented that he was forced to retire before he was ready when his eyes and legs failed him.

Over the course of his life, Don Anastasio received medical care in each of Puerto Rico's health systems: the regional health system in his youth, an employer-based plan as an adult, and through La Reforma and a Medicare HMO upon retiring. During the life history interview, Don Anastasio explained how he navigated these changing systems; I focus here on "choices" he made about his health care, his self-presentation as a worker rather than a consumer, and the association he made between work and health.

Don Anastasio grew up in the interior of the island, near Caguas. In those days, he claimed, people got sick less frequently. Months and years would go by without illness. He explained how things used to be:

> In those days, people were raised to be healthy. Well, one went to the hospital, was treated and prescribed something. The cost of living wasn't what it is now because before you would pay the doctor and the doctor would say pay only if there's money, if not, you wouldn't pay anything. Now it's not like that, now you have to pay.
>
> And if someone cut themselves at home, when they stuck themselves with a nail, anything like that, one didn't go to the hospital. I remember. I once sliced my foot open, right here. And my dad what he did was grab the leaves of a guava tree, chewed them and then he put them on me and tied them with a bandage. And by the next day when I woke up, the wound was closed. Nowadays, no one does that. But if it was a really bad injury, they would take you to the hospital, yes for really big cuts. There they would sew you up and send you back home. They wouldn't keep you in the hospital. The doctors, what they would do if they had to was go to your house. Well, that's how one would go through life.

According to Don Anastasio, medical care during his youth was less mediated by the cash economy. Doctors were only consulted in very serious cases and accepted payment only if the family had the ability to pay. Home visits by physicians were common and one did not go to the hospital for minor cuts and colds. Medical care was also less necessary because people knew the curing properties of plants and herbs. He described many *remedios caseros* (home remedies)[5] for an assortment of common ills: headaches, digestive problems, and colds.

A cold, for example, was easily cured with cod liver oil. It was tough to get down, but it knocked the cold and fever out. The next day he could swim in the river. Boys in those days were peaceful and hardworking, he explained. They drew water from the well and gathered firewood. Even if he woke up feeling sick, by the time he returned home with a stack of firewood, he felt fine.

Don Anastasio's narrative was upbeat and optimistic; he transformed a question about illness into a reminiscence about accomplishing household chores and playing in the river. This stands in contrast to the multiple complications that Don Anastasio was currently experiencing from his diabetes and the seriousness with which diabetics must treat minor cuts and ailments. As a boy, good health was associated with productive work and physical activity.

We know from other sources that the Puerto Rico of Don Anastasio's youth (the 1940s and early 1950s) was also a time of political transformation, rural to urban migration, industrialization, and economic dislocation.[6] More than a realist depiction of how things were, Don Anastasio's story is interesting in the way that the distant past is framed in relation to the present.[7] He described his youth as a simpler time of working in agriculture and respect for one's family. Don Anastasio talked about how healthy life was then; the family ate viandas[8] and grew their own food on his father's finca. He also described life as less isolated—there were parties with neighbors during the zafra[9] when they roasted a pig, played the cuatro, and sang.

His memories of a close relationship to nature were tempered by a sense of loss over a falling out with his father over going to college. He cut cane and saved money to pay for his studies, but when he went to get the money from the bank to study engineering in Mayagüez, it had been spent on one of his siblings. At that point, he moved in with his grandmother and began looking for work.

Like many Puerto Ricans during this time period, Don Anastasio did not follow his father's example and make his living from agriculture. He left the countryside to work in the wage labor force. At 18, he married and moved in with his wife's family in Trujillo Alto. His working years (43 years from about 1959 until his retirement in 2002) were spent laboring at a variety of jobs such as an electrician, truck driver, and operator of heavy machinery.[10]

For Don Anastasio, becoming disabled was a struggle against the realities of aging and was particularly difficult for a man accustomed to doing physical labor well. In his mid-fifties, he missed his first day of work for illness. He remembered the incident vividly. His leg began swelling uncontrollably so he went to the hospital in Carolina where the doctor diagnosed cellulitis and wanted to amputate immediately. Don Anastasio asked for 20 minutes to think it over and then he left the hospital. His leg was so swollen that his pants could barely contain it. He went to Centro Médico—the largest medical center on the island that is also affiliated with the University of Puerto Rico—where they operated and were able to save his leg. Don Anastasio still sees the doctor who saved his leg at Centro Médico. His physicians advised him to go on disability after this incident, but Don Anastasio returned to work.

Six years later in 2002, he finally decided to retire. At the time, he worked with heavy machinery in Culebra clearing the tops off hills,[11] but his legs wouldn't allow him to push the controls on the machine anymore. He described the moment he decided to retire:

> I started to knock down a mountain, but my feet were not helping me, I had to give up work because you have to push down on the clutch really hard and the machine was just too big, enormous. Every time I was going to make a cut I had to look through some mirrors to see the tips of the blade and my vision was not helping me. That's when I decided to retire. That was in 2002, around then. I left home one day in the morning to go to work, on the fifth of April, I left for work and when I got to the workshop, my work had to do with the workshop, I saw that I was losing my vision. And everything was hurting, everything. And I said: "Man, this is how it is. Now's the time."

He called his American boss and told her what has happening. She gave him the address of a doctor and told him to go there, that she would pay for it, but Don Anastasio insisted that he would use his Reforma card even though it meant that he would have to chase down referrals and authorizations for his care.[12] Don Anastasio recalled that he retired on the 5th of April. This was the only instance in the interview where an event was associated with a specific date. Don Anastasio insisted that he chose when to retire and where he would receive treatment. He was already in his 60s when this happened and he went on Social Security for disability shortly thereafter.

Don Anastasio described his retirement as a loss of autonomy and purpose. He continued to wake up every morning before dawn as if he were going to head off to work.

> I have always gotten up at two in the morning and I've continued waking up at two in the morning. I haven't broken that habit. I get up at two, I go and brush my teeth, I read the newspaper. . . . She leaves for work and I

stay here sitting out on the porch until the sun comes up. That's how it is, it's been very difficult.

Earlier he had mentioned that his eyesight was impaired, that he could barely see me and only registered shadows. So, stating that he got up at two in the morning to read the newspaper was more a gesture of self-presentation than a testament to his daily habits. It speaks to the importance of work discipline in his life—he did not want his retirement to be seen as sloth or laziness. At this point in the interview, the nostalgic stories from his youth about working outside and attending family parties gave way to melancholy. His body was succumbing to age. I asked if he became depressed after retiring and he answered:

> I guess I would have to say yes. For me, yes. It's really hard when one is used to working. I tried, I tried to do things, but I just couldn't. And then, they told me about the, the losing my balance and I'm here by myself and sometimes I fall and have to get myself back up. That's why I hardly ever go out to the yard. I almost never go out to the yard, or if I do, I sit down over there and then come back inside. They hung a hammock for me in the garage, but the last few times I went out to the hammock, I always fell right there.

He could not leave the house for fear of falling. He was no longer the breadwinner in the household while his wife was still working. She left during the day and he did his best to take care of himself. I asked if he visited his relatives often or if they came to see him. But he said that he cannot go out much anymore due to his inability to ambulate well and so sometimes he receives visitors, but not often. Usually, he sits alone in his home all day while his wife is away at work.

In old age, Don Anastasio complained of a lonely, solitary existence. However, he was largely content with the medical care that he was receiving and was knowledgeable about plan rules and how to navigate the managed care system. He enrolled in a Medicare HMO after seeing an advertisement on television and calling the number. He stated that he was extremely satisfied with the service that he was receiving; he paid very little out of pocket and still used La Reforma to cover his medications. His initial experiences with La Reforma were difficult, especially with the enrollment process: many of his doctors did not take it, and it was hard to obtain referrals to specialists such as when he needed to have his eyes operated on. Yet he preferred both the Medicare HMO and La Reforma to the private health plan that he had while employed, because the copayments and deductibles were so high—he cited $15 every time he went for an office visit. He could name his primary care physician and said that he sees him once a month, sometimes every 15 days. The one instance where he was not satisfied with care was in a public hospital (Carolina) when he almost had his leg amputated. Instead, he left the hospital and went to another public hospital, Centro Médico, where they were able to save his leg.

He had been taking insulin for 30 years and was initially diagnosed with diabetes when he lived briefly in the United States.[13] To control his diabetes, he took insulin twice a day but sometimes when he has cravings for food that he should not have, he eats it anyway. He said that this has not cost him much. He tries not to eat salt and fat and said that he eats a lot of salad. He takes one medication for his high blood pressure and another so as not to retain water. The only care that he was not currently receiving that he thought necessary was diabetic shoes.

Research in the United States with retired and disabled veterans with diabetes showed a similar orientation toward work in the management of diabetes—the anthropologist Steve Ferzacca terms this "a humoral biology that marks health as work, productivity, and self-discipline" (2000, 37). In Ferzacca's study, the reintroduction of work discipline through self-care was an annoyance to study participants. For Don Anastasio, self-care was not an annoyance; it represented a disruption from his productive life. He experienced his illness as an inability to work and so there was a confluence of good, productive, and healthy versus ill, nonproductive, and diabetic.[14] In the first few minutes that I spoke with him, he told me that he had never been unemployed in Puerto Rico.

Don Anastasio spent his life engaged in physical labor. He harvested cane, laid power lines, and bulldozed hills. He was a product of and contributed to the economic and political transformations that remade the island in the second half of the twentieth century. Yet even after a productive life in a two-income household, he still qualified for benefits through La Reforma. In other words, his income was still below 200% of the poverty line. His dream of class mobility through higher education never materialized as he worked to support his family. However, his children have gone on to service-related jobs and his wife worked for a medical supply company.

If Don Anastasio is a health care consumer, he is also a former worker, a diabetic, a thwarted engineer, and a solitary person confined to the house. Don Anastasio did not behave in ways predicted by neoliberal health policy. He had fond memories of the health system from his boyhood when household remedies were common and medical care was not all about money. As an adult, he spoke of himself not as a consumer, but as a former worker. As shown by the quotes from George W. Bush and Karen Ignagni that opened this chapter, creating more choices for beneficiaries is an essential aspect of neoliberal health reform. Don Anastasio did make several important choices about his medical care. However, the degree to which these were market-based choices remains unclear. In part, Don Anastasio was interpolated as a health care consumer: he enrolled in a plan, learned how to navigate the managed care system, and walked away from a hospital when he thought that something else could be done to save his leg. He described his decision to leave the hospital in Carolina, however, as the product of fear and an instinct for self-preservation rather than the result of carefully weighing costs and benefits. Ironically for proponents of marked-based care, his other choices took him to the public system and away from private-plan choices where his out-of-pocket costs would be higher. He engaged in self-care (taking insulin and changing his diet), but only to a point, and did not follow his doctor's advice to retire or to amputate his leg. The choices that seemed to matter most to Don Anastasio involved autonomy in his working life and specifically that he—not a medical condition, not doctors, not his employer—would decide when he could no longer work.

Doña Carmen: Caring for the New Health Consumers

Don Anastasio recalled the health system from his childhood in nostalgic terms—herbal remedies were common, healthy food was more readily available, and curing did not depend on only money. Doña

Carmen's story, in contrast, was devoid of nostalgia. She was profoundly disappointed in the health system, the government, and herself.

Doña Carmen was the primary caretaker for her two sons, Manuel (43) and Enrique (44), who were diagnosed with schizophrenia. For 30 years, she had struggled to access appropriate and effective treatment for her sons. Their current treatment consisted primarily of regularly scheduled "med checks" with their psychiatrists who were in private practice and who accepted the Medicare HMO and Reforma insurance plans. Doña Carmen explained that to obtain treatment for her sons, "*siempre ha habido algo con el gobierno* [there has always been something with the government]." Doña Carmen was well aware of the government's role in providing and paying for her sons' health care services. But with that recognition came responsibility—when she was unable to obtain adequate care for her sons, she held the government and not just herself accountable.

Doña Carmen lived in a Section 8 apartment on the second story of a cement house in Villa Carolina.[15] Villa Carolina consisted of block after block of cement houses packed up against one another: lettered houses on numbered streets with only an occasional sign to help decipher the code. I doubled back so many times that it felt like I was driving on windy mountain roads rather than in the concrete grid of an urban housing development.

Doña Carmen let her sons smoke one cigarette an hour. She kept the pack of cigarettes in her pocket and handed them out when it was time, though she didn't check a watch. Manuel, her younger son, asked at least two or three times before she gave him one. Her older son, Enrique, was more responsive. He asked a lot of questions, insisting that I was a doctor whom he had met previously. Manuel hardly spoke. Doña Carmen said that the only thing he knew how to talk about was cigarettes. On other topics, he could not respond. Or, if you asked him something, his answer would be unrelated to the question. We sat on the front porch drinking juice while her sons watched television inside. It was summer and mangoes were in season. Toward the end of the interview, Doña Carmen's sister came over and Manuel went down to the car and picked up a box full of mangoes.

The story of her sons' illness was intertwined with the dissolution of her nuclear family, the loss of her husband's livelihood through gambling debts, and the murder of her youngest child when he was 18. At the time when her son was murdered, Doña Carmen had left her husband and was living with a close female relative. The death affected her opinion of herself as a mother and is perhaps related to her total devotion to her two disabled sons: "*descuidé a mis hijos, te digo que yo tuve culpa en esa parte . . . además de la enfermedad de Manuel fue la otra cosa que nos destruyó* [I neglected my sons, I have to tell you that I am guilty of that . . . besides Manuel's illness, that was the other thing that destroyed us]."

Manuel's story (as told by his mother) was also linked to state institutions and their inability to honor the trust put in them by common citizens.[16] When Manuel was 14 and in the ninth grade, he started skipping school and was not focused on his studies. Doña Carmen's neighbor at the time suggested that she enroll him in Job Corps.[17] Doña Carmen thought that Job Corps would offer more structure, keep him in school, and eventually lead to a job opportunity. Manuel had to be at the school all week but could come home on the weekend.

In retrospect, Doña Carmen said she should have known better than to leave him at that school. She described a generalized sense of delinquency at the school and in the country at large in those years (1973 and 1974). The kids in Job Corps could not be trusted, she claimed, because they had no parents. She lamented leaving her son at a place where the children were disobedient and out of control.

A week after leaving Manuel at the school, she was told to come pick him up:

> They said you need to come and pick up your son because he is crazy, crazy. That's the word the nurse used when she came to my house, or the social worker. And, well, you can imagine, when she said that, it destroyed my soul because I took him somewhere that was supposed to make him better, and they made him sick.

Doña Carmen took Manuel to the doctor who said that Manuel had ingested acid. The doctor began treating her son and she was instructed to leave him at the Clínica Juliá (a private in-patient psychiatric facility).[18]

Doña Carmen blamed herself for putting her son in a school where this could happen to him. However, she also ascribed the onset of his condition to outside forces. She claimed that some boys at the school gave her son a cup of coffee that had been laced with LSD. I asked if she thought that genetics might have contributed to both of her sons being diagnosed with schizophrenia and she said, no, her oldest son was poisoned as well. Her eldest son got sick at a time when he frequented bars where LSD could be slipped into a drink. Schizophrenia was something that had been done to her family, not a condition they carried with them in their DNA or an illness that recurred in the family. She also related it to a generalized sense of disorder and delinquency that gripped the country at that time. In the anthropologist Kim Hopper's (1991) work on the cross-cultural study of psychiatry (which focused on schizophrenia), he summarizes Janis Jenkins's research with Mexican Americans in Southern California: "Relatives were found to embrace more than one belief about the problem, and they did so in tentative, even contradictory terms, making it all but impossible to classify their responses as belonging to any one category" (315). Likewise, Doña Carmen did not ascribe to a single cause—an amalgam of delinquency, drug use, and malicious acts triggered the onset of schizophrenia in her son.[19]

When Manuel was hospitalized, his condition only worsened. The treatment that Manuel received at the hospital further provoked Doña Carmen to lose trust in the institutions that were supposed to be caring for her son:

There were a lot of veterans at that time and this clinic was full of veterans, and, well, no one gave them permission, but they smoked a lot of cigarettes. And my son, he's crazy about cigarettes, they seem like they've been smoking their whole lives, since he was 14. So when I went to go see my son, he was covered in burns. He had made a cross here [she pointed to her forehead], here [to the mouth, on lips], here, here [to both cheeks] and like this [to the chest], even here behind [to the back]. And, well, his face, I looked at it and looked at it and he was . . . and I, oh God, I couldn't believe the condition that he was in. Well, my husband got so enraged, and he said I can't understand how it's possible that here there is so little supervision of the patients, how can it be that he's been burned like that. The only thing they told us was that if we were not satisfied, that there were not enough people to supervise him and, well, they told us if you are not satisfied, look, unfortunately, we're going to have to discharge him and you'll have to find another clinic to take him to.

This is one example from the many she mentioned in which treatment proved more harmful than therapeutic for Manuel. At that time, there were no inpatient psychiatric facilities for adolescents in Puerto Rico. Therefore, Manuel was mixed in with a general population, with many veterans, and his safety could not be guaranteed. When the family complained, they were told that Manuel should be discharged. The family decided to care for Manuel at home rather than leave him in a hospital or clinic where he could inflict harm upon himself or be negatively impacted by the other patients.

And so we took him home and that was really terrible because that night he was so disoriented and he wanted to kill himself, he wanted to cut his penis off because he said that he had, he had disrespected God. I don't know how, but in his mind that's what he thought. And it was a question of, well, we spoke to a friend who knew a doctor that could treat him. So then we brought him to Golden Gate in Guaynabo. And in Guaynabo, this man treated him well, he stayed and talked with him for hours, he had time, he didn't have, how do you say, time like doctors do now that they speak to you for a moment and then take out the prescription already filled out. Well, no, he had time for the boy. And, look, thank God he got better. He got better and Manuel was able to study again, he studied body work. But with such bad luck, I couldn't, I couldn't. So he was going to work, but they put him to work in Cataño and Cataño for me is just so far away and I didn't have a way to take him to the place.

I include these lengthy quotes to give a sense of the struggles the family went through to keep Manuel from harming himself. When Doña Carmen was able to attain effective treatment for her son, the job placement was on the other side of the metropolitan San Juan area. For a poor person without a car, the journey would entail changing *público* or bus several times and would take at least two hours one way. Again, Doña Carmen took the blame on herself. This was the one course of effective treatment that she described during our conversations where Manuel received lengthy therapy and was able to work.

In the early years of his illness, Manuel was hospitalized several times and also attended different outpatient-based treatment programs. However, by the time of the interview, his treatment consisted primarily of regular visits to receive his medication and the care that his mother provided at home. Most of his doctors, his mother explained, write out the prescription before the patient is even seen.

An examination of the label placed on Manuel's diagnosis further reveals the social and moral circuits through which Doña Carmen made sense of her sons' illness. When asked about Manuel's diagnosis, Doña Carmen answered that he had schizophrenia.

> Schizophrenia, at first it was chronic schizophrenia. Then it turned into a schizophrenia that I see as, later they called it undifferentiated [*indiferenciada*]. But I don't see that, he is a good person, he's very affectionate, very respectful of people, he doesn't get involved in the neighbor's business, he can be calm, he is a calm boy.

Her description of the diagnosis reacted to the stigma placed on sufferers of schizophrenia. She did not like the label *indiferenciada* that she said was put on the diagnosis later. Hence, she contrasted the medical language with her own assessment of his character as a person: he is a good person, loving and respectful; he does not get involved in other people's business. Doña Carmen's understanding of her sons' schizophrenia differed markedly from biomedical framings of the disease. Her story traverses emotional terrain marked by guilt, stigma, and responsibility. Doña Carmen felt betrayed by the school system, medical system, and specific providers. She also felt partially responsible for not protecting her son adequately from getting sick. She worried about who would care for her sons when she was gone. Finally, she insisted that her son was inherently a good, moral person who behaved respectfully.

After 30 years of treatment in the health system (remember her statement: "*siempre ha habido algo con el gobierno* [there's always been something with the government]"), Doña Carmen believed that schizophrenia was caused by LSD and that her sons should not be held culpable for their disease. She wished that she had more money to cover their expenses, but mostly she wanted a guarantee that they would be cared for at least as well as she could do it after she passed away. There is a great distance between the specialized biomedical knowledge that diagnosed Manuel as "undifferentiated" and Doña Carmen's own understanding of his illness. This difference between biomedical and lay knowledges as well as the real economic constraints faced by the family represent a further limit on their ability to exercise "therapeutic and economic self-determination" (Tomes 2006).

Clearly Manuel and Enrique are not the ideal rational and informed decision-making consumers described in the Medicare Modernization Act. The family does not fit the model of the neoliberal consumer in several respects. First, Doña Carmen saw the government as the legitimate provider of her sons' care. Second, Manuel and Enrique were not independent decision makers in the sense envisioned in market-based reform policies. Though Doña Carmen was not opposed to making choices, she had few real options. She tried a whole series of different care settings, but they proved dangerous or inadequate. She never became an empowered health care consumer, and she was batted about by the currents of public policy and tried to do what she thought was right (at great personal cost). Third, decisions about care were made as a family (not as individuals) with the unpaid labor of some supporting the care of others. Fourth, illness was understood socially rather than individually or biomedically—schizophrenia was done to the family by social delinquency.

When the integrity of the self is precisely what is affected by conditions like schizophrenia, market-based health reforms transfer responsibility from the state onto the individual and his or her family. One reason the system worked for Manuel and Enrique was that they had a caretaker who ensured that they made their medical appointments, took their medication, and ate their meals. Doña Carmen spent her life performing the unpaid labor of caring for her disabled sons. They may never be able to take care of themselves, reapply for their Reforma benefits, or choose the highest-quality health care provider. Doña Carmen expressed affective attachments to the state characterized by a sense of betrayal. In so doing, she also spoke of the government as a caretaker, which is precisely the government role that neoliberal health programs attempt to undo.

Teresa Ramírez: Disability and the Precariousness of Class Mobility

Teresa Ramírez's story chronicles how her class mobility was cut short by mental and physical disability.[20] It is also a story of refashioning oneself in the wake of a life thrown off course. At 43, she was the youngest person I interviewed. An accident at work left her permanently physically disabled, which in turn precipitated severe depression. She worked with advocacy groups to press for changes in the health system, forge new kinds of community among the disabled, and fight her depression by engaging in activities that she found meaningful and important. She spoke about the violent dislocations of debilitating illness and the small measures one can take to bear it.

Since Teresa had just moved into a new apartment, I picked her up and we conducted the interview at my kitchen table. She said that her place was still a mess and not fit to have anyone over. I began by asking about her family. Though Teresa has eight brothers and sisters, she did not grow up with any of them. She was adopted by her grandparents. This, she added, made her mother her sister. She attended a public high school in Caguas that she described as a very violent school. She got good grades and was the teacher's pet. While she was growing up, her grandparents used medicinal herbs to treat most common ailments. Also, her feces and urine were regularly examined at home. In her case, this was particularly necessary because she ate dirt. Her grandfather worked in the sugar cane fields and then joined the army. Following his discharge, he was a janitor at a cigar factory in Caguas for the rest of his life. Both of her grandparents were extremely healthy and did not visit the hospital until they went there to die. Her grandmother was from Gurabo; she sewed and rolled tobacco leaves.

After high school, Teresa studied English literature at the University of Puerto Rico in Río Piedras. She did not graduate. In her fourth year, when strikes were occurring at the university, she traveled to Israel. At this point in the interview, she interrupted me and wanted to know why I was asking about these things if I was interested in studying health plans. I explained that I was getting a sense of her as an entire person by trying to understand her social context. She stared at me for a moment, accepted this explanation, and continued with her story. She stayed in

Israel for 8 months and then traveled to New Jersey where she lived with an aunt. She returned to Puerto Rico in 1983 when her grandfather fell ill with cancer. I asked her if she would like to finish her degree and this was when we began to discuss her experiences with anxiety and depression. She said that she would like to finish, but she was afraid.

> Well, I had severe depression. I still have it. And at first when I got it, I lost the ability to read. . . . I love to read and then all of the sudden I couldn't do it. It was, like, I would pick something up and say, "Equilibrium is eq, eq, . . . Oh! Eq, equili . . . Forget it." I could not read. You know, it was a complete blur. I could not pay attention. I couldn't concentrate on anything for more than a few seconds, it was very difficult. I'm afraid that if I study again, that the same thing will happen.

The onset of her depression was marked by her inability to do one of the things she most enjoyed. As a literature major, her identity and class mobility were tied to reading. The fear of the reappearance of this symptom prevented her from completing her degree.

Upon returning to Puerto Rico, Teresa held a series of part-time jobs that she did not like, such as telemarketing. She also took up photography and began to develop film. Eventually, she obtained a job with a local newspaper as a photographer on a contractual basis but it did not include health insurance. She described two accidents: one where she cut her fingers and another where she injured the meniscus in her knee. In both cases she had to pay out of pocket for treatment and did not know that she could receive treatment through the Industrial Hospital.[21] These accidents both occurred before the implementation of La Reforma. In the incident involving her fingers, her supervisor told her to wrap her fingers up and go back to work; there were pictures that needed to be taken.

The major accident that resulted in her disability occurred in 1997. By then, she was a full-time employee at the newspaper with a private insurance plan. She described herself as a successful professional, someone whose social life revolved around work and she had considered moving to the United States for a higher salary and better opportunities. Her physical accident led to severe depression and a series of hospitalizations in psychiatric facilities.

I had an accident. I injured my leg, the left leg. I injured the ligaments. And I thought that I would return to work quickly, because this is what had happened in the past, when I hurt my ankles and had to get the cast. They sent me to the Industrial Hospital because the accident occurred in the newspaper plant. I left work and went there. And I was limping, but I made it there. I left in a cast and I never returned to work. Because then after spending months and months in my house, I began to get depressed. Because I thought I have made my whole life revolve around work, my entire social life, everything was about work. And then all of the sudden I discovered what a bad idea it was to do that because when there is no longer any work, I was left with nothing. And I was stuck with that and it depressed me a great deal. To go from having such an active life and then having to be like, I am at home, I cannot move.

Through the accident, her life became immobilized. The physical complaint was almost immediately accompanied by mental distress. As her principal complaint was physical and stemmed from the accident, she was treated through the Fondo del Seguro del Estado. When her nerves started to bother her, she sought treatment using the insurance, Triple-S, provided by her employer. At that point, she was on leave from work and so still eligible for insurance. She began seeing a psychiatrist.

I started in October or November; I'm not sure but I started about 3 months after the accident, and I continued to see her. But I felt worse and worse and worse. I wanted to commit suicide; I wanted to die first. No, no. You know this happens in phases. Well, I wanted to die and the doctor asked me if I would consider hospitalizing myself. At first I was like nah-ah, I don't want to do that. But finally I agreed and they hospitalized me in Panamericano.

This hospitalization was a bad experience, not just because of the severe depression that brought her there, but because of the care she received. Since she had private insurance, Teresa went to a private hospital that enjoyed an aura of prestige. However, her perceptions about higher-quality care in private versus public hospitals were quickly disrupted. She described complications with her physical injury that were not treated properly and resulted in a stress fracture. She was restrained and denied pain medication that had been prescribed by the ortho-pedist. The doctors were gruff and indifferent to her physical symp-toms. She also recounted experiencing ongoing conflicts with the nurses, being ignored by the staff, and observing violence toward other patients.

> I asked to go to the Panamericano, because I had photographed it. I thought, this does not seem like a mental hospital. This doesn't look like what you see on the soap operas. This looks like a hotel. And it is very pretty, you know. Beds, rooms that look like a resort. Gardens, a pool, a basketball court with a covered roof, air conditioning, a gym, it had everything. But the treatment was horrible. The treatment was very bad, very bad, very bad.

Teresa contacted a friend who was a lawyer for help. He worked with PAIMI: Protection and Advocacy for Individuals with Mental Illness. She met with a lawyer from this organization regarding the treatment she received at Hospital Panamericano. This lawyer worked directly from the Office of the Procurador del Impedido [as a disabled person's ombudsman]. She said after this visit that the care improved, but she still wanted to leave the hospital. So she was transferred to another mental hospital: San Juan Capestrano. There she described the treat-ment as being much more humane. One of her symptoms was that she pulled out her hair in clumps. She said the nurse would sit with her for hours and immobilize her hands; when it got really bad, she would be restrained.

Over the years, Teresa had been prescribed a variety of medications. I asked about the medications that she had been given for her psychiat-ric symptoms and she described a litany of prescriptions that she could not keep straight. She began to describe herself as an object experienc-ing drastic side effects.

> I do not remember. Honestly, with so many changes in my medication. I've been hospitalized 26 or 27 times already. I could tell you if you name a new medication, maybe I could tell you if I have not taken that one yet. But I've tried, almost, I've tried Prozac, I've tried Efexor, I tried, um, antidepressants, Zoloft, Paxil, ah, all of the antidepressants there are.

I've taken other medications for psychosis. I started to have hallucinations. And for anxiety. I've taken many, many things, many, many, many things. At one point, I took Ciprexa, that is for . . . they give it to people who have schizophrenia. They give it to people with different conditions. They gave it to me mostly for the psychosis, because I had hallucinations. I saw things that did not exist, and the bad thing wasn't that they didn't exist. The bad thing was that you didn't know if they were real or not. So I would have them sometimes when I was driving. So I had to stop driving for a while. But this Ciprexa it made me . . . I weighed 300 pounds. And then I could not walk. I'm not thin, obviously, but I weigh 200 and some odd pounds. But, then, I weighed almost 80 pounds more than I do right now. It was really bad. I couldn't sweep the floor of my house.

When I asked about her current medication regimen, she mentioned that she was trying to take fewer prescriptions. She said that she began to feel like she was secreting medicine from her pores and became too indifferent to what was happening around her. Teresa was struggling to differentiate between the symptoms of treatment and the symptoms of her depression and anxiety. She made a concerted effort to reduce her medication intake because of these side effects, what the anthropologist Sue Estroff (2004) has termed "treatment as sensate torture" (287). During other parts of the interview, she discussed looking for alternative therapies through natural and holistic medicine. However, she had found some of the practitioners to be too commercial; she compared them to Amway. Teresa attempted to take control of her prescription regimen by seeing different kinds of providers and requesting that her dosages and medicine be changed.

Right now they are giving me Wellbutrin and Clonopin for anxiety. Wellbutrin is for depression. And I was taking it when I got out of the hospital; I was taking sleeping pills, too, but I did not like them. I would like to keep the medication to a minimum. I want to take less. I don't want so much medication. At one point, I was taking 14 different medications a day. It was a lot. It was a lot of stuff. And I thought that if I did like this and licked my skin, it would taste like medicine. It was horrible. And the side effects were like—I could wait on line for 3 hours and it wouldn't even bother me. But I felt like a piece of wood.

Part of the difficulty in adjusting her medication so that the side effects were not worse than the symptoms being treated is that she had to change psychiatrists on multiple occasions. Psychiatrists go in and out of insurance plans, which has a huge impact on patients who are covered by Medicare and La Reforma. It is also difficult to find a psychiatrist who participates in public programs and conducts therapy sessions. Most appointments are only for adjusting medication. Therefore, Teresa also saw a therapist who was a master's-level social worker. In her current plan, the therapy sessions were covered if and when they were preauthorized by the company that had been subcontracted to manage mental health services (also known as a mental health carveout). However, she had to stop seeing the psychiatrist under whom she found her treatment to be most effective, because the psychiatrist did not participate in her current plan. Having to switch providers was an extremely common complaint for beneficiaries who received their medical care through an HMO. This is the flip side of choice. Providers often choose not to participate in the more onerous HMOs that have excessive paperwork or delay too long in paying claims. The beneficiary is left with the "choice" to pay out of pocket or seek care with someone else. In this hierarchy of choice, choices made by providers create the conditions under which consumers in turn make theirs.

When Teresa described going on disability and qualifying for Medicare, she referenced her mental condition and the electric shock treatments that she said had affected her memory. However, her story was similar to those of other interviewees in the sense of being shepherded through state bureaucracies without a clear idea of what one qualifies for, why, and what benefits would be received.

> Look, I have to explain something. I have a little bit of a void around a certain period of time. I also received ECTs [electroconvulsive therapy]. And there are a lot of things that I can't remember. Details. I know that I had long-term disability, an insurance policy, that they considered in order to put me on long-term disability, they required me to apply for Social Security. And in one of these situations when I was at Social Security to deal with the paperwork and everything, it was over there at San Patricio Plaza, I know that they had me fill out papers for Medicare, that it was time for me to fill them out and they asked me if I was going to

sign up for Part B. And, well, I looked into it and what did I know. And, well, I decided it was in my best interest. And more or less around that time, I think it was around then I had already used up the COBRA benefit, the COBRA plan. I had already had to buy private insurance, to sign up with the retailers, with the Centro Unido de Detallistas,[22] in order to be able to buy a private insurance plan that included medicine, because I was no longer covered then. It was, you know, I was already using up my benefit with El Fondo. Then El Fondo approved my disability case for mental, for emotional, and for physical. But after 2 years they kick you off the treatment. They give you disability. They give you some money. And then it's go home. So that's when I signed up for Medicare.

Instead of making choices as a rational, informed consumer, she was shuffled between one program to the next: a private insurance plan, COBRA, El Fondo, Social Security, and Medicare. To navigate this array of agencies requires knowledge of the bureaucracy and much patience and persistence. Given her severe depression and anxiety, it is surprising that her case was resolved at all. I asked if she had ever applied for La Reforma. Her narrative gives a sense of the bureaucratic quagmire involved in qualifying for these programs. The process requires applying at a Medical Aid office, which involves verification of one's financial condition so as to be officially classified as medically indigent. If one qualifies at the Medical Aid office, then the beneficiary must go to the insurance company assigned to where they live in order to complete the inscription process. Teresa claimed that after the 2 years it takes to be officially considered disabled, she had absolutely nothing left economically. Nonetheless, she was denied the benefit of La Reforma three times only to find out years later that the system had listed her as approved. During the story, she acted out the role of the bureaucrat:

Yes, yes, I applied on various occasions when I was—when the COBRA plan was ending. But they never approved me. And then to my surprise when I went a few months ago to apply for MediMed,[23] "Oh God, you have La Reforma approved." And I said, "No." And they told me, "Yes, you asked for it and it was approved." And I said, "But I went three times and three times was denied and I got tired of applying and they never gave it to me." La Reforma, I was applying for it because I could not pay any more. I did not have any money. I had already used up all my vacation pay and the money I had saved in the bank. You know, I didn't have anyone left to borrow money from. So I had to take care of my situation somehow. But they never approved my application for La Reforma. I never had the benefits of La Reforma.

Before the implementation of La Reforma, anyone could receive care in the regional system. However, the privatized HMO system implemented eligibility procedures so that only those who met the criteria of the program received a Reforma card, which in turn allowed them to access publicly financed care. Technological innovations like the electronic eligibility system were supposed to objectively determine who qualified for La Reforma and in so doing bring more efficiency and transparency to the health system. However, in practice, these new eligibility procedures created additional barriers to accessing care, even for those who met the program's eligibility criteria. Maintaining accurate eligibility files and ensuring access to them proved an onerous task for the Commonwealth's Medicaid office, as Teresa's case illustrates. Anthropologists have long raised objections to enrollment procedures in Medicaid because they lead to "de facto disentitlement" by creating barriers and bureaucratic hurdles to enrollment (L. López 2005; see also Horton 2004; Horton et al. n.d.; Lamphere 2005). Puerto Rico's experience with Medicaid managed care proved no exception; I heard story after story of qualifying for La Reforma and then having to attend an interview every year and begin the process anew. Several interviewees let their coverage lapse rather than go through the time-consuming and often humiliating interviews.

Because Teresa was educated and formerly of the middle class, she had to deal with the incredulousness of government functionaries when she applied for aid in government offices. We discussed the difficulty of adjusting to being disabled:

> One is in limbo. Especially in those first months when this happens, one doesn't know what to do and you end up getting sucked further under. And I see other people who are like me. I say, we're like the new poor. Because we are not accustomed to going to government agencies and asking for things. We are used to being the ones who see to things, or

who maintain the family or take care of the house, to being "heads of household." And then, all of the sudden, it's food stamps. Food stamps? How on earth can you tell me that I need to go apply for food stamps? You know, it's very strange. Very strange. And you go to the government offices and they mistreat you, they verbally, you know. And they would treat me like, "Ma'am, you earn $900 from Social Security, why are you here?" You know. And I would start to cry. In public! It was, like, I had already lost all sense of humiliation. . . . They say things to you, they say things like "Oh, go home, you don't qualify." And you sit there, trembling, or you start to cry or you just leave. You do what they tell you. You don't do what you need to do to make things better. If I, now I'm more clear in the head. If someone tells me no, I say to them, "No, no, no, no, no, no. Find me your supervisor and you will explain it to me with hairs or signs why not. You're going to tell me in writing." But when you really need a service, like when I needed La Reforma, you see? I was treated horribly. It's really bad. Most of the people who work for the government couldn't care less. I went to sign up for public housing and they told me, "Oh, you earn how much?" And I just sat there, like hyperventilating. And I was like, "But, why would you do that?" or "I have the right to . . . " "No, you earn too much. Get out of here." And so I would go to these places and it was always "You earn too much or you earn too little, you earn too much, or you—"

Teresa Ramírez described her position as one of "limbo" and went on to say that others like her, whom she termed "the new poor," were going through a similar process. Her disability revealed how precarious upward mobility is in a society where medical care is not available to everyone, employment is increasingly flexible and contingent, and the social safety net is inadequate and difficult to access. Yet the traces of having been a professional—her speech, her $900 Social Security payment, her clothing—all signaled to government bureaucrats that she did not belong on relief programs. Disability had undone her not just physically, but also socially. She found ways to reinvent herself through activism and working with patients' rights organizations. In particular, groups that worked on developing assertiveness and life skills were helpful in learning how to exist within this maze of bureaucracies and the isolation of not working. The "no, no, no, no, no" with which she now challenges bureaucratic refusals is not just the product of having her head in a better place, but also of talking with those other "new poor," exchanging information with advocacy agencies and learning to assert her rights.

Conclusions: Consumers, Citizens, and the State

What do these particular stories of becoming disabled and receiving government assistance reveal about the ways in which citizens are becoming consumers of health care under neoliberal reform programs? This chapter opened with the claim that the relationship between government, citizens, and public services has become unsettled. In the United States, 30-plus years of market-based reforms to the public sector have privatized public services in the name of making government more efficient and in the process have treated citizens more like consumers. In Puerto Rico, the full force of neoliberal reforms arrived later than in the United States—the most radical changes were undertaken by the pro-statehood administration of governor Pedro Rosselló (1993–2001), who implemented market-based reforms to the provision of utilities, education, policing, and, of course, health care.

The unique sociopolitical and historical trajectory of market reform in Puerto Rico partially explains why Don Anastasio, Doña Carmen, and Teresa Ramírez continue to see a strong role for the state in the provision of health services. The government in Puerto Rico is larger and more centralized than most state governments, has historically taken an active role in providing social services, and serves as one of the island's largest employers.[24] With roughly half of the island's population living in poverty, public programs are directed at a much larger proportion of the population than in most mainland states. Recent islandwide protests against laying off government workers and a 2-month-long strike by university students against neoliberal reforms to public higher education speak to the continued relevance in the popular imagination of a strong role for the government—a role that encompasses far more than contracting with and regulating private firms. In sum, the relationship between government, citizens, and public services has indeed become unsettled, but not to the same degree as on the mainland.

The historical importance of the state in Puerto Rico as a provider of services and as an employer partially explains why the beneficiaries whom I interviewed did not transform seamlessly into information-processing, neoliberal, health care consumers as a result of health care reform. But there were other factors at work. One of the more intractable factors was that the rational, decision-making consumer did not prove to be a great metaphor for how people actually behaved when seeking medical care. In the life histories recounted here, people were workers and family members; they expressed disappointment and betrayal by public institutions, did not always listen to their doctors, disputed stigmatizing labels like "undifferentiated," worried that their skin secreted medication, avoided using their private insurance, insisted that their mentally ill family members were essentially good people, and so on. They made sense of their health care according to nonmarket logics including familial obligations, notions of what made a moral person, their own self-perceptions and how illness altered that sense of self, and, finally, through the fog, pain, and symptoms of illness itself. They primarily used moral frameworks, not economic ones, to make health care decisions.

If neoliberal health policies presume that consumers make calculating economic decisions about their care, these policies also presume that the subject doing the calculating is essentially rational, independent, and fully able. Recent work on disability has challenged some of the assumptions implicit in able-bodied notions of citizenship and the theories of human behavior that undergird many market-based health programs. In their research on caring for disabled children in the United States, the anthropologists Rayna Rapp and Faye Ginsburg observe the following:

> Progress in legal arenas has problematized the presumption of American citizenship as the exclusive entitlement of a normative, able-bodied, nondependent, wage-earning individual. At best, this model of personhood describes only a portion of the normal human life cycle. At worst, it systematically erases the rights of the disabled and their caretakers to have their fundamental needs addressed in the public arena. (2001, 552)

In other words, being a full citizen is tied to being able-bodied and employed.[25] This is clear, for example, in how social service and welfare programs determine eligibility and allocate benefits. Most safety-net and social-insurance programs in the United States and Puerto Rico assume that one is able to work: the reliance on an employer-based health care system ties health coverage to employment status; Social Security payments are pegged to one's previous participation in the labor force; and welfare benefits are now limited and contingent on moving into the workforce.

Recall that when George W. Bush signed the Medicare Modernization Act into law, he actually erased those with disabilities by addressing the speech solely to "seniors." This erasure, which is symptomatic of the able-bodied bias of market-based health policies, has concrete negative effects for recipients of public services. Teresa Ramírez, for example, struggled to navigate the health system and its new eligibility procedures through the fog of depression. She acutely felt the rights and pleasures she formerly enjoyed as an employed member of the middle class evaporate with her disability. Doña Carmen received very little in Social Security because she did not work in the wage labor force— her lifework was caring for her disabled sons.[26] Manuel and Enrique's story presents the clearest example of how the able-bodied assumptions about health care consumers are out of place in a health program *for* the elderly and disabled. To what extent can Manuel and Enrique ever act as rational, informed, health care consumers? If they cannot behave the way that policies ask them to behave, then what happens to their care? Do they have rights? Who will guarantee them?

The policy focus on decision-making consumers in health care excludes those who fall outside of the able-bodied "norm"; however, for other reasons, imagining patients as consumers might be problematic for everyone. According to neoliberal policy makers, consumers should be able to exercise control over their treatment and choose among competing care providers. The historian Nancy Tomes (2006) explores this problem by showing how consumer advocacy movements in health care from the 1960s and 1970s were co-opted by for-profit hospitals, HMOs, and pharmaceutical companies as they attempted to market their products to the affluent. Tomes argues that the popularity of policies and programs targeted at health care consumers marks a retraction and not an expansion of the consumer's ability to participate in his or her medical care:

My skepticism about the latest generation of so-called consumer-controlled policies reflects two conclusions based on my historical research. First, that modern conceptions of patients'—and consumers'—rights are best understood as responses to long-term *contractions*, not *expansions*, of patients' powers of therapeutic and economic self-determination. Second, that models of consumer "sovereignty" based on patients' ability to discipline the health-care marketplace through individual choices have historic limitations that will likely never be overcome. (2006, 84–85)

One of these "historic limitations" is that health care is an incomplete and imperfect commodity. One cannot make choices about health care in the same way that one chooses which soda to buy. A variety of factors limit the choices available in the health care marketplace; these include the strong role of regulation, the influence on medical care exerted by professional associations like the American Medical Association and the pharmaceutical lobby, the lack of competition for many kinds of care, the lack of public information about pricing, and finally the importance of nonmarket criteria like trust and respect, not to mention geographic proximity, in selecting providers. Another limitation on the ability of consumers to truly exercise therapeutic self-determination involves the structure of medical knowledge—patients must rely on the advice of trained, professional physicians. Patients often do not have the knowledge or medical literacy to assess health risks, navigate the health system, and choose the most appropriate treatment. Alternatively, their understandings of illness (as with Doña Carmen) are likely to go unrecognized by biomedical practitioners. As medicine becomes more specialized, this knowledge asymmetry will only grow. Finally, access to health coverage in the first place is often determined by economic factors. Consumers' "powers of therapeutic and economic self-determination" are increasingly limited by their lack of control over their own working lives as employment becomes more flexible and temporary and as benefits like health insurance are not guaranteed.

Examining market-based health policy from the perspective of the sick and disabled is a useful way to interrogate the assumptions of neoliberal personhood. It allows us to listen to those who are struggling to make their way through a health system that has been transformed by market-based policies. What people actually seemed to want in the interviews that I conducted was to be treated with respect and to be cared for competently in moments when they were vulnerable and in distress. Don Anastasio refused the medical advice to have his leg amputated due to fear and his belief that his doctor did not really know best. He also avoided going on disability after his operation because working was meaningful for him and he felt like he still had some productive years left. However, he did not carefully weigh his treatment options based on quality indicators. He made a rash decision to flee a hospital when his instincts told him that he was not going to get the best possible care. Doña Carmen wanted her sons to be treated with respect, to be spoken to by doctors and not to be herded through treatment only to have their prescriptions refilled. She tried several live-in treatment facilities for her sons but always pulled them out because they were mistreated or neglected. In vain, she sought some assurance that her sons would be cared for when she died. Teresa Ramírez struggled to navigate the relief bureaucracies and found herself learning to assert herself. She demanded care that was at least decent and that she be given denials in writing, and that the rationale be explained to her. All of the interviewees in this chapter challenge any simplistic notion of a health care consumer. If we were to rethink health programs from the perspectives of the people they are intended to serve, how might we be able to reimagine the system? This chapter suggests that a modest starting point would be to part with the ahistorical and asocial health care consumer as the fundamental social unit that animates health systems.

PART II

The Business of Care

Market Values and Management Strategies

4

Quality

Managing by Numbers

Dr. Benedetti would not listen to stories. Soon after starting work at the Medicare health plan in Puerto Rico, I learned that the U.S.-born medical director would not entertain anecdotes or rumors. His office door was always open and he would meet with anyone in the company, but they had to bring numbers. As a new manager in the Compliance Department, I wanted Dr. Benedetti to take action to resolve a sudden increase in members' complaints about delivery delays for medical equipment. He was not impressed when I recounted the story of the woman in Guaníca whose oxygen was delayed, who decompensated, and whose daughter rushed her to the emergency room. He instructed me to create a log of the complaints. I should tally and aggregate the data. A graph would be better to capture the magnitude of the increase and to pinpoint when the trend began. Is the growth in a particular kind or category of complaint? Are there changes across all categories? Dr. Benedetti did not think that empathy would remedy the delivery delays. But once convinced by numbers that a problem existed, he would gladly discuss how to resolve it.[1]

Unlike this particular physician-administrator, as a cultural anthropologist, I have been trained to traffic in stories. Ethnographic writing would hardly be recognizable without pithy anecdotes, arrival tales, and thick descriptions. Dr. Benedetti's aversion to stories, or worse, "anecdotal evidence," struck me as a highly restrictive sieve through which to filter what one is willing to hear. In order to talk with Dr. Benedetti, I created tables and graphs. I was forbidden from using explanatory text on the PowerPoint slides of my department's weekly reports. A quick glance at this report allowed company executives to monitor how efficiently the department performed, but the report conveyed little about the people doing the work or if it had been done well.

Dr. Benedetti's penchant for quantification and his insistence that complex problems be presented in numerical form were anything but aberrant. Instead, he must be seen as part of a larger trend in American medicine toward administering health care according to business logics that value efficiency, profit maximization, and performance measurement (Donald 2001; Horton 2006; Lamphere 2005; McIntyre et al. 2001; Wendland 2007). From evidence-based medicine to quality improvement and accreditation programs, both the U.S. and Puerto Rican health systems have been swept by a craze for measurement. The same faith in understanding complex health-delivery systems through graphs and charts, report cards, "dashboard" readings, and rankings underwrites a systemwide effort to quantify quality and performance data for use by health plan administrators, regulators, and consumers.

The production of quality data is currently so important in the Medicare program, because patients are supposed to use quality statistics to make informed plan choices. Legislation that amended the Medicare program in 2003, by adding more private plan options, described its intention to "advance the goal of *improving quality and increasing efficiency* in the overall health care system. Medicare is the largest payer of health care in the world. Medicare can drive changes in the entire health care system" (*Federal Register* 2005, 4587, emphasis added). Quality and efficiency are linked in this vision—the availability of quality statistics should "drive" improvements to the health system because beneficiaries will choose to enroll in higher-quality plans, thereby creating more competition and efficiency. In addition to enabling consumer choice and spurring corporate competition, the production of quality data in health care is part of a standardization process that allows comparisons to be made across health systems, delivery settings, or health plans. Quality measurements can rank the performance of an employer group plan in Silicon Valley versus an insurance company with a Medicaid contract with the government of

Puerto Rico. Quality studies are compiled, published, and interpreted in the larger political field to demonstrate the successes and failures of health programs. Quantified quality then is instrumental in guiding policy.

This chapter examines quality measurement's place within market-based health policy. Quantifying quality is supposed to unite regulators, health plans, and health care consumers in a circuit of constant improvement. But examining this proposition ethnographically reveals significant differences among how policy makers, health plan administrators, and health plan members write and talk about quality. The differences in how these actors understand quality merits critical attention, especially as improving quality has become both the justification *for* and the putative result *of* the market-based health care delivery model currently in place in the United States and Puerto Rico.

This chapter begins by analyzing policy documents that define the methods and administrative rationale for conducting quality measurement. I then draw on my ethnographic research at Acme to examine how the day-to-day work of compiling quality data departed from the stated objectives of health policy. Much of what I observed was targeted at maximizing revenue and complying with regulatory requirements, rather than engineering changes in clinical practice to improve patient care. I close the chapter with interview excerpts from health plan members regarding how they imagine quality care, so demonstrating some of the disconnects between the quality-measurement efforts of policy makers and health maintenance organizations (HMOs) and the kinds of quality concerns raised by consumers. These interview excerpts cast doubt on the claim made by health policy experts that consumers will operate first and foremost as rational economic actors and choose to join higher-performing plans, thereby driving the system to compete on quality.

Quality Measurement and Governing from Afar

Though quality-measurement initiatives in health care are now ubiquitous, the widespread concern with quality is of surprisingly recent origin. A national conversation on quality in the United States began to coalesce in the late 1990s. Some key events are illustrative: the first nationwide quality reporting and monitoring focused on hospitals and began in 1998 through the Joint Commission (Chassin et al. 2010, 683); the first federal agency charged with monitoring and improving quality in health care was created in 1999 (AHRQ 1999); and in 2001, the Institute of Medicine published a landmark report, *Crossing the Quality Chasm*, which claimed that "health care today harms too frequently and routinely fails to deliver its potential benefits" (1). By the mid-2000s quality reporting had become common throughout the health care system, including at hospitals, physician practices, skilled nursing facilities, and health plans. This timing is significant for at least two reasons. First, the focus on quality emerged from the ashes of the HMO backlash of the late 1990s. Thus, it represented an attempt to reinsert a concern with patient care and outcomes into a health system that was widely accused of overemphasizing cost containment and utilization control.[2] Second, quality measurement gained prominence at a moment when market logics were already entrenched as political common sense in the United States and market-based reforms had already restructured government services and welfare programs. For example, "by 1997 nearly 50 percent of all Medicaid recipients nationwide were members of MCOS [managed care organizations]" (Engel 2006, 237). Quality as practiced by regulatory agencies emerged as a tool for monitoring the performance of these newly privatized health plans.

The movement toward privatized models of service delivery prompted important changes in the form and function of government. These changes were not unique to Medicare and Medicaid or even to the United States—they are part of widespread transformations that occurred across service domains (including in education, the military, welfare programs, and international development) and in multiple national contexts. As discussed previously, the privatization of government services creates a need to reinvent government bureaucracy so that it is possible to "govern from afar" (Clarke 2004; Miller and Rose 1990; Rose 1996, 43). The distance denoted by "afar" refers to the administrative gap that is created when government transforms from being the direct provider of services to financing and overseeing service provision by private corporations or nonprofit organizations, but it also signals how governing has become increasingly indirect as corporations are required to self-regulate through activities such as establishing compliance programs, internal auditing, and creating extensive policies and procedures. In the case of Puerto Rico, this distance takes on an additional valence because the regulatory agencies in Baltimore and New York are physically and culturally quite distant from the island.

In addition to creating new pathways for government oversight, neoliberal assessment technologies such as quality reporting, auditing, and accreditation are said to promote transparency and aid consumers in making informed choices (Clarke 2004; Giri 2000; Strathern 2000). For example, *Crossing the Quality Chasm* (Institute of Medicine 2001) argues that in the current health care system, there is a "need for transparency":

> The health care system should make information available to patients and their families that allows them to make informed decisions when selecting a health plan, hospital, or clinical practice, or choosing among alternative treatments. This should include information describing the system's performance on safety, evidence-based practice, and patient satisfaction. (8)

Publicly available quality measures are supposed to make visible the hidden differences between how doctors practice, hospitals function, and insurance plans operate. Transparency, however, merits critical examination: it presumes that "particular forms of disclosure equate with the exposure of absolute truths otherwise concealed" (Schumann 2007, 854). The problem is that quality measurement does far more than make public a preexisting truth; quality measurement is better understood as a truth-making rather than truth-revealing practice. Quality measurement has transformed how health care is valued and what aspects of care count. It has also prompted significant changes in how health care delivery is organized through the creation of new processes for tracking, recording, and reporting quality data. For example, most major health care organizations, whether a hospital, large-group practice, or insurance company, now have quality departments led by quality managers. Many graduate programs in health administration now offer degrees in health care quality. And so quality measurement has taken on a social life that far exceeds its role to make visible how health care organizations perform.

An important characteristic of quality measurement's epistemology is that it aspires to objectivity and neutrality (Porter 1995). Like Dr.

Benedetti's insistence that conversations begin with the numbers, the practice of quality measurement is concerned with demonstrating its own objectivity. Upon closer inspection, it is clear that quality measurement is itself a moral project. In the discussion of policy documents from the Medicare program here, I show how an emphasis on objectivity and expert knowledge obscures quality measurement's own moral attachments to a value system that emphasizes efficiency, privatized service delivery arrangements, and cost-effectiveness above all else. Ironically, this concern with expertise and objectivity creates a distance between health care consumers and the highly technical quality data they are supposed to draw on to make informed health-related decisions.

Rather than view quality measurement as a transparent window into how a health plan serves its members, delivers care, and shepherds public resources (or as the path to perpetual improvement), this chapter explores three interrelated questions: How is knowledge about quality generated? How is that knowledge used? How is quality measurement a moral project?

Quality measurement within health policy is a specific way of knowing that sheds light on certain quantifiable aspects of care. It is hard to argue against the work that quality measurement has done to draw attention to error in medicine and health disparities (NCQA 2007, 10).[3] Nonetheless, like other forms of performance measurement, quality measurement runs the risk of being "the latest version of how to take 'politics' out of policy and practice choices" (Clarke 2004, 133). What is essentially a political decision (quality is something that can be measured, it is not subjective, it is related to values like efficiency and economization) is often presented as a value-neutral and technical designation made by experts. Though proponents assert its objectivity, critics portray performance measurement as a knowledge-making practice that is deeply linked to a moral vision of government that values market-based solutions to social problems.

Anthropological Accounts of Quality and Health Policy

An emerging body of empirical work in medical anthropology examines the unexpected consequences of implementing market-based health policies. The most comprehensive of these projects studied the privatization of the Medicaid program in New Mexico and showed that market reforms initially improved access to care through the use of primary care physicians (Boehm 2005; Horton et al. 2001; Lamphere 2005; L. López 2005; Nelson 2005; Wagner 2005; Waitzkin et al. 2002; Willging 2005). However, privatization also entailed a number of less positive unintended consequences, including enrollment difficulties, more bureaucracy and rules for providers, an added burden on safety-net providers, access barriers for rural clients, and decreased access to mental health care (Lamphere 2005, 13). The New Mexico study showed how market moralities that emphasize efficiency and controlling costs became part of the daily practices of providing health care services. Where beneficiaries did not suffer access barriers, it was often because safety-net providers assumed additional unremunerated responsibilities in an effort to fill the gaps left by privatization.

Several articles from the New Mexico study mention quality explicitly. William Wagner, for example, reports that while managed care administrators argued that utilization review and other forms of standardized care protocols would increase the quality of care available to Medicaid beneficiaries by ensuring that they received the best, medically necessary care available (2005, 76–78), mental health care providers maintained that changes ushered in by managed care "resulted in the downgrading of the types of services and quality of care available to New Mexico's children" (68). Likewise, Cathleen Willging was critical of attempts to oversee clinical decision making in which "the push for profit surmounts the desire for quality care for Medicaid recipients" (2005, 99). In an article that interrogated the relationship between quality and market reforms to publicly financed health care in Philadelphia, the anthropologist Jeff Maskovsky similarly argued that quality of care worsened after the introduction of managed care even though "politicians, policy makers, and pundits have justified this shift on the basis that it will cut costs and improve the quality of care for the poor" (2000, 121–122). Each of these researchers shows how privatizing Medicaid negatively impacted access to care. However, they fall short of interrogating quality as a kind of epistemology or specific way of knowing. Instead, quality of care (itself left undefined) is seen as being negatively affected by managed care arrangements.

Others have examined quality measurement (and parallel forms of performance measurement) as a way of knowing about health care systems. These studies argue that quality measurement and monitoring programs emerged out of a broader capitalist concern with regulating industrial production and have more recently been shaped by neoliberal forms of governance. Alasdair Donald's research at psychiatric hospitals highlights how quality assurance is justified by "a conviction on the part of managed care proponents that good clinical treatment is equivalent to efficient cost control" (2001, 427). Quality measurement takes what was an individual focus on the patient in psychiatry and transforms it into a focus on the population—the right care is what is effective according to population-based quality studies so that "industrial efficiency" is now "equated with efficacy" (430). Sarah Horton found that performance measures of provider productivity, in evaluating the performance of clinicians and time-management practices in a safety-net hospital serving Latino patients in the northwestern United States, were problematic because "provider efficiency may be elevated as an end in itself, displacing the goal of improving the quality of services rendered" (2006, 2704). Finally, Sabina Stan, in her study of reform to the Romanian health care system, argues that policy must be seen in epistemological terms: "Transparency policies claim they enhance the visibility of public services systems by producing essential knowledge on the way in which systems work. The production of transparency is thus also a production of knowledge" (2007, 258). Donald, Horton, and Stan show that quality measurement is a knowledge-making practice that creates information *about* the health system and *for* managing the system in new ways.

Each of these empirical studies demonstrates how market values have come to displace competing notions of what is "good" or "right" in health care, through practices like quality and performance measurement. Though policy makers advocate for "consumer choice" and "high-quality care," such pronouncements do not guarantee that market-based health care programs are designed, enacted, or administered in ways that further these aims. For these reasons, it is critical that medical anthropologists examine policy makers' claims ethnographically. This chapter contributes to the emerging literature on health care reform and performance measurement, by providing a case from inside an HMO that focuses on the disconnects between policy pronouncements about quality and their enactment.

Quality Measurement and Health Policy

Measuring and improving quality is a mandated activity for Medicare health plans—it is part of the legislation that authorizes managed care in the Medicare program as well as the Government Performance and Results Act (Jencks et al. 2000). The regulatory agency that oversees the Medicare program (the Centers for Medicare and Medicaid Services, or CMS) must be able to demonstrate to the current administration and Congress that the agency is improving the quality of care in addition to expending its enormous budget.

To carry out this mandate, CMS works closely with the National Committee for Quality Assurance (NCQA), a nonprofit organization that develops and administers nationally recognized quality measures. The NCQA is not a federal agency, but the results of its measures are closely followed by CMS, and its patented methodologies for customer satisfaction surveys and quality measurement are required of health plans that are contracted with the federal government. The NCQA's own statements about why quality measurement is vitally important are based on an assumption that health policy makers, health plans, and consumers are all engaged in a mutually beneficial partnership to exchange information and improve quality. The NCQA's website asks: "Why is it so important to measure performance? The answer is simple. It gets better if you do" (NCQA 2006). As if weighing yourself made you thinner, the NCQA argues that tracking performance on standardized quality indicators will drive improvements in the health system. This tautological view elevates measurement itself to a moral good— quality measurement is necessary in managed care because measurement guarantees improvement.

But what gets lost in policy makers' and bureaucrats' exhortations about the importance of quality measurement is the lack of agreement regarding how quality is defined. Among professional associations that specialize in quality measurement, the definition of quality varies, including the degree to which a patient's subjective assessment of good care is taken into consideration (Burhans 2007).

The ambiguous definition used by CMS breaks quality down into several components, none of which involve a patient's subjective assessment: "good quality health care means doing the right thing at the right time, in the right way, for the right person and getting the best possible results" (CMS 2008a). The adjectives "good" and "right" appear repeatedly in the definition but are not themselves defined. Instead, "quality" is broken down into constituent parts—the right person, the right time, the right way, and so on. The patient is a passive object to whom the "right things" are done. If all of the preceding parts of the definition are achieved, "the best possible results" would seem to follow.

In addition to the definition used by CMS, a second definition that influenced work processes at Acme was one used by the NCQA. The NCQA defines quality more broadly than CMS in order to encompass access to care and the utility of performance measures to consumers:

> Quality health care can be defined as the extent to which patients get the care they need in a manner that most effectively protects or restores their health. This means having timely access to care, getting treatment that medical evidence has found to be effective and getting appropriate preventive care. Choosing a high-quality health plan—and a high-quality doctor—plays a significant role in determining whether you'll get high-quality care. (2008b)

The NCQA explicitly links quality of care and consumer choice. Its definition is addressed directly to the consumer who is called upon to choose high-quality health care providers. Like CMS, the NCQA emphasizes the importance of evidence-based care and following certain standardized treatment protocols. Interpersonal aspects of care are largely absent—the patient may not feel cared for, but if his or her health is protected or restored, then quality is, by definition, present.

Both CMS and NCQA definitions establish quality as a substance amenable to quantification and scientific study. Quality-measurement initiatives track certain key indicators as proxies for how well a health plan, hospital, or physician is performing. In so doing, quality programs operationalize "the right thing" or "best results" into standard assessment tools (Atkinson 1993) that produce numerical ratings. For example, 75% of patients who were diagnosed as diabetic received an eye exam, or 35% of Medicare beneficiaries received a flu immunization. These indicators are interpreted as providing information about how well the health plan is managing chronic conditions (based on the measure for diabetics who receive eye exams) or delivering preventive care to at-risk populations (based on flu immunization rates). Quality measurement does not monitor every aspect of a plan but instead focuses on certain measures that are selected to be relevant, scientifically sound, and feasible (NCQA 2008a). The NCQA describes the steps involved in selecting quality measures:

> Developing a measure is a multi-step process. It involves identifying the clinical area to evaluate; conducting an extensive literature review; developing the measure with the appropriate MAP and other panels; vetting it with various stakeholders; and performing a field-test that looks at feasibility, reliability and validity. (2008a)

The process of developing quality measures then is portrayed as being done through professional consensus, careful research, and taking into account logistical factors such as the ease with which the data can be collected. For example, in assessing a health plan's cardiac care, all aspects of the cardiac program are not evaluated. Instead, two or three measures may be used such as the administration of beta-blockers after a heart attack, providing aspirin upon admission to the hospital, and the in-hospital mortality rate (Lambie and Mattke 2004). Much like the process of implementing population-based treatment protocols for psychiatric care (described by Donald 2001), quality measures track whether or not population-based "best practices" are being carried out in a particular setting. The quality-measurement process is used to establish national benchmarks or acceptable thresholds that plans can aim to achieve. Increasingly, quality measurements are compiled into "report cards" and will list an overall "grade."

This process is incredibly good at producing data that allow rankings to be developed and comparisons to be made across plans. But the measures are a kind of attenuated representation, a short hand for a much larger entity: "quality." As with any truth claim, it is important to understand the limitations of what is known; in this instance, the numbers do not measure quality itself, but very specific processes for which data are easily available. Aspects of care delivery that are not easily quantifiable (and therefore do not meet the feasibility criteria) are often not chosen as points of data collection. Because health plans understand which measures count, plan executives have learned to game the system by introducing efforts to improve only the indicators being measured and by hiring consultants to "massage" the data (Dalzell 1998).

In and of itself, one could hardly object to quality measurement, but when quality is mobilized as part of larger policy agendas, it can become a proxy for discussions about what is desirable or good in health care. As foreshadowed in the story about Dr. Benedetti with which I began this chapter, something important gets lost when quality is understood only quantitatively. My concern here is twofold. First, the language of quality implicitly lays claim to the moral authority to determine what is right in health care, without having to justify these claims on moral ground. And, second, the language of quality measurement is extremely limiting; it does not easily allow for subjective perspectives and it is deeply invested in imagining what is good in health care according to market logics such as efficiency and economization. When professional associations and regulatory agencies utilize the definitions above as the basis for creating quality-measurement instruments, these concerns with moral claims and subjective assessments are papered over by a process that is presented as objective, technical, and professional.

The Quality Meeting

We sit around the modern-styled, pressed-wood table in ergonomic rolling chairs, waiting for the doctors to arrive. Though food has been banned from meetings at Acme, for doctors, an exception is made. We pick at the spread of *quesitos*, *croquetas*, and *pastelillos* and gossip about the day's earlier meetings.

The Quality Committee meets quarterly. A contracted doctor from each area of the island participates, along with the corporate medical director, the quality manager, a member, and me, because I represent the Compliance Department. I am the only gringo in attendance, so the meeting is held in Spanish.

Once everyone filters in, the quality manager, who is also a registered nurse, asks us to introduce ourselves. I introduce myself as the compliance manager and a researcher interested in studying quality of care in Puerto Rico. The member explains that he has been enrolled for a little over a year, is very satisfied with the services, and is happy to attend the quality meeting. He mentions that he is trying to get everyone he knows to join the plan.

The agenda is passed around with the minutes from the previous meeting. We read the minutes and the doctor from Ponce motions to accept them; everyone agrees. The quality manager reviews a recent audit; she explains that the company began requesting progress notes when physicians would bill for office visits of longer than half an hour each. She asks whether the physicians were aware that this was being done (they were) and how other physicians in the market were reacting. The doctor from the West says if anyone complains too vociferously about it, they are probably committing fraud. The quality manager dims the lights and shows a graph of how visits of this length have declined since the policy was implemented.

The next agenda item is to review the recent customer satisfaction survey that was required by the federal government. Satisfaction is high. The quality manager points out that members are particularly satisfied with their physicians. She then mentions that the company has to pick a quality improvement project soon. There is no discussion of it.

A doctor from the interior gives an update on a quality-of-care complaint that had been discussed in the previous meeting. Since then, he has conducted peer-to-peer review on the case and urged the physician in question to better document diagnoses and interventions. A letter will be sent to the physician as evidence of the call, with a copy placed in the provider's file, and this physician will be monitored for future incidents. The committee agrees that no further action need be taken at this time. The quality manager takes notes and then reads her summary back to me. Is this okay, she asks? She is writing the notes for federal auditors and also with an eye to a potential lawsuit.

With no further agenda items, the meeting officially ends. However, it is another 45 minutes before anyone leaves the table. The doctor from Ponce gathers his things to go and then asks about what is happening with the durable medical equipment. The other physicians join in a chorus of agreement. Each doctor brings specific complaints to the table—a member was delivered the wrong blood glucose monitor, the wait for psychiatric appointments was too long, a patient hadn't received her walker. I jot down the information and promise to pass the cases on to the Appeals and Grievance Department. The physicians say if these problems are not straightened out, the plan will surely lose members, especially with so much competition out there.

Performing Quality Management at Acme

The committee meeting shows how producing and interpreting quality data at Acme took place according to the organizational needs of the HMO, not necessarily in order to achieve the health policy objective of providing higher-quality care for beneficiaries. At least three features stand out: the importance of documentation, the focus on cost-saving strategies, and the marshalling of sensitive issues like complaints into postmeeting conversations. A meaningful, if implicit, distinction was made at the meeting between official and unofficial business. The official business represented an instance of what John Clarke terms "performing performance" (2004, 136), in which an organization must exhibit and document its commitment to achieving compliance for outside evaluators.

Official business was documented—it became part of the minutes that were both submitted to the board of directors and reviewed by auditors. The meeting agenda was also crafted to satisfy regulatory requirements without volunteering any additional, and potentially sensitive, information. It was during the unofficial portion of the meeting that managers and physicians expressed their concerns about patient care (though the informal activities were set in motion by the requirement to hold a formal quality meeting).

Employees at Acme generally took pride in providing high-quality care; many had encouraged their own family members to join the plan. However, Acme had recently contracted with a single U.S.-based company to replace a complex network of local providers of durable medical equipment. Many Acme providers and managers disliked working with the new durable medical equipment provider, but the upper management had made a business decision in an effort to control costs. The single provider was supposed to simplify ordering, increase efficiency, and reduce costs through bulk purchasing. Nevertheless, the transition created a host of logistical and administrative obstacles as the newly contracted company struggled to fill orders with little knowledge of local delivery routes or prescribing customs. By addressing these cases, participants in the quality meeting were able to do something for individuals even if the larger order and delivery problems remained unresolved.

In contrast to the candid tone of the unofficial business, the committee's official business was more formal in nature and largely geared toward documenting progress on federally required quality measures. The meeting included review of two different kinds of quality measures: audit results and a customer satisfaction survey. The quality improvement project was essentially an exercise in profit maximization aimed at investigating physician billing practices. Claims for every appointment of longer than half an hour had to be submitted with progress notes that medically justified such a lengthy interaction between a doctor and patient. The audit ensured that physicians were billing for shorter appointments (whether or not the actual length of appointments changed was not investigated). Though the likelihood that this project would improve quality of care in terms of clinical outcomes or access to care was minimal, it was reviewed and approved by government regulators as a quality improvement project. Hence, quality became part of the organization in the form of controlling costs and standardizing appointment lengths.

The other quality measure discussed at the meeting, the customer satisfaction survey, was always the focus of enormous organizational energy at Acme as interdepartmental committees labored to pull the data together. The brief discussion of the survey results at the meeting belied the quite lengthy process that was necessary to assemble the data in the required formats. For example, a few months earlier, I had listened to an hour-long conference call about the customer satisfaction survey and how to submit data correctly. This was part of a longer series of calls centered more on the proper preparation of data rather than offering quality care. Weekly meetings were held to review the process for obtaining the data and subsequently a data auditing firm was used to verify that the information had been gathered correctly prior to its submission to federal regulators. This narrow but necessary attention to process diverted both time and resources from other kinds of quality projects.

Acme's concern with managing how quality data were recorded and extracted was part of an industrywide trend. As described by a senior editor for *Managed Care*, an industry magazine, how measurement was conducted was at least as important as what was being measured:

> Today, plans can turn to a growing army of consultants, auditors and software manufacturers who are ready, willing and able to help them corral and domesticate this beast. And these lion-tamers-for-hire are finding a receptive audience—because where HEDIS [Health Plan Employer Data and Information Set] scores are concerned, the perception of a plan's quality of care is only as good as how well it can "do" HEDIS. (Dalzell 1998)

The industry insider makes an important assertion—quality for the plan is directly related to how measurement takes place.[4] Quality scores are based on how well the plan can do measurement, not necessarily on the quality of care offered by the plan, hence the growth in the consulting industry to help improve scores. Dalzell is clearly concerned with the "perception" of quality, not with quality as an objective characteristic of the care provided. This is a very different epistemological orientation to quality measurement than that promoted by health policy makers.

In addition to the quality initiatives discussed at the committee meeting, the quality program at Acme was also subject to biannual audits by CMS. During the on-site audit, CMS reviewed documentation from the quality program and interviewed the quality manager. Subsequently, CMS sent a report to the plan detailing the findings that required corrective action. After one such audit, I reviewed the quality findings, the most serious of which was a lack of evidence that the quality program had been approved by the corporation's board of directors. CMS's concern was with what they call "governance issues," meaning they wanted clear lines of authority and responsibility drawn within the organization. The audit findings did not address quality of care for patients, but the mechanisms within the corporation for ensuring that the board of directors approved the quality program and were informed of its activities.

When quality measurement is examined from the vantage point of health plans, it appears considerably less neutral and objective than the description by the NCQA of a process that is field-tested for "feasibility, reliability and validity" (2008a). Instead, Acme understood that the processes through which quality data were produced could be "massaged." Since quality programs are a point of contact between government regulators and private health plans, the health plan attempted to manage impressions and mold the quality review process in directions it deemed desirable. For example, Acme selected a quality management project based on shortening appointment lengths and paid very careful attention to what was officially recorded in the minutes. As can be seen from this description of the quality activities at Acme, improving clinical outcomes was not usually the target of the quality initiatives undertaken by the health plan. Quality was not important primarily because it was the right thing to do (as in health policy), but because it was necessary and required. Even though many individuals who worked at the plan were concerned with improving quality (as evidenced by the informal conversations at the quality meeting), the daily practices of the quality program at Acme were largely oriented toward managerial imperatives such as meeting regulatory demands, improving data collection methods, and controlling costs.

Health Plan Members Talk Quality

According to market-based health care legislation like the 2003 Medicare Modernization Act, recipients of privatized health care need quality-of-care data in order to make an informed choice to join the highest-performing plan. Consumer choice is said to drive the whole system toward ever-increasing quality and efficiency based on the assumption that people behave as rational, economic actors. Scholars of Michel Foucault have termed this consumer "the prudential subject" (O'Malley 1996, 203) or the neoliberal "homo economicus" (Gordon 1991, 43). Neoliberal theories imagine the subject as constantly engaged in cost-benefit calculations aimed at optimizing his or her health. Ethnographic attention to how consumers use quality data and make decisions, however, suggest that neoliberal subject-making projects remain largely unrealized (Kingfisher and Maskovsky 2008).

In this section, I use life history interviews to examine the proposition repeatedly forwarded by health care policy makers and other proponents of market-based health systems that beneficiaries of publicly funded health care use quality-of-care data to make informed health plan choices. These interview responses are not offered as representative of Medicare beneficiaries as a whole. However, the views do present a counterpoint to definitions of health care quality that focus on population-based clinical protocols, efficiency, cost-effectiveness, and complying with federal regulations.

During open-ended life history interviews, I asked Acme beneficiaries two questions about quality: "Are you satisfied with the quality of medical care that you receive?" and "What would most improve the quality of care that you receive?" The interview methodology is described in greater detail in chapter 3 and appendix 1. None of the 44 health plan members (in 35 interviews) expressed familiarity with publicly available quality scores (which were occasionally reported in the press but are primarily available on the Internet). Quality as a technical way of assessing and understanding the appropriateness of one's medical care was not a terribly meaningful evaluation for the health plan members I interviewed. When interviewees expressed dissatisfaction with the health care they received, they mentioned wanting more generous prescription-drug coverage, shorter wait times, and fewer problems getting authorizations (particularly on La Reforma). Some interviewees brought up particular care episodes in hospitals or at doctors' offices where they felt like they could have been treated better. Table 4.1 contains a complete list of interviewee responses to the two quality questions and demonstrates that most respondents held both positive and negative assessments of their health care.

When I asked directly about beneficiaries' levels of satisfaction with the quality of care that they were receiving, most of them reported satisfaction, which is consistent with findings from other anthropological studies of patients' attitudes where interviewees "did not express their likes and dislikes in terms of satisfaction or dissatisfaction, had no criticisms of the health services if asked generally but expressed positive and negative views on specific aspects of care" (Atkinson 1993, 286). A phrase I heard frequently in answer to the quality questions was "*hasta la fecha, lo encuentro bien*" or "*hasta la fecha, no me quejo*" ("up until now, it's been fine" or "up until now, I can't complain"). Nonetheless, elsewhere in the interviews when informants recounted their specific experiences with the health care system, they were far more likely to describe instances in which they felt that they were not respected by a medical care provider or did not receive care that they

Table 4.1. Responses to the Quality Interview Questions

Positive Assessments	Proportion Who Gave This Response
Up until now, it's been fine/Up until now, I can't complain	33%
My doctor is very good or a good person	27%
Very satisfied	24%
Satisfied	15%
Doctors are good, up to their abilities	3%
I pay less with Acme	3%
I'm satisfied; what choice do I have?	3%
Very well-cared for	3%
Negative Assessments	**Proportion Who Gave This Response**
Need more medication coverage	27%
Lengthy wait times	21%
Had problems getting prescriptions or referrals on La Reforma	15%
Had a bad experience at a hospital	9%
Had a bad experience at a mental hospital	9%
Need help with transportation to medical appointments	9%
Provider network is not adequate	9%
Missing medical equipment	9%
Need more home care	6%
Doctors in a rush	6%
Want better mental health care	6%
Diabetic shoes should be covered	6%
Plan poorly administered	3%
Issues coordinating a primary care physician for La Reforma and Acme	3%
Not treated with respect in La Reforma	3%
Poor people treated badly	3%
Want to be listened to instead of treated like I am crazy	3%
Want help at local office getting authorizations and explaining plan communication	3%
Want better explanations of coverage, benefits, and the provider network	3%

Table 4.1. Responses to the Quality Interview Questions (Continued)

Negative Assessments	Proportion Who Gave This Response
Doesn't want medication appointments with psychiatrists—it's too impersonal	3%
Wanted alternative therapies to be covered	3%
Quality of services used to be better	3%
Too much paperwork	3%
Doctors too concerned with computers	3%
Difficulty getting an out-of-network authorization with Acme	3%
Did not like it when La Reforma patients came to the doctor's office—it was too crowded	3%

Multiple responses possible. Most interviewees gave both positive and negative assessments. Out of 35 interviews, the table represents 33 responses. In interview 10, I did not explicitly discuss quality because the conversation veered off-course. The recording for interview 3 was damaged and my notes did not include responses to the quality questions.

thought was necessary. This tendency to express complete satisfaction and withhold criticism when asked directly about quality raises doubts about the validity of satisfaction surveys (which are the primary way in which patients' subjective assessments are incorporated into quality-measurement programs) as measurement tools that accurately capture patients' evaluations. Open-ended interviews revealed that the same patients who said that they were completely satisfied also experienced significant access barriers, found it difficult to pay for prescription drugs, and were confused by plan rules.

Doña Socorro illustrates this pattern; she expressed complete satisfaction when asked directly about quality, but she then revealed that she struggled to access needed care, pay for prescription drugs, and be seen in a timely manner in physicians' offices. At the time of the interview, Doña Socorro was 48. She grew up in Arecibo and boasted that she was *una mezcla americana* (an American mixture); her mother was black and her father was white with blue eyes. Doña Socorro married at 15, had a child, and finished the 12th grade by attending night school. She wanted to keep studying to become a secretary but was not able to achieve this dream. Instead, she worked at a food-packing plant for 21 years and went on disability due to a repetitive strain injury. Her youngest daughter had Down syndrome and lived with her.

Though Doña Socorro's income qualified her for La Reforma, she left the program to join Acme and did not know that she could combine the two benefits. She left La Reforma because she was paying out of pocket for most of her prescription drugs and found it increasingly difficult to get the authorizations that she needed for specialty care. La Reforma stopped paying for most of the things that she needed, so she decided that it was not worth it to continue on the program. She wished that she still had drug coverage and dental care, but she really liked her new doctor with Acme; he listened well and gave her in-office injections for her pain.

When I asked Doña Socorro directly about the quality of care that she received, she answered *"no me quejo"* ("I can't complain"). She recently underwent surgery and had to pay very little out of pocket: "I can't complain because one has to work a little bit to look for referrals and documents, but this is part of the process, right? They can't make things too easy for you, right?"

I asked if she always received all of the care that she needed. "Yes," she answered, "but there are some medications that the plan [Reforma] did not cover and I had to pay for those myself. And now that I'm on Acme, the plan without prescription drugs, I have to pay for all these things myself." She answered yes but went on to explain that she meant no.

I asked Doña Socorro what could improve the quality of services that she received. She prefaced her answer with "I don't know if this is what you're asking me, but . . . I don't really know." She then explained that she wished that the wait was shorter in doctor offices. The wait can take hours and hours. With her health condition, she cannot stay seated for long periods of time, so it is particularly difficult. She ended her response by asking, "Am I doing a good job answering the question that you asked me?"

Clearly, the language of quality felt foreign to Doña Socorro and she was timid when it came to criticizing her health plan or doctors. When she did mention that she would like appointments, she added that this would probably be nice for the doctors too. They could have a less chaotic schedule and would probably like it. She was hesitant to criticize and hedged her opinions in phrases like "I can't complain." In this sense, she did not act like an empowered decision-making consumer, and she expressed discomfort when asked to assume that role. Furthermore, her cost-benefit calculations prioritized noneconomic decision-making criteria. Doña Socorro made decisions about her health care coverage that weren't in her best financial interest (like giving up her prescription-drug coverage) but that were related to her desire to be treated with more respect and to avoid the hassle of chasing down referrals and authorizations.

In expressing her general level of satisfaction, Doña Marta, whom we met in chapter 1, was also typical. However, her interview suggests that medical care was significant to health plan members in a way that quality evaluators might not appreciate. Doña Marta lived in a modest cement home in the interior of the island and had gone on disability from her garment factory job in the 1980s due to *nervios*.[5] She qualified for La Reforma in addition to Medicare (meaning she was at 200% or below of the poverty line), was in her late 60s, and had a fifth-grade education. Like everyone else I interviewed, she did not have access to the Internet at her home. Doña Marta reported a recent heart attack and a history of heart troubles but stated that she had not gone to the cardiologist, though she was aware that she should. She did, however, see her primary care physician on a regular basis. I asked if she was satisfied with the quality of care she was receiving and she responded that she was, up to that point. I asked her about her physicians and she said that they were good people. Then I asked her if there were long waits at the doctor's office and she said,

> Yes, of course. Two or three hours, depending on your number. Some-
> times you call and she says to come at a certain time and so I go at that
> time, more or less, or a little bit before. If they tell me to go at three, I'll
> go at two so I can spend some time socializing with the people in the
> waiting room who sometimes I know.

I asked if there was anything that would improve the quality of the services and she answered, "Again, I would have to tell you that up to this point I have found it to be fine." Doña Marta's answers to the quality questions were rather terse, especially compared with other topics we discussed. She had a lot to say about changing conceptions of respect in society, her jobs at various factories, and her experiences going on disability. As discussed in chapter 1, Doña Marta spoke freely about the previous health system in which patients were treated at government health centers. Now, there were specialists for every part of the body and even poor people could see them: she saw this as a sign of progress. But when asked what could improve the quality of care that she was receiving, she did not feel like she had anything to complain about or wanted any specific improvements. When I fished for complaints about waiting times (which is an NCQA and CMS quality measure and an item that many interviewees found frustrating about accessing medical care in Puerto Rico), she had none. Instead, she showed up an hour early to socialize at the doctor's office. Significantly, the criteria that Doña Marta used to evaluate her health care were interpersonal and social in nature—her doctors were "good people" and waiting gave her the opportunity to socialize. I suspect Doña Marta's answers, like those of Doña Socorro, stem in part from a class-based hesitancy to criticize doctors. Nonetheless, it is hard to imagine how her actions would spur the system to compete on quality.

Another interviewee, Doña Carmen, whose story was discussed at length in chapter 3, had struggled over many years to obtain adequate health care for her two disabled sons. She described their diagnoses as schizophrenia and that her younger son developed his symptoms after consuming drugs at school. We spoke about quality a couple of hours into the interview and she was slightly tired and emotionally drained. Both sons were present and drifted in and out of the conversation. Doña Carmen's husband had problems with alcohol and gambling and did not live with the family. She struggled with depression—she could not leave her sons in the house alone, so she was rarely able to spend time on her own. She was 66, and she worried about what would happen to her sons when she died. Like the Brazilian informants in Sarah Atkinson's study (1993), the beneficiaries whom I interviewed reported high satisfaction with their personal physicians and did not seem comfortable criticizing doctors in general. Nonetheless, when asked about specific care incidents, they described situations that a quality specialist would consider indicative of low-quality care. For example, Doña Carmen described taking her youngest son out of a hospital because, when she went to visit him, he was covered in cigarette burns. But when I asked her if she was satisfied with the quality of care that she and her sons had received, her answer was not about substandard care. She responded, "Yes, I have to be satisfied because there is nothing else that I can do." She then described the process of qualifying for disability. She said that when her sons began to receive medical care through disability benefits, she didn't worry about filling out any papers for herself, because she was not sick at that time and her husband was working. She later regretted this decision as she attempted to manage her household on public assistance totaling $558 a month while taking care of two disabled adults. I asked about quality of care and she answered with reference to her household accounts: "I have to do what I can because now they'll take away even that, what's it called, Social Security. So, I'm satisfied. What else can I do? Maybe if I had married a rich man things would work out."

Doña Carmen did not talk about quality in the same terms used by quality specialists at the NCQA or CMS—there was nothing in her answer about delivering the right care to the right person at the right time (CMS 2008a). Instead, when I asked about quality, she described her Social Security payments. The answer was also inflected by gender—it was her husband who filled out the Social Security papers and who worked in the formal economy and therefore paid into the Social Security system. Doña Carmen spent most of her adult life performing the unpaid work of taking care of her two disabled sons and therefore did not collect much Social Security. She said that she was satisfied but simultaneously pointed out the impossibility of making things right.

The quality industry is geared toward measuring specific indicators, developing projects to improve performance on those indicators, and circulating that information to decision-making beneficiaries. The quality enterprise does not fathom the way that Doña Carmen talks about quality in terms of the inadequacies of her household economy and conflicts with her husband. Nor does it allow for Doña Marta's tacit acceptance of the system. She is not out seeking the highest-quality care—instead of seeing a cardiologist, she attends the local doctor's office and hopes to socialize with old friends and acquaintances. Doña Socorro claimed that she could not complain, but she then described joining a private Medicare plan where she forfeited her prescription-drug benefits and struggled to pay out of pocket for her medications. Clearly, there is a disjuncture between how quality professionals and beneficiaries of publicly funded health programs understand quality. The aspects of health care quality that plan members valued—good

relations with the provider, a social waiting room, economic security—
would not give rise to a more-efficient or cost-effective health system.
A personal, unhurried interaction with a provider is time-consuming,
and under Acme's new billing policy the time would likely not be
remunerated for the doctor. A sociable, comfortable waiting room
where one might encounter lifelong friends and acquaintances is
superfluous to quality-of-care measures. In fact, the quality-of-care
measures used by CMS call for health plans to keep the waiting time to
less than a half hour. Finally, more coverage and governmental support
for the elderly and disabled run counter to the downsizing impetus
of neoliberal health policy. Rather than a seamless synergy between
consumer demands and efficient care, this ethnography reveals some of
the cleavages between how neoliberal health policies imagine consumer
behavior and the ways in which health care consumers actually behave.

Conclusions: The Moral Qualities of Market Medicine

"Studying through" health policy illuminates how distinct actors
conceive of and value quality health care differently. Health policy
makers and Medicare regulators understand quality as a quantifiable
entity that is knowable through objective measurement and ongoing
performance monitoring. The moral project of quality measurement
in health policy was epitomized in the assertion by the NCQA that
measurement leads to improvement; quality was seen as a public good
linked to transparent government, greater efficiency, and the promotion
of consumer choice. At the health plan where I worked, quality
measurement was conceived of as a formal, bureaucratic enterprise
aimed at satisfying government requirements. Rather than an objective
indicator of the plan's performance, quality numbers were something
that could be shaped and improved upon by "massaging" the data. In
terms of a moral project, at the health plan quality monitoring was a
necessary requirement that worked best when quality of care and
cost efficiency were synonymous. For health plan members whom I
interviewed, quality was much less quantifiable, clinical, and codified. It
emerged experientially and had to do with the ability to obtain enough
care, to be treated well (interpersonally), to feel comfortable, and to
have access to adequate resources (not just health care). These broad

differences between how each group understood quality as a way of knowing and as a moral project attest to the fragmented nature of the market-based health system currently in place in Puerto Rico and in the mainland United States. Though the system is premised upon the circulation of information among actors in order to make decisions in the health care marketplace, in practice, members of these three "organizational and moral worlds" (Shore and Wright 1997) do not share a common understanding of what quality is or why it is important.

My intent is not to dismiss quality measurement altogether. Quality measurement has some useful, if limited, application in curbing error rates, standardizing care procedures, and holding health plans and doctors accountable to minimal levels of care. However, the problem arises when quality, and quantitative performance measurement programs in particular, become the only language available to discuss what is equitable, right, and appropriate in health care. Just as what I could say to Dr. Benedetti was seriously limited by his insistence on numbers, the public-policy conversations that revolve around quality inevitably take place in a language that is concerned with efficiency, standardization, and, more often than not, economization.

Recall the neoliberal tautology mentioned earlier: "Why is it so important to measure performance? The answer is simple. It gets better if you do" (NCQA 2006). Ethnography reveals that measuring quality does not necessarily lead to improved quality, just as an obsession with weight has not made Americans thinner. One of the fundamental problems with linking quality measurement to quality improvement is that market-based health policies are often based on spurious assumptions about how institutions and individuals behave.

As this book goes to press, quality is again a buzzword in conversations about health reform in the United States and Puerto Rico. Policy makers would do well to understand how previous performance and quality-monitoring programs were implemented and the shortcomings of investing so much time and energy into measurement for measurement's sake. Because relying on satisfaction surveys is clearly inadequate, in order to recalibrate quality toward the goal of meaningful reform, we must actually listen to what patients value in health care.

5

Complaints

The Wrong Glucometer . . . Again!

Recall the story from the introduction about the two brothers from Río Grande, Don Ignacio and Don Enrique. The brothers repeatedly requested a glucometer from Acme with an extra-large print display so they could manage their diabetes, but the company kept sending them the standard model. Each time the brothers called Acme to complain, a member of the Customer Service Department opened a grievance in the electronic complaints system and a new glucose monitor was sent to their home. When I met with them, several blood glucose monitors that they could not read were gathering dust on a shelf in their small concrete home. Both of the brothers' diabetes were not well controlled, and Don Enrique had developed gangrene from a small, untreated cut on his foot.

In Don Ignacio and Don Enrique's case, order authorizations were processed incorrectly, the delivery of their medical equipment was delayed, and the wrong glucose monitor was repeatedly sent. But the brothers' case was no anomaly. At this time, the most common complaint reason at Acme was a delay in delivery of medical equipment. Ironically, the drive to save money and deliver the cheapest glucose monitor backfired. Acme spent far more on delivering the wrong monitor, and, in the process, the company aggravated the brothers' health condition.

This situation developed for a variety of reasons. The Miami-based durable medical equipment (DME) company with whom Acme had subcontracted was unfamiliar with the topography of the island and it lacked the local knowledge to navigate unnamed streets and unnumbered houses (especially in rural areas). The DME company also expected that physicians in Puerto Rico would be very similar to those in South Florida; after all, they spoke Spanish in both places. They did not realize, however, that significant differences existed in prescribing customs between the island and Florida. When the new DME company received an order that contained what they deemed "insufficient" information (for example, if the order lacked a diagnosis code or medical justification for nonstandard equipment), the order languished while overwhelmed customer service representatives tried to obtain the missing information from physicians' offices that were not used to having their orders questioned and did not have the staff to deal with the added administrative burdens imposed by managed care. These problems arose in part because Acme decided to do business with a company from the mainland. Acme had determined that local DME companies were overbilling, too costly, and inefficient. Ultimately, Acme's attempt at economization and increased efficiency produced a barrage of complaints at the organization, and, too often, this left beneficiaries receiving suboptimal health care.

These unintentional consequences stem in part from the contradictions inherent in transforming the medical care of the poor, the disabled, and the elderly into a profit-generating enterprise. Clearly, there was a misfit between market goals (saving money through a more standardized approach to product delivery) and health objectives (getting the brothers a glucometer that they could read and use in order to manage their diabetes). But this example is also interesting because it illustrates how market-based reforms to public services increasingly call on citizens to behave as consumers; the only redress available to the brothers was to complain to Acme through their corporate complaints process.

The Right to Complain

The question of how privatization reconfigures the manner in which citizens can register discontent and pursue resolution is ultimately a question about how privatization transforms citizenship. Privatization entails more than the transfer of formerly state-run services and industries into private ownership; it also occasions transformations in practices of citizenship so that acting as a citizen increasingly resembles acting as a consumer.

In a market-based health care system, the ultimate way to register one's complaint is to join the health plan that the competition is offering. Consumers are supposed to express dissatisfaction through purchasing decisions like opting to join a higher-performing health plan or to visit a better-rated doctor. But members of private Medicare plans can and do complain with more than their feet. Significant regulations are in place at Medicare health plans that govern the receipt and processing of consumer complaints. The Centers for Medicare and Medicaid Services (CMS) explicitly uses the language of rights to describe the kinds of protections that Medicare beneficiaries are entitled to: "You have certain rights and protections designed to do the following: protect you when you get health care, make sure you get the health care services that the law says you can get, protect you against unethical practices, and protect your privacy" (CMS 2009, 7). In order to protect beneficiaries' rights, the federal government has mandated that private Medicare Advantage plans create extensive complaints processing procedures that are subject to regular audit and verification.

This chapter explores how private corporations actually go about protecting beneficiaries and the contradictions created by a system in which the corporation is at once the alleged violator and guarantor of one's rights. In managing a corporate compliance department that was responsible for processing complaints and in interviewing Medicare beneficiaries, I found that the complaints system exhibited a paradoxical quality. The consumer complaints system *appears* to foster a democratic means for beneficiary voices to be heard and due process to be protected. But in practice, the complaints system actually hollowed out, or severely limited, beneficiaries' rights and avenues to redress because it narrowly channeled (1) *how* beneficiaries were permitted to complain, (2) to *whom* they may complain, and finally (3) *what* kinds of issues were deemed legitimate and actionable. Frequently, the reasons that motivated a beneficiary's complaint—issues such as a desire to be treated with respect or to have their unique health-related needs be

recognized (like needing more than the standard blood glucose monitor)—were not addressed or recognized within the corporate complaints process. The complaints system also served as a safety valve for
containing member and provider dissent, which in turn allowed the
health plan to continue rationing care through utilization review.

Citizenship and Privatizing the Colonial Welfare State

Relationships between individuals and governments are undergoing
profound changes in the new millennium under the influence of
globalization and neoliberalism (Gledhill 2005; Nguyen 2005; Ong
2005; Petryna 2002; Rose and Novas 2005).[1] In this context, new
medical knowledge and technology, infectious disease outbreaks, and
the restructuring of public health systems (often along market lines)
have become particularly fertile terrains for crafting new citizenship
practices. For example, research on HIV treatment programs in Brazil
(Biehl 2007) and the Ivory Coast (Nguyen 2005) and on populations
seeking access to disability payments in the wake of major disasters
(Fortun 2001; Petryna 2002) argues that such programs tie access to
state and international aid resources to disability and medical diagnostic
categories, thereby segmenting citizenship along medical lines (those
with a politically recognized diagnosis may gain access to more state or
international aid resources).[2] A similar process is occurring in Puerto
Rico as those who meet the eligibility criteria for public insurance
programs (criteria based on age, disability status, and/or income)
gain access to publicly funded, though privately administered, health
insurance coverage.

These beneficiaries of public programs are at once citizens who are
entitled to certain health care benefits and protections under the law
and consumers who are clients of private corporations. For proponents
of market-based reforms, this change is celebrated as an expansion of
citizenship into new domains because beneficiaries gain access to services from corporations that were formerly only available to private
customers. However, there is a less optimistic way to make sense of
how citizenship is transformed by the marketization of public services.
Rather than creating more agency for citizens and greater access to
social protections, anthropologist John Gledhill argues that these new

forms of citizenship display "the paradoxical quality of both expanding the ways in which citizenship can be defined and "hollowing out" its substance" (2005, 88). Hollowing out happens as economic insecurity increases, social welfare programs retract, and violence (often from para and extra state sources) increases. In the case of Acme, the right to due process in health care is hollowed out by a corporate, bureaucratic system that narrowly defines what is a legitimate and actionable complaint.

Citizenship is already a hotly contested political issue in Puerto Rico: "Questions of citizenship, migration, and identity in Puerto Rico acquire a sense of urgency seldom found in well-established nation-states that do not have to justify their existence or fight for their survival" (Duany 2000, 8). Currently, market-reform programs are transforming the relationship between U.S. citizenship and access to welfare programs on the island. Residents of Puerto Rico were included in federal social welfare programs beginning with the New Deal (though aid to Puerto Rico came later and at reduced levels than on the mainland) and continuing with the establishment of the Commonwealth government in 1952 (Colón Reyes 2002, 27; Morrissey 2006). The extension of social welfare programs to Puerto Rico had a profound effect on the local government, creating a "colonial welfare state that has become a crucial actor in the economic and social life of the community" (Rivera Ramos 2001, 227). Federal social welfare programs (including nutritional assistance, Medicare, Social Security, housing assistance, and education) as well as the ability to migrate freely to the mainland have all underwritten American colonial hegemony on the island (Rivera Ramos 2001). Nonetheless, because Puerto Rico is a *colonial* welfare state, many federal programs are available in some form on the island, but they are not administered in the same way, and residents of Puerto Rico have no voting representation at the federal level that could influence policy.

Currently, privatization and government downsizing are dismantling parts of the colonial welfare state (Colón Reyes 2005; Silver 2007), potentially troubling the relationship between American citizenship, access to social welfare programs, and the political status of the island. The social and political contract on which the Commonwealth status is predicated is undergoing profound restructuring through neoliberal policies, including downsizing the government workforce, creating more public/private partnerships, and prioritizing fiscal reforms that cut government debt and deficits. New citizenship practices like complaining to corporations provide a window onto how citizens are making sense of these changes and how corporations have gone about taking on new governmentlike responsibilities. Directing ethnographic inquiry at the multiple ways in which individuals talk about and interact (or fail to interact) with a corporate complaints department reveals how people are attempting to exercise their rights to health care and how they understand the obligations that the government retains toward them as citizens.

While a growing consensus of public health bodies and social critics argue that national governments should assume a stronger role in establishing, maintaining, and funding public health and national health insurance systems (Garrett 2007; Pfeiffer and Chapman 2010; Smith-Nonini 2006; WHO 2008), the health systems in Puerto Rico and the United States continue to be dominated by consumerist models and market-based reform projects. This chapter illustrates some of the consequences of that position for beneficiaries seeking care in Puerto Rico.

Novel Forms of Liability and Their Complaints

The Customer Service Department at Acme sprawled over half a floor of the modern, mirrored glass office building. Arranged in rows, the customer service representatives answered calls piped directly into their headsets and entered customers' information into computers. Many of the calls were prompted by the receipt of written communication from the health plan. The plan was required by law to issue denial notices to members if a physician submitted a claim and the health maintenance organization (HMO) decided not to pay. The denial notice included a description of the member's rights and instructions on how to file an appeal. The denial notices were often confusing for beneficiaries and ended up generating complaints even when no payment was being sought from the member by either the health plan or the service provider. The process also inadvertently created an adversarial relationship between providers and patients. The following complaint illustrates some of the ironies of these processes that were put in place to safeguard consumers' rights.

Doña Hermina called Customer Service and complained about a notice she received in the mail. She was liable for $55 for a procedure that Acme had determined was cosmetic and not medically necessary (and therefore not covered by Medicare). Doña Hermina claimed this was a mistake—the podiatrist, Dr. García, never told her she would have to pay out-of-pocket. The customer service representative phoned Dr. García's office and asked for his version of events. The provider, annoyed, said he had already been called about the case. The customer service representative could not reach a quick resolution, so she transferred the case upstairs to the Appeals and Grievance Department. In contrast to the customer service representatives who were packed into a large room with small cubicles arranged side by side with no dividers in between, the appeals and grievance coordinators worked behind much larger cubicles on expansive desks where they could spread out the case files and enjoy a modicum of privacy. Upstairs, in the Appeals and Grievance Department, the complaint was classified as an appeal and was resolved by sending a letter to the member. The letter stated that the doctor would not charge the member for the service but that Medicare does not cover cosmetic procedures and next time, she would have to pay.

The podiatrist, Dr. García, after receiving multiple calls from the health plan regarding this case, became quite angry and vowed to file a grievance against the member. He sent a letter to Doña Hermina with a copy to the HMO written in all capital letters. Dr. García claimed that he was referring the case to his lawyer and would sue Doña Hermina for libel and defamation of character. The letter was handed from person to person at Acme, but no one was quite sure what to do. However, no complaint file was created and tracked in the system, because the government only audits consumer, not provider, complaints—only certain types of cases are handled through official channels.

The letter found its way to me and as lawyers were being invoked, I asked the manager of the Provider Relations Department to speak with Dr. García. She pulled me into her windowed office, shut the door, and dialed his number with the phone on speaker. We spoke to the doctor for 25 minutes. His primary complaint was that his reputation had been insulted. When the patient came to his office and tried to pay the $55, he refused to see her and much less take her money. He said his daughter can spend that amount on makeup in a weekend. He does not need the money. He includes a reminder of the amount owed on patients' appointment cards, but if they cannot pay, he writes it off at the end of the year on his taxes.

The physician was insulted by the idea that he would go after a patient over $55. Ironically, had the HMO not been mandated by the government to protect consumers' rights by sending out a denial notice, the conflict would never have erupted. Protecting the member's rights caused the complaint because new billing practices and notions of liability supplanted the customary practices that many doctors in Puerto Rico employed in their offices.

To resolve the issue, the provider relations manager complimented the physician, assuaged his ego, and explained that the HMO was only investigating because the organization was compelled to do so by federal law. After venting his frustrations, Dr. García agreed to call off his lawyer.

Doña Hermina phoned that day, agitated and crying. She couldn't sleep for her nerves since receiving the doctor's letter. The appeals and grievance coordinator told her that the doctor would drop the issue and would she please pick another podiatrist from the provider list. She agreed and vowed to never visit Dr. García again. The appeals and grievance coordinator made a note of the outcome and closed the case in the electronic tracking system.

The complaints process in this example was both dysfunctional and overzealous. The corporation attempted to protect the rights of its members in compliance with federal regulations, but the complaint investigation itself aggravated the situation as multiple Acme employees called the doctor and the member, thereby transforming what was a minor billing misunderstanding into a much larger problem. The physician's reaction—though rare—draws attention to how the initial denial notice and the subsequent investigation ignored local norms for handling billing discrepancies and re-scripted the interaction between the provider and the patient into the idiom of complaints, which created a newly adversarial and litigious relationship. Was Doña Hermina meaningfully protected in this interaction? Unfortunately, she ended up more aggrieved at the conclusion of the process than she was at the beginning.

Regulation of Complaints Processing

As intimated in the stories above, the Medicare program defines complaints through extensive regulations.[3] The rules surrounding how complaints are addressed are designed to protect the rights of Medicare beneficiaries who elect to enroll in private plans, but the rules themselves can be overwhelming. Consider the variety of complaint options available to beneficiaries. The types of complaints that beneficiaries may use to express their dissatisfaction are grievances, expedited grievances, quality-of-care grievances, standard appeals, expedited appeals, fast-track appeals, immediate quality improvement organization (QIO) reviews of discharge decisions, formulary exceptions, expedited formulary exceptions, prescription-drug coverage redeterminations, and prescription-drug coverage expedited redeterminations.[4] Each of these complaint types requires different processing procedures and time frames. Some of these complaints are received and processed by the health plan, while others must also be reviewed by independent agencies under contract with Medicare. Why this dizzying array of complaint options? To understand what may appear overdone, we have to look back at the history of managed care in Medicare. The current system for processing complaints is largely the result of a lawsuit.

In 1993, a group of beneficiaries from New Mexico who were enrolled in a Medicare health plan filed a class action suit known as *Grijalva v. Shalala*. The plaintiffs argued that the HMO had violated their constitutional right to due process by denying coverage for a medical service or claim and refusing to make an appeal available in a timely manner. The plaintiffs also claimed that the insurance company never made clear its reason for denying services.

The procedural history of *Grijalva v. Shalala* reveals that the extension and codification of beneficiaries' due process rights were initially linked to the court opinion that HMOs were "federal actors." Though this position was later reversed, the case shows that the question of whether or not HMOs were state actors was at the center of debates about the rights due to Medicare beneficiaries who were enrolled in private health plans. In 1996, the district court ruled on the case and mandated that Medicare HMOs establish new procedures that would protect beneficiaries and provide appeal rights; these new procedures included the fast-track appeal and additional member notification requirements for service terminations. The government appealed, but the appeals court agreed with the district court that "organization determinations" by the government-contracted health plan constituted government action. Hence, in the opinion of the appeals court, the HMO was a federal actor. Of particular importance was the possibility that the HMO could deny necessary medical care, thereby causing "a high risk of erroneous deprivation of medical care to the beneficiaries" (*Grijalva v. Shalala* 1998).

In 1999, this decision was overturned. In an appeal before the Supreme Court, *Grijalva v. Shalala* was remanded back to the district court for two reasons: the first concerned a similar case and the second had to do with new legislation that created appeal regulations for Medicare health plans (*Grijalva v. Shalala* 1999). In the similar case (*American Manufacturers Mutual Insurance Company v. Sullivan*), the Supreme Court also considered a utilization review issue and ruled that the utilization decision *did not* constitute state action. The Balanced Budget Act of 1997, which was referenced by the Supreme Court as a rationale for remanding the case, contained more stringent appeal and grievance regulations for Medicare health plans. The Balanced Budget Act had been passed by Congress after the initial class action lawsuit was filed in 1993. In fact, these regulations went further than the recommendations of the district court (*Grijalva v. Shalala* 1998). For example, the Balanced Budget Act defined the conditions under which beneficiaries could grieve or appeal a plan decision as well as the timeframes within which the case had to be processed.

Ultimately, the plaintiffs were granted their rights, but not because the HMO was a state actor. There was then a real ambiguity in the court's position—the beneficiaries were entitled to the same rights they would receive if the services had been delivered by the state, but the court would not recognize the private plan as the state. Through legislation, new due process rights ultimately became part of the law that authorizes and regulates private Medicare health plans. This legislation extended the reach of government practices—like extensive notification

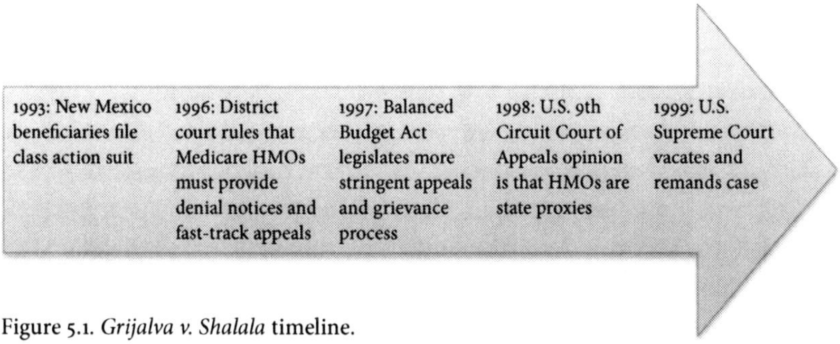

| 1993: New Mexico beneficiaries file class action suit | 1996: District court rules that Medicare HMOs must provide denial notices and fast-track appeals | 1997: Balanced Budget Act legislates more stringent appeals and grievance process | 1998: U.S. 9th Circuit Court of Appeals opinion is that HMOs are state proxies | 1999: U.S. Supreme Court vacates and remands case |

Figure 5.1. *Grijalva v. Shalala* timeline.

procedures, standardized denial reasons, appeal rights, and verification through audit—without ceding that the HMO was a state actor. This is the legal framework that creates Medicare beneficiaries' dual roles as consumers with a choice of health plans to join in the marketplace and as citizens entitled to certain rights and protections. The complaints stories that appear in this chapter illustrate the difficulties that beneficiaries encounter while trying to navigate their dual roles as consumers and citizens.

A Fast-Track Appeal

One of the new complaint types created as a result of the *Grijalva v. Shalala* ruling was the "fast-track appeal." When a member is discharged from a skilled nursing facility (SNF) or if services from a home health agency or comprehensive outpatient rehabilitation facility are terminated, the member must receive a notice regarding the discontinuation of such services. The member must sign the notice, which also describes appeal rights. To exercise one's appeal rights, a beneficiary must request another, more detailed notice that explains why the services are to be discontinued. Upon receipt of this longer statement, the beneficiary may then file a fast-track appeal with a QIO (which is an independent review organization under contract with the Medicare program). If the member opts to appeal, the QIO medical staff reviews the case and makes a determination as to whether they agree with the plan or if the care should be continued.[5]

The first fast-track appeal case that I worked on at Acme involved Doña Regina, whose SNF stay was being discontinued because she had exhausted her benefit, which is Medicare-speak indicating that her services would no longer be paid for because she had exceeded the maximum number of 100 covered days. The independent reviewer at the QIO said that she would not handle the fast-track appeal because the issue was exhaustion of benefits, not medical necessity. The QIO reviewer and I disagreed about whether or not Doña Regina's appeal should even go through the fast-track process (demonstrating confusion about the process even on the part of the professionals who were charged with implementing the law). The QIO worker was reluctant to accept the case because it did not appear to require a medical necessity review, and she also had difficulty obtaining the medical records because it was the weekend. From Acme's perspective, I was concerned that if we did not process the appeal, then we would be found noncompliant by CMS. After many phone calls back and forth, the QIO reviewer was able to obtain medical records and she faxed me the decision on Saturday. The reviewer upheld Acme's initial decision, and Doña Regina's stay at the SNF was discontinued.

A staff member at the SNF delivered the notice to Doña Regina and read it at her bedside, explaining that she was financially responsible for her continued stay. Doña Regina was originally from Cuba; she suffered from paralysis and had no family in Puerto Rico. Of course, her complaint of having nowhere to go, of being isolated from her family, of being paralyzed was not addressed by the fast-track appeal process. I doubt she felt grateful that her due process rights were being protected.

Though the fast-track appeal rules were designed to protect beneficiaries' rights by creating an expedient process that would be available seven days a week, the process suffered from several practical challenges, including that the process itself was difficult for beneficiaries to understand, complicated to administer, and provided narrow definitions for what was "appealable." The only question that the appeal process could answer was whether the beneficiary was entitled to any additional covered days (which she was not). Other aspects of her complaint and the ultimate problem of her predicament were unprocessable, and ultimately unrecognizable, through the official complaints process.

The Vigorous Processing of Complaints at Acme

Part of my work at Acme was to ensure that the plan complied with the new federal complaints regulations, which even in the mid-2000s were sometimes referred to as *Grijalva*. Being found in compliance hinged on establishing a process for the receipt and resolution of complaints—it did not necessarily involve making a fair or just determination in any particular case. The techniques for managing dissatisfaction and protecting due process according to the *Grijalva* rules involve properly classifying the complaint, sending the correct acknowledgment letter, investigating the issue, applying established decision-making criteria, documenting the response, and notifying the member of the outcome. Records must be kept for 10 years, and proper tracking of all cases is essential in order to pass a government audit. That said, the process works exceptionally well on paper, but often ineffectively in practice.

One of the most difficult aspects of the appeals and grievance process was correctly classifying a member complaint. Members rarely, if ever, called and requested to invoke their right to a fast-track appeal. In other words, they did not complain using the technical language and categories of the government. They were upset and worried about their health and wanted the plan to do something. The customer service representative who listened to the member complaint then tried to match it to a complaint category. Days of training were dedicated to understanding the various kinds of complaints and there were always many errors, as well as differences in interpretation. This problem was compounded by high turnover rates in Customer Service. Every week some customer service representatives quit or were fired, and others began working at Acme.

Even the highly trained customer service managers struggled to distinguish between an appeal and a grievance. During a CMS audit, I sat in on an interview with Margaret, a CMS reviewer, and three customer service managers—Julio, Maritza, and Usbaldo. Margaret asked about a hypothetical situation: a patient goes to a doctor's office but is refused care, and the patient believes he or she is entitled to that care, so how should the complaint be handled? Julio, Maritza, and Usbaldo began bickering back and forth. It's a grievance. No, it's an appeal and they need to submit it in writing. No, it's just an inquiry as to whether a service is covered. Margaret took notes as they disagreed with one another. My face turned red (I was the one responsible for training them). Julio, Maritza, and Usbaldo looked in my direction, embarrassed. Finally, I answered Margaret that this was an appealable situation, but we accept appeals in writing. The member should have been oriented about his or her appeal rights and if the member requested an expedited appeal, the case should be transferred to Compliance immediately. Though I was confident of my response at the time, in retrospect, I'm not sure which answer Margaret considered correct.

In my time at Acme, individual reviewers were not rewarded for denying coverage, nor were staff instructed to ignore complaints. Instead, complaints were processed vigorously. I did not witness the kinds of predatory practices that were depicted by Michael Moore in the film *Sicko* (2007), where expensive claims were intentionally denied and due process rights were routinely violated. This is partially because Medicare is more stringently regulated than the employer group and self-insured plans that Moore exposed.

But even when a plan earnestly endeavors to receive and sort complaints well, the maze of categories, definitions, and timeframes impedes navigation. Add to this the incommensurability of the member's story with the complaint category and we can begin to see the difficulty that the beneficiary experiences in exercising his or her due process rights. This is an example of the kind of hollowing out of citizenship that happens under market-based systems for administering public services—on paper, rights may be protected, but in practice the situation is far more difficult to manage. In this example, the thoroughness and complexity of the regulatory requirements contributed to challenges in administering complaints processes and also created a disconnect (or misrecognition) between members' stated complaints and the categories available for pursuing resolution. Further, as a result of the exigencies of "governing from afar," government audits and oversight focused on easily quantifiable and procedural aspects of complaints processing, such as when an acknowledgment letter was sent and the timeframe for a resolution. The content of the complaints and the appropriateness of the resolution were of secondary importance. Too often, the resolution process was driven by the demands of audit rather the unique health needs of beneficiaries, as in Doña Regina's fast-track appeal case discussed earlier.

Complaints as Safety Valves

Acme's vigorous processing of complaints could be seen as an attempt to safeguard the due process rights of members. But the function of the complaints area might be better understood as reinforcing—not challenging—Acme's utilization review and care-rationing practices. Appeals allowed *individuals* to receive payments for services that were initially denied (assuming that the case was received in the correct format and classified appropriately), but appeals also allowed the entire utilization review *system* to continue denying services for beneficiaries and providers.[6] The exceptions strengthen the rule.

By joining a Medicare Advantage plan, a beneficiary agrees to follow the plan rules. Four paragraphs of legalese directly precede a beneficiary's signature on a Medicare Advantage enrollment form (itself four pages long). This legal text contains the following crucial clauses:

> I understand that beginning on the date Acme coverage begins, I must get all of my health care from Acme, except for emergency or urgently needed services or out-of-area dialysis services.
>
> If I move out of the area that Acme serves, I need to notify the plan so I can disenroll and find a new plan in my new area.
>
> Once I am a member of Acme, I have the right to appeal plan decisions about payment or services if I disagree. I will read the Evidence of Coverage document from Acme when I get it to know which rules I must follow to get coverage with this Medicare Advantage plan.
>
> Services authorized by Acme and other services contained in my Acme Evidence of Coverage document (also known as a member contract or subscriber agreement) will be covered. Without authorization, NEITHER MEDICARE NOR ACME WILL PAY FOR THE SERVICES.[7] (CMS 2010, emphasis in original)

Members are made aware of plan rules in several ways, the most extensive being a document numbering almost 150 pages called the Evidence of Coverage (or Member Handbook). Unsurprisingly, a common reason for appeal was that a claim for a service was denied when a member did not follow the plan rules. The most frequent rule violations were visits to out-of-network physicians, failure to obtain prior authorization for certain services, receiving routine care off the island, and receiving noncovered services.

Before paying a claim, a managed care organization will ask two questions: Is the service covered? Is it medically necessary? But as the enrollment form excerpt makes clear, plan rules can be difficult to understand. For example, what constitutes a "covered service" can be mystifying. Covered services are defined by the Medicare program, and each Medicare Advantage plan may offer some additional services that are not covered by Medicare (like eye glasses, gym memberships, or hearing aids). Don Ignacio and Don Enrique thought their blood glucose monitor should be covered, but Acme decided otherwise. This is because covered services are only truly covered when they are also deemed medically necessary. Just because a service is received from a physician, that does not mean that it will be considered medically necessary (as Doña Hermina learned after her visit to the podiatrist's office). Medicare defines medically necessary as "services or supplies that are needed to diagnose or treat your medical condition and that meet accepted standards of medical practice" (CMS 2012b).

As in other ethnographic studies of utilization review processes, I found that Acme employed "strategic ambiguity" in defining medical necessity for beneficiaries and providers (Wagner 2005, 64). In his study of utilization review procedures in Medicaid managed care in New Mexico, Wagner (2005) found that utilization review served as a care-rationing mechanism and created a bureaucratic apparatus that was virtually impossible for beneficiaries and providers to navigate. Current controversies over evidence-based medicine likewise demonstrate that defining an "accepted standard of practice" can be quite contentious. While the medical necessity and other plan rules provide the rationale for issuing denials, Acme enforced these rules with a great deal of flexibility, which created a safety valve for containing dissent and appeasing disgruntled members and providers.

Increasingly, health plans use automated payment software to determine whether or not a claim for services is covered by Medicare and medically necessary. This sector of the health care industry is growing rapidly. One example of a health technology company that specializes in helping managed care organizations deny claims is iHealth Technologies, which bills itself as a "payment policy management" company. iHealth developed a tool that analyzed diagnostic and procedure codes on DME, professional, and other outpatient claims, looking for reasons to deny, based on research that the company had conducted into constantly evolving standards of medical practice. iHealth provided Acme with a denial rationale for each claim that included references to Medicare payment policy, clinical trials, and professional associations like the American Medical Association in order to make its denials, in its words, "defensible" (see www.ihealthtechnologies.com). For example, iHealth had payment rules (called iHealth "logics" at Acme) that generated denials for things like receiving too many therapies in a week (such as physical therapy or cardiac rehab). A favorite of the appeals and grievance coordinators were denials produced by iHealth logics for unpleasant procedures such as penile tests or too many colonoscopies in a 2-year period. As with most denials at Acme, iHealth denials were usually overturned on appeal. Most of the cases were shown upon review to have medical merit (not many people would subject themselves to an unnecessary colonoscopy). But more generally, Acme preferred to pay the claim in order to keep members and providers from becoming angry.

Companies like iHealth have their parallels in the provider world; the claims denial practices of HMOs have spurred the creation of companies that sell their coding services to providers so that they can avoid unnecessary and costly denials. Other e-health vendors specialize in products that allow providers to "upcode" by automatically populating claims forms with data from electronic medical records in order to ensure that providers maximize their compensation from payers. Though denying unnecessary services is supposed to reduce waste, the "payment policy management" arms race creates less, not more, efficiency in the health system. Recent reports also suggest that it contributes to escalating overall costs (Abelson, Creswell, and Palmer 2012).

Another common denial reason that illustrates the tendency to decide cases in favor of members is seeking care out-of-network. In theory, provider networks are an essential tool of managed care: they limit who a member can see and ensure that only providers who have agreed to the plan's reimbursement rates and management protocols see patients. However, at the time of my study, Acme only selectively enforced its provider network rules.[8] In one of the many unwritten policies at Acme, the Executive Committee decided to pay for out-of-network doctor visits if they occurred in Puerto Rico because the volume was huge, but on a per-service basis, the cost was minimal. In one 3-month period, an executive explained to me that there had been around 900 visits per month for elective services, costing roughly $180,000. If Acme denies all of those claims, we'll have 900 pissed-off members a month, I was told. This would dramatically increase the number of appeals and probably would not save much money once all the administrative costs and disenrollments were factored in. So, the executives made what they described as a "business decision" to pay the claims, but only when they were submitted by the doctor, not the member. Acme was trying to expand its provider network at this time and wanted to maintain good relations with the physician community on the island.

When the Compliance Department received an appeal for payment for an out-of-network service (either because it was delivered in the United States, paid for by the member and submitted for reimbursement, or submitted by a nonphysician provider), the appeals and grievance coordinators would try and find a reason to overturn the initial denial (thereby siding with the member). One of the most common ways to do this was to determine whether the member perceived that an emergency had occurred. Services can be obtained out of network in an emergency if that care meets the criteria established by Medicare:

> An emergency medical condition is a medical condition manifesting itself by acute symptoms of sufficient severity (including severe pain) such that a prudent layperson, with an average knowledge of health and medicine, could reasonably expect the absence of immediate medical attention to result in:
> - Serious jeopardy to the health of the individual or, in the case of a pregnant woman, the health of the woman or her unborn child;
> - Serious impairment to bodily functions; or
> - Serious dysfunction of any bodily organ or part. (CMS 2011)

CMS employs a subjective definition where a "prudent layperson" only needs to perceive that an emergency exists (irrespective of whether examination by a medical professional determines that an actual medical emergency exists). Many appeals cases were resolved this way (it allowed for considerable leeway on the part of appeals and grievance coordinators to argue that such claims should be paid).

Cases that could not be resolved in favor of the member administratively in the department had to be presented to the Appeals and Grievance Committee (which contained intimidating executives like the chief medical officer). The cases that went before the committee and were upheld were typically for very expensive services like motorized wheelchairs and bariatric surgeries. In these instances, Acme submitted the case to an independent review organization that determined whether or not Acme's denial was valid.

Ethnography reveals that the appeals and grievance area served as an escape valve that released the pressure created by managing care and denying claims through the application of plan rules. This way, Acme could continue to deny services and ration care, but if any individual got too upset, the decision could be reversed. Dissent was effectively contained, but the underlying utilization review practices remained unchanged. Several times, this intention was stated directly by Acme executives who, when implementing a new utilization review process or iHealth payment logic, would say, let's just see what happens. If we get a lot of complaints, we'll deal with the appeals.[9]

When the Safety Valve Fails: Mental Health Complaints

In both Medicare managed care and La Reforma, mental health services were contracted out (delegated) to a managed behavioral health organization (MBHO). At the time of my research, there were only two MBHOs (and then one) on the island. Therefore, Medicare plans and Reforma plans contracted with the same companies. At Acme, this delegation relationship made processing complaints for behavioral services particularly challenging. While delegation allows companies that are specialized in a particular area (dental, behavioral health, prescription drugs) to deliver services to members, it also introduces an added layer of organizational and administrative complexity that can create barriers to coordinating care. As in La Reforma, Acme's delegation agreements were risk-based; Acme paid the delegated entity a capitation (premium) per member per month in exchange for providing access to delegated services, maintaining a provider network, monitoring quality, processing appeals, and paying its own provider claims.

Acme received many complaints regarding accessing care through its delegated MBHO. Processing times were slow and members often struggled to obtain approval for care at the intensity that they thought necessary, for example, for an appointment with a psychiatrist rather than a social worker, or for an inpatient hospitalization, rather than ambulatory care. When these complaints were received at Acme, they were transferred to the MBHO for resolution. Because behavioral health was delegated, there were no psychiatrists on staff at Acme, and so none of the medical staff felt qualified to interfere in the MBHO's utilization management decisions. Therefore, it was left up to the MBHO's expertise to decide what level of care was most appropriate and suitable for Acme members. Likewise, when CMS conducted an audit, the auditors were not clinical staff and did not interrogate clinical decision making.

In other contexts where utilization review was employed in a managed care setting for behavioral health services, downgrading of services was common:

> While expressly intended to instill professional accountability among clinicians, utilization review limited expenditures for care by closely limiting length of residential treatment stays and number of outpatient counseling visits. Clinicians also observed that utilization review channeled Medicaid recipients requiring highly specialized services into less specialized services. (Willging 2005, 93)

The beneficiaries whom I interviewed also expressed concern about short medication-based appointments (Don Luis, interview 13; Doña Carmen, interview 27; Teresa Ramírez, interview 31), lack of adequate institutional care (Doña Carmen, interview 27; Teresa Ramírez, interview 31), too much burden on family members to care for the mentally ill (Doña Carmen, interview 27; Doña Candelaria, interview 28), and being treated disrespectfully by Reforma doctors (Don Luis, interview 13).

Underutilization of privatized mental health services was a prominent problem throughout the health system in Puerto Rico (Comisión Para Evaluar el Sistema de Salud 2005; PAHO 2007, 46–47; Rivera Mass et al. 2004). In the only major study evaluating the impact of La Reforma on the health system, investigators found that three-quarters of adults and children who needed mental health services did not receive them (Comisión Para Evaluar el Sistema de Salud 2005, 24–25). The system is also fragmented and separates mental from physical health services, and there is "documented evidence of deficient care in the private system" (PAHO 2007, 47). The commission also found from speaking with providers and patients that there was a "generalized dissatisfaction" with mental health services and there were many problems with unclear service denials and lack of an effective appeals process (25). Additional problems mentioned in the report include outdated prescription practices and formularies, low reimbursement rates for mental health professionals, and precertifications that created barriers to service. Dr. José L. Galarza Arbona, the head of the Administration for Mental Health and Anti-Addiction Services (ASSMCA), offered these conclusions:

> The problems with low reimbursement rates, delayed payments, and a pre-authorization system that creates barriers to care have only been addressed with indifference, not seriousness, by these companies who operate with considerable earnings, and whose priority has been the generation of earnings, and not the just treatment of providers and patients. Then they have the audacity to characterize providers who protest as only interested in their own personal gain. (Quoted in Comisión Para Evaluar el Sistema de Salud 2005, 92)

This same practice of blame shifting—when managed care organizations blame providers for being too greedy or providing too much care—was found in research on privatization of the New Mexico Medicaid system (Willging 2005).

Finally, beneficiaries complained about the limited and constantly changing MBHO provider networks. The public health researcher Ruth

Ríos Albizu-García and her colleagues (2004) have documented that mental health providers dropped out of the managed care network at a rate of 31% over the course of a single year (the year was 1999) in Puerto Rico. "A majority (86%) attributed their departure to some contention with the MBHO. Among these, nearly one half indicated that they primarily dropped out of the network because of concerns with the effects of care management on quality of care, because of tardiness in reimbursements, or revenues lost because of unsettled claims" (261). These findings contrast markedly with explanations I heard the MBHO give to CMS reviewers during a site visit. When the issue of a limited network was brought up, the MBHO medical director argued that this must be understood within a general shortage of mental health practitioners and especially psychiatrists on the island. No mention was made of low reimbursement rates or provider complaints during the interview.

Given the widespread, systemic problems with the MBHOs, how did patients resolve their disputes? The next two examples are illustrative.

Unregistered Complaints

Some of the complaints I encountered while conducting life history interviews never figured in the official registers of managed care organizations. Consider how Don Luis from Caguas discussed his dissatisfaction with La Reforma. Don Luis did not want the interview to be recorded, so his story is excerpted from my notes. We spoke in his immaculately clean living room, but outside in his front yard overgrown blades of grass reached as high as the windowsill. He explained it was the only way to keep his neighbors' dogs out of the yard.

Don Luis was previously on La Reforma but had nothing good to say about it. The main thing that La Reforma did, in his view, was humiliate poor people. He told a story about a blond psychiatrist from San Juan. She kept an office in Caguas that she visited once a week. Don Luis made his appointment and was told to be there at least by 8:00 a.m. He arrived at 7:30 and waited for the doctor who showed up at 2:00. When finally Don Luis was called to be seen, the doctor did not look him in the face. She did not examine him. She simply pulled out her prescription pad and started writing. So Don Luis asked her if she was planning to examine him. She said, oh, so you must be a doctor if you know so much about medicine. He said, I'm not a doctor, that's why I have to come to you. But I do deserve a proper examination. Throughout his story, he spoke to the doctor with the polite, formal address, *usted*. By the way, he asked, do you know how long these people have been waiting for you? The situation escalated and Don Luis ripped up the prescriptions and made a scene in the packed waiting room. He said that the doctor also yelled at those people and told them if they're not happy, they can leave. Don Luis defended the people gathered there: just because we are poor, he said, we do not deserve to be treated like this.

Don Luis explained how this experience and his other troubles obtaining mental health care caused him to leave La Reforma. When he received notice of his annual coverage renewal appointment at the medical aid office, he never went. He said it was just as well. One psychiatrist under La Reforma expected patients to line up starting at three in the morning to see him. Then, they might have to wait half the day to actually be seen. He didn't like any of his psychiatrists—they gave him too many medications.

Here we can see another avenue in market-based health systems for patients who are not content with their health care. They have the choice to leave public programs and may elect to pay for private health services instead or forego treatment altogether. In her research on Medicaid managed care in New Mexico, anthropologist Leslie López calls this "de facto disentitlement" (2005); beneficiaries fall off the roles of public programs due to the barriers created by annual recertification procedures or other bureaucratic hurdles. In some ways we can see what Don Luis did as a protest against La Reforma. However, he never filed a formal complaint, even though he insisted that his rights had been violated. Therefore, his grievances about being disrespected, needing more than medication management, or his inability to obtain timely access to care were never heard by the private plan or the government. The actions he took were severely circumscribed and individual in scope. Instead of seeking redress as a citizen, he acted like a customer and took his "business" elsewhere. Although there is obviously a conflict between the physician and Don Luis, they have one important thing in common. If people are unhappy with their medical care, they are "free" to choose another provider. Unfortunately, this freedom is limited by the fact that, as in many U.S. states, mental health providers who accept public insurance programs like La Reforma are in scarce supply in Puerto Rico.

Don Luis said now he just receives his mental health care from his primary care physician (PCP). He likes his PCP—the man knows how to listen. He currently takes Xanax for his mental health problems. Sometimes he still falls into depressions, but he makes it through okay. The doctor told him to leave the house when he feels something coming on, go for a walk or a drive, just change his environment. Don Luis said this usually works for him. He has a pickup truck and sometimes he'll start driving and end up an hour away in Ponce.

While Don Luis seems at peace with leaving La Reforma since it allowed him to maintain his dignity and self-respect, this is a man who was once hospitalized against his will and diagnosed with schizophrenia. When he left La Reforma, he no longer received coverage for his prescription drugs. And so his unregistered complaint has also resulted in unmet health needs.

Complaining as a Citizen

The problem of complaints left unaddressed has recently been repoliticized and recollectivized in Puerto Rico. Changes to the mental health system occurred because patients and their advocates went outside of the prescribed complaint channels and instead sought accountability by other means including press conferences, protests, and coalition building among unions, academic researchers, professional associations, and patients' groups. In other words, they acted more like citizens and less like consumers.

One such story involves the suicide of a 22-year-old man. The man sought care at the offices of his government-contracted MBHO complaining of severe depression. He also reported a suicide attempt the previous week. He requested to be hospitalized or to speak with a psychiatrist on February 11, 2005.[10] The social worker at the insurance company gave him an evaluation appointment for February 25 (2 weeks later) and an appointment with a psychiatrist for March 3. A week before his appointment, he committed suicide. A photograph appeared in the newspaper of his mother attending the scheduled appointment, clutching a box that contained his ashes (Sosa Pascual 2005d). This event mobilized public criticism, and protests were held outside the office of the MBHO. Eventually the government imposed fines of $375,000 and the event helped to galvanize support for a university-led commission to evaluate the health reform (Sosa Pascual 2005b, 2005f, 2005h).

When I returned to Puerto Rico in the summer of 2007, I attempted to track down the young man's mother, but I was told that she does not want to sue the company or discuss the case further because she fears the attention that will be focused on her personally and her remaining child. The gross delays in service, however, became a powerful symbol of what was wrong with the privatized health system. The case provided public legitimacy for a temporary reversal of privatization. In 2007, the Puerto Rican health agency that regulates mental health and addiction services reassumed responsibility for delivering mental health services in the municipalities of Mayagüez and San Juan. Amid widespread criticisms that privatizing mental health care unduly limited access to care, the government was seen as an alternative that would likely improve access and quality. This pilot project was discontinued after only 8 months, because it was deemed not cost-effective by the newly elected pro-statehood (and by extension pro-privatization) governor and legislative majority in 2008. As a result, the government re-contracted with the same behavioral health managed care organization that was involved in the suicide. This case clearly points to the inadequacies of acting solely as a consumer to seek redress and the potential of complaints that circulate outside of corporate complaints departments for transforming the system itself. However, it also shows that reversing privatization is politically precarious and likely to meet with much opposition.

Conclusions: Complaining as Citizenship?

I have selectively pulled excerpts from some of the many complaints I heard in the field. In each example, the stakes differed. However, each beneficiary marshaled innovative combinations of citizenship and consumer practices in order to make demands for access to care, to dispute charges, or to be treated with greater respect. As publicly funded health care is increasingly privatized by contracting out service provision, complaining to the insurance company is one of the only mechanisms available for seeking redress for a wide variety of perceived wrongs. Few options exist for consumers beyond lodging a complaint when the HMO denies care or increases costs, when staff behave rudely, or when providers commit medical errors.

For appeals that fit squarely within the corporation's complaint system, the health plan member stands a good chance of having the initial denial overturned. For example, if a member was denied payment for a service but could show that the service was medically necessary and covered by Medicare, then the claim would in all likelihood be paid. However, for complaints that fall outside of these bounds, the consumer's demands are far less likely to be met. Consider the complaints discussed in this chapter. Each one shows how consumer dissatisfaction is narrowly channeled along bureaucratic pathways that comply with regulatory standards (except in the case of the MBHOs) but that often fail to address the issues of access, rationing, and humane care that motivated the complaint in the first place. The brothers eventually received their blood glucose monitor, but only because I went outside of the established mechanisms and asked the company to send it as a personal favor. Problems with durable medical equipment delivery continued to be the top source of member and provider complaints at Acme. This high volume of complaints was tolerated by company executives because ultimately the services of the new DME company were more cost-effective. Doña Hermina, who had the billing dispute with her podiatrist, was more aggrieved at the end of the complaints process than she was before the corporation tried to protect her rights. She also had a newly adversarial relationship with her provider. Doña Regina, whose fast-track appeal was upheld, was responsible for paying her bills at the SNF, but she did not have the means to do so or any alternative form of care at her disposal. Technically, her rights had been protected. But in actuality, she continued to have legitimate medical needs and no way to meet them. Don Luis did not expect his care to change significantly under La Reforma. He did not expect to be treated with respect, receive timely appointments, or get psychiatric care that consisted of more than medication management. He accepted his role as a consumer and voted with his feet. Unfortunately, this decision left him without a regular source of psychiatric care and he forfeited coverage for his medications. Finally, the young man who committed suicide did so only after he was unable to obtain care through his mental health plan. Though he followed established procedures, the plan failed to recognize his acute care needs.

These examples illustrate how corporate complaints systems are a highly circumscribed and limited domain for the exercise of due process rights in health care. The system is designed to contain and channel complaints, not to empower citizens. One of its primary functions is to establish due process mechanisms that ultimately serve to protect the insurance company and CMS in the event of a lawsuit. The result is that you can appeal a decision made within the system, but you cannot change the system itself. The new procedural requirements that emerged out of the *Grijalva v. Shalala* lawsuit clearly created new kinds of rights. Nonetheless, one must be attentive to the limits of those rights when acting as a citizen becomes increasingly synonymous with acting as a consumer.

6

Market Values

Partnering and Choice

For any way of thought to become dominant, a conceptual apparatus has to be advanced that appeals to our intuitions and instincts, to our values and our desires, as well as to the possibilities inherent in the social world we inhabit. (Harvey 2005, 5)

A great deal of symbolic and cultural work has gone into transforming "the market" into the solution for the social problems that ail us. As I argued in chapter 1, markets in health care are a relatively recent phenomenon in Puerto Rico. Proponents of privatized managed care had to contend with a previous consensus that health care was a human right best provided by the government. But market reforms came to make sense to Puerto Rican policy makers and their constituents because they resonated with, upheld, and created values that were compelling and commonsensical.[1]

Market values naturalize and valorize a market-based approach to economic life, government, and human relations. For example, market values:

- Celebrate market-based activities like competition, choice, and efficiency as intrinsically good, whereas government regulation, taxes, and social welfare programs are condemned as bad and a drag on economic progress;
- Respect atomized individuals as entrepreneurs, independent decision makers and creators of economic growth while they vilify the poor, sick, and disabled for being dependent or in need; and
- Closely identify the free market, private property rights, and consumer choice with other values that are important in society such as democracy, equal opportunity, freedom, and patriotism.

This chapter explores how two market values—partnering and choice—were deployed to accomplish the cultural work of making market-based reforms seem natural, desirable, and good in Puerto Rico's Medicare and Medicaid programs. Partnering references a more business-friendly way to conduct government regulation in the context of contracting out government services to private firms. Choice is thought to be what health care consumers want and value above all else—choice in their doctors, treatments, and insurance plans. A discussion of partnering and choice brings us full circle to the question of market moralities that was explored in the introduction. Recall that market reforms are not just about managing people and things in new ways but also are about valorizing and legitimating certain forms of economic activity and ways of being. The upshot is that market values become more than just another policy choice among many; when effective, these values transform into common sense and the right thing to do.

This chapter looks at partnering and choice as they were discussed in policy circles and then interrogates ethnographically whether those market values lived up to their promises. Did the focus on "partnering," which relied on notions of transparency, efficiency, and accountability, really transform the relationship between federal agencies and private corporations? Were these new partnerships egalitarian and democratic enterprises? What kinds of choices did market reforms actually afford consumers? In my research, I found that the much-celebrated market values of partnering and choice did not translate well into practice and instead were characterized by hidden constraints, deep contradictions, and persistent and growing inequalities.

Part 1: Better Business Partners

In testimony before Congress in 2002, Thomas Scully, the administrator of the Centers for Medicare and Medicaid Services (CMS), stated:

> Since I took over as CMS Administrator, *my number one priority* has been to improve the Agency's responsiveness and make it a *better business partner*. At CMS, we are committed to simplifying our rules, making them easier to understand and less burdensome. (Scully 2002, emphasis added)

CMS is the division of the U.S. federal government charged with providing health care coverage through the Medicare and Medicaid programs to the elderly, disabled, and those living in poverty. The "better business partner" slogan invoked by Scully recurred on the agency's website, punctuated the beginnings and ends of speeches by agency officials, and was often held up as the rationale behind new administrative procedures. The "better business partner" slogan succinctly and optimistically described an attitude toward government that by the early 2000s had become institutional common sense. Under the administration of President George W. Bush, the better business partner initiative went hand in hand with seeing the "private sector as the way forward for Medicare" (Reinhardt 2003). This is an example of the amalgam of new attitudes and practices that have been termed "entrepreneurial governance," because they seek to transform government into an efficient and streamlined enterprise where public/private partnerships thrive (Holland et al. 2007). Whereas chapter 2 explored the role of enforcement and oversight in public/private partnerships through the prism of auditing, the better business partner metaphor is positive, not punitive. This rebranding campaign portrayed CMS as responsive, concerned, available, and eager to collaborate with its fellow business partners.

This effort at reframing the purpose and tone of regulation in Medicare merits closer inspection. At first blush, partnering appears to advance democratizing impulses and contribute to greater citizen participation in Medicare. However, the partnering practices that were actually embraced by CMS led only to increased involvement by corporations and specialized stakeholders such as professional associations and well-organized patient advocacy groups. This chapter considers two uses of the term "partner" by CMS: (1) the recasting of regulation as a business relationship and (2) the designation of individual citizens and organizations as "partners" in the work of providing government-sponsored health care. How does recasting regulation as a partnership change the way in which CMS interacts with private health plans? What happens when a health agency makes goals such as simplifying rules and easing burdens on corporations its "number one priority"? Do corporations and the beneficiaries of publicly funded health insurance programs act as partners? Do they want or expect the government to do so?

As described in previous chapters, the politics of privatization in Puerto Rico must be read through the island's colonial relationship to the United States. The Puerto Rican government and its citizens are subjected to federal health policy that is promulgated and enforced without their formal political participation, a political reality that strains the partner metaphor. Furthermore, health plans with federal contracts are exempted from following most local regulations (the only exceptions being in financial reserves and licensing). Scully's vision of government as essentially cooperative, pro-business, and efficient obscures the ways in which colonial relations of rule usher in market reforms on the island without formal participation by the island's citizens or government. Partnering, in this instance, is a compulsory process that occurs between nonequals even as it produces opportunities for new kinds of collaboration.

Regulation as Partnership: Commenting on Proposed Rules

The better business partner mode of regulatory oversight emphasized increased transparency and promoted the participation of "stakeholders" in the rollout of the new Medicare program. When Congress passes legislation that creates a new government program, the legislation contains the broad outline of the program, but it usually lacks specific details and technical requirements that are necessary to actually implement the legislation. Regulatory agencies like CMS are therefore called on to draft rules to implement the legislation—the rule in turn carries the force of law. As stipulated by the Administration Procedure Act (APA), draft rules are published in the *Federal Register*[2] for public comment at least 30 days before the rules are to take effect. While I conducted fieldwork at Acme, Congress passed a major piece of Medicare legislation (known as the Medicare Modernization Act [MMA], which added a prescription-drug benefit to the program). Shortly thereafter, CMS called on its partners to participate in the rulemaking process. Compliance departments at Medicare managed care plans all over the United States and U.S. territories read the draft rule, and many insurance companies, pharmaceutical manufacturers, pharmacy benefit managers, and professional associations submitted comments to CMS. Once CMS received the comments, the agency revised the rule. The final rule was subsequently published with a discussion detailing and justifying the rationale used by the agency in arriving at its final determinations. During this process, CMS held conference calls at least weekly (often two or three times a week) with the industry to communicate regarding the development of new requirements and to answer questions. On several occasions, I emailed or phoned administrators at the central office in Baltimore and received prompt answers.

The promulgation of the rules featured opportunities for comment that promoted transparency in government rulemaking processes. However, as several recent studies have indicated, the contemporary policy emphasis on transparency and participation warrants critical examination (Lockhart and Durey 2004; West and Sanders 2003); in practice, open, transparent processes tend to have a very narrow field of application and can conceal as much as they reveal. In this instance, the overall shape of the new prescription-drug program was already decided upon in the legislation (legislation that was largely authored by individuals with documented connections to insurance and pharmaceutical companies). Nonetheless, the opportunity to comment on CMS rulemaking did enable certain limited kinds of participation—particularly by corporations and professional associations who advocated for minor modifications. Partner comments were largely directed at clarifying or changing certain administrative processes such as the appeals and grievance procedures or the rules for developing a plan that operated in multiple regions. These decisions stood to greatly impact the financial bottom line at companies that were planning to participate in the new prescription-drug program or expand their Medicare managed care offerings. But the broader public did not participate in this process as it was highly technical and required a sophisticated understanding of the Medicare program (as well as the willingness and time to read hundreds of pages of legislation and proposed rules).

To give a sense of who was able to comment on the proposed rule, it is important to keep in mind that there were 43,404,885 Medicare beneficiaries in 2005 in the United States and its territories, all of whom were impacted by this legislation (KFF 2005). However, according to CMS, they received only the following:

186 items of correspondence containing more than a thousand specific comments on the August 3, 2004 proposed rule. Commenters included MCOs and other industry representatives, representatives of physicians and other health care professionals, beneficiary advocacy groups, representatives of hospitals and other providers, insurance companies, employers, States, accrediting and peer review organizations, members of the Congress, Indian Health Service (HIS), Indian Health Service, Tribal and Urban Health Programs (I/T/U), American Indians and Alaska Natives (AI/AN), and others. (*Federal Register* 2005, 4591)

CMS went on to state that it responded in detail to most of the comments. However, comments that did not directly address the proposed rule were not responded to, thereby illustrating the limited nature of (1) who actually participated in the process and (2) the kinds of comments that were recognized as worthy or appropriate by CMS. Despite the proliferation of language suggesting that stakeholders participate in modernizing Medicare, these partnerships should not be taken to imply that there was a relationship of equals or that stakeholders were able to significantly alter the course of the implementation process; all partners are not created equally.[3]

Calling on CMS to Be a Better Partner

Every Medicare Advantage plan has a plan manager at CMS through whom it must conduct all official "business": submit inquiries, receive investigation requests, and provide information. This person participates in audits and makes recommendations to his or her superiors regarding the organization's compliance. A former plan manager whom I will call Carla was the visible, human face of federal regulation at Acme. Though Carla was based in New York, her mother was a member of the plan in Puerto Rico; when her mother fell ill, Carla would place a call to let the plan know. Carla would occasionally neglect to return phone calls, emails, or answer questions. As in many bureaucracies, Acme's documents were often lost and had to be re-sent. My boss suggested that I keep a log of all communication with Carla in order to have evidence that required documents were sent in or an inquiry answered. The Compliance Department strategized on how to get her to answer our calls and questions right away. The department tried weekly conference calls and sent follow-up emails documenting the conversations, but these trailed off after the first few sessions. Finally, the department complained to Carla's superiors. The complaint applauded the agency's efforts to become a "better business partner" and explained that Acme, too, valued transparency and efficiency and wanted to work with the plan manager to achieve that goal. Afterward, Carla started to call me Ms. Mulligan instead of Jessica and I still had to re-send things that she lost.

Shortly after this incident, I received an email from Acme's CEO. The email warned that Carla was upset that members of the Compliance Department were going around her to get questions answered. She said it made her look bad to her bosses and could endanger the good relationship between Acme and the CMS regional office. I was reprimanded by the CEO and lectured on how to improve my people skills. In the email that Carla sent to the CEO, she described the problem as one about relations, impressions, and respecting her authority. The CEO urged my boss and me to figure out how to get back into her good graces.

In this example of how regulatory relationships functioned on a day-to-day basis, smooth social relations were of far more importance to the corporation than transparency, efficiency, or professionalism. My boss and I made the mistake of taking the "better business partner" slogan at face value. The market values encapsulated in the notion of partnering had not come to supplant other values like showing deference and respect to regulators, the importance of trust in interpersonal relationships, and the need for warm, friendly communication. Though the "better business partner" mode of regulation did change some aspects of CMS—conference calls became regular activities, more information was available on the website, more data were exchanged electronically—the enormous federal bureaucracy was not seamlessly remade (quite the opposite). In the context of a changing regulatory environment and increased auditing from afar, personal, not professional, relations with plan managers were more crucial than ever for navigating the morass of regulations and the constantly changing priorities of the agency.

Health Activism as Partnership

The final example of "partnering" that I will discuss involves new forms of activism that are enabled by the "better business partner"

186 << MARKET VALUES

mode of government. Partnering was not just encouraged on the part of corporations who did business with CMS, it was also promoted in consumer education initiatives surrounding the new prescription-drug benefit. For example, CMS maintained a partner section on its website directed at a broad array of stakeholders, including "Employer Partnerships, Faith-Based Partnerships, Federal and State Partnerships, Fee-for-Service Provider Partnerships, Financial Planner Partnerships, National Medicare Education Program Partnerships, [and] Racial/Ethnic/Cultural Partnerships" (CMS 2005). Groups as diverse as churches, local governments, financial planners, health educators, and racial minorities were referred to as partners. So how did these "partners" try to cultivate relationships with regulatory agencies and advance their agendas?

When I returned to Puerto Rico in 2007, I was interested in learning more about the kinds of health activism that were emerging to change the health system on the island. Many of the figures I encountered were women who became active when they, but more often a loved one, received low quality or inadequate care. One such activist, Roxana Velazquez, became politically engaged in health activism when her son was diagnosed with a serious anxiety disorder and she had to struggle to obtain adequate care for him. Roxana serves on several boards and is now a prominent citizen-representative on government panels. She has traveled to the United States to represent Puerto Rico at conferences and has appeared numerous times in the local press as a spokesperson on mental health issues. I first met Roxana at a meeting at the School of Public Health. She sought me out afterward and suggested that I interview her. During our interview at her middle-class apartment in Hato Rey, she showed me her collection of press clippings. When I explained that I was having difficulty locating doctors who were willing to be interviewed, she phoned a prominent psychiatrist and arranged a meeting. Then, she called the president of the Medical Association and got me on her calendar. When it came time for the interviews, Roxanna picked me up and drove me to the interviews. She is an extremely savvy activist who has been effective in raising awareness about her son's condition and advocating for parity in mental health care. In the process, she has taken full advantage of the "partnering" opportunities offered by government agencies and various corporate entities from insurance companies to pharmaceutical firms.

Roxana engages in a distinctly middle-class form of activism that requires one to volunteer vast amounts of time, maintain extensive cell phone communication, sit through meetings and presentations with professionals and academics, create organizations, forge coalitions by cultivating extensive contacts, and publicize one's work. It is a coalitional and cooperative form of activism that seeks to modify the current system in the name of broadly acceptable social values such as "better health" or "equitable treatment." As such, health activism through partnering tends to be tactful and polite so that conflict and explicit conversations about politics are often avoided. Many health activists whom I encountered were engaged in numerous coalitions and moved between patient advocacy groups, support groups, university-led coalitions, government meetings, and corporate-sponsored health education activities. Activism created social capital, a forum for making community, and solidarity through the exchange of stories of suffering. Partnering with government agencies and corporations was just one strategy among many that activists used to advocate for better care.

Government initiatives that recast regulation as a partnership open up new space for the kinds of activism that Roxana Velasquez was able to engage in. However, in order to be heard, she had to participate in decidedly classed ways that are out of reach for many beneficiaries of public health insurance programs. Significantly, she was able to obtain better care for her son and create support networks for those with similar diagnoses. Nonetheless, activism as partnering has some intrinsic limitations; though incremental modifications may be possible when working within the system, changing it completely is not compatible with "partnering."

Revaluing the Better Business Partner

The "better business partner" slogan was adopted by the federal agency that administers the Medicare program in order to project a more business-friendly and efficient image. The adversarial regulator and enforcer was deemphasized in favor of the reciprocal partner. This shift produced opportunities for corporations to call on the agency to be professional and transparent and for activists to make new kinds of claims and gain access to decision makers within organizations. The better business partner mode of regulation valorized efficiency, transparency, and participation. But when examined in practice (rather than solely as political rhetoric), partnering appears both less unobjectionably good and less influential than Scully might have hoped. In the examples I have considered, the partnering metaphor enabled new forms of collaboration even as it channeled participation along narrow pathways that privileged certain groups over others and tended to avoid conflict and explicit discussions of "politics."

The better business partner approach must be understood as an example of "regulatory capture," which occurs when the government bodies responsible for regulating a specific industry see their primary mission as advocating on behalf of that industry instead of ensuring that rules are enforced and that public safety and well-being are protected. Regulatory capture has been a consistent feature of the regulation of managed care, not least because managed care organizations invest a considerable amount of money into lobbying efforts aimed at influencing regulatory processes (Rochefort 2001, 130). We saw this process at work in chapter 2, when industry insiders authored the MMA legislation and again during the rollout of the Medicare Advantage program when CMS overlooked marketing violations that confused Medicare beneficiaries (discussed later in this chapter).

By examining market values ethnographically, we also see that market values are not as powerful and compelling as they sometimes seem; in practice, they are always contested. For many people (some of whom may work at CMS) market values do not transform into common sense. Most people are excluded from the process of offering comments on new regulations at CMS, given the very technical nature of the formal comment process. The type of partnering available at this level is for highly educated stakeholders who are both incredibly familiar with the work of the agency and cognizant of how regulatory changes are likely to impact their bottom line. Transforming the day-to-day regulatory interactions between CMS and health plans into a relationship characterized by "partnership" is likewise fraught with limitations. On the one hand it is likely to devolve into "regulatory capture" in which the agency becomes beholden to the corporations it supposedly regulates, thus diluting CMS's ability to fulfill its fiduciary obligations. The other obstacle to partnering is that bureaucracies are slow to change and operate according to their own traditions and social practices such as maintaining good social relations and saving face. Finally, the kinds of community partnerships that CMS seems to cultivate are again highly classed and professional in nature. They assume a certain education level, amount of free time, and professional pursuit of a cause in order to be effective, as evidenced by the activist's story I recount above. The poorer beneficiaries whom I interviewed did not envision themselves as "partners" to regulators, nor were they treated as such by government or HMO workers. This raises important questions about the ability of public/private partnerships to enhance democratic participation. Ethnographic research into public/private partnership initiatives in North Carolina likewise found the following:

> The heavy reliance on partnerships is frighteningly devoid of guarantees that all segments of the public will be served. If a particular segment of the population is for some reason unable to organize itself into associations that can effectively partner with the government, then it most probably will experience neglect, and even real social harm. (Holland et al. 2007, 234)

In these examples, policy conversations about partnering utilize democratic and egalitarian language to characterize a set of relationships that are in practice quite hierarchical and unequal.

Part 2: Choosing Choice

Though partnering clearly falls short of many of its promises, can the same be said for choice? In their influential treatise on the consumer, Gabriel and Lang argue that "choice lies at the centre of the idea of consumerism, both as its emblem and as its core value" (2006, 26). By this they mean that choice is seen as inherently desirable and good; it is linked to political freedom and democracy; it is said to lead to more efficiency and competition in the marketplace; and it is thought to be essential to human happiness and well-being. In short, choice is

6

the moral foundation on which market reforms to public services like health care are often justified.

The MMA extended the role of private health plans in the Medicare program, and it did so with explicit reference to the importance of choice. I include here a rather lengthy excerpt from the introduction to the legislation because it reveals the legislation's ideological underpinnings:

Beginning in 2006, the MA program is designed to:

Provide for regional plans that may make private plan *options* available to many more beneficiaries, especially those in rural areas.

Expand the number and type of plans provided for, so that beneficiaries can *choose* from Health Maintenance Organizations (HMOs), Preferred Provider Organization (PPO) plans (the most popular type of employer-sponsored plan), Fee-for-Service (FFS) plans, and Medical Savings Account (MSA) plans, if available where the beneficiary lives.

Enrich the range of benefit choices available to enrollees including improved prescription drug benefits, other benefits not covered by original Medicare, and the opportunity to share in savings where MA plans can deliver benefits at lower costs.

Provide incentives to plans, and add specialized plans to coordinate and manage care in ways that comprehensively serve those with complex and disabling diseases and conditions.

Use open season *competition* among MA plans to improve service, improve benefits, invest in preventive care, and hold costs down in ways that attract enrollees.

Enhance and stabilize payments to organizations, improve program design, introduce new *flexibility* for plans, and *reduce impediments* to plan participation.

Advance the goal of improving quality and increasing *efficiency* in the overall health care system. Medicare is the largest payer of health care in the world. Medicare can drive changes in the entire health care system.

With these *new and improved choices*, Medicare beneficiaries, like Federal employees and retirees in the Federal Employees Health Benefits (FEHB) Program, will have the opportunity to obtain improved benefits, improved services, and reduced costs. (*Federal Register* 2005, 4589, emphasis added)

The legislation posits a system where what is good for business and what is good for the consumer are in harmony. The reform also contains a vision for changing the global health system, since Medicare is the largest health care payer in the world. It offers a utopian promise: more benefits, better service, and lower costs for everyone. Choice is seen as what Medicare beneficiaries want—they need more options so that they can select the plan that is best for them, and when all the plans in the market are competing, the beneficiary ostensibly gets better prices and more services.

In chapter 3, I explored the life histories of three Acme beneficiaries and argued that their ability to make choices and act as free information-processing consumers in relation to their health care was quite limited. This chapter shares that same overall premise, but I focus on the more narrow issue of choosing a health plan with its attendant rules, benefits, and provider network. Understanding how consumers select a health plan is particularly important because giving consumers a choice of health plan has become one of the primary policy prescriptions for making the health care system function more like a marketplace. In the 1990s, "managed competition" was the Clinton administration's health reform buzzword.[4] Managed competition emphasized the importance of choosing a health plan (rather than health care providers) because "plan selection took place under less stressful circumstances, packaging services and providers together for easier comparison, managed competition was expected to lead to more effective consumer decision making" (Schlesinger 2005, 100). The Bush administration shared this belief that allowing consumers to choose their health plan was key to creating a more market-based, efficient health system that valued consumer choice and competition. Under Obama's Affordable Care Act, the newly insured likewise have to choose their health plan from a variety of options available in the health insurance exchanges. But what does choice mean for beneficiaries of public insurance programs who must decide which private plan to enroll in?

Shopping Problems

The primary way in which the MMA legislation created more choice for beneficiaries was by increasing funding levels to private Medicare

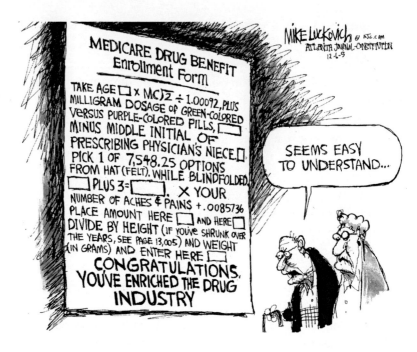

Figure 6.1. Mike Luckovich, editorial cartoon used with the permission of Mike Luckovich and Creators Syndicate. All rights reserved.

health plans and authorizing the establishment of new plan designs, such as special needs plans, fee-for-service plans, and regional preferred provider organizations.[5] One of the ironies of opening the Medicare program to the participation of private health plans is that the program creates choice in terms of which plan a beneficiary might choose to enroll in, but the actual benefits offered between plans do not vary greatly. Plans were required to offer actuarially equivalent benefit packages that include all of the services covered by traditional Medicare. Differences in the benefits between plans were in the provider network available to enrollees and the supplemental offerings such as vision, hearing, dental, and prescription drugs. The premiums and cost sharing varied slightly.

As the MMA was implemented in Puerto Rico, many new HMOs joined the market. On January 1, 2006, there were 54 Medicare Advantage plans offered by 11 different companies (CMS 2006b). In addition, there were also 10 standalone prescription-drug plans offered by 6 companies that beneficiaries could enroll in to receive the Part D prescription-drug benefit and continue receiving medical services through Original Medicare (CMS 2006d). So the MMA clearly created new choices, but on what basis were beneficiaries to make a decision?

The information that beneficiaries received about their plan options came through various channels; beneficiaries learned about the plans from media coverage, advertisements, friends and family, their doctors, and plan sales agents. They also received copious amounts of documents in the mail. The vast majority of information sent by plans and CMS to beneficiaries was in writing, some in complicated book-length formats. This, even though more than half (52.6%) of those over 65 in Puerto Rico have less than a ninth-grade education (U.S. Census Bureau 2000).[6] The most sophisticated and informative tools to compare plan options were available on the Internet, but none of the beneficiaries whom I interviewed had access to the Internet.[7] One problem with health policies that focus on consumer choice is that they assume that all consumers are middle class; these policies

> require health knowledge outside the scope of the average citizen as they attempt to restructure the traditional hierarchy in the doctor-patient relationship, recasting patients as "middle class activists" and ignoring issues such as literacy and psychological feelings of powerlessness that make activism especially difficult for working class and low income populations. (Hill, Zimmerman, and Fox 2002, 44)

Even the staunchest supporters of market-based health policies agree that choice works only when consumers have adequate information; for example free-market health care enthusiast David Dranove believes that patients have a "shopping problem" that is the product of imperfect information about price and quality (2000, 3). My research suggests that in addition to this "shopping problem," beneficiaries confront obstacles that cannot be overcome with simply more information. Choosing the optimal Medicare Advantage plan requires that a beneficiary access search tools on the Internet, understand complicated plan structures and benefit packages, accurately predict his or her medical expenditures and medication needs, and join a relatively stable provider network. In practice, much of the information necessary to make an informed decision is unknowable (Will I get sick next year? Will my doctor remain in the network?) and what is known (plan structures, covered benefits, coverage rules) can be quite difficult to digest. The following examples from my fieldwork illustrate these points.

Medicare health plans simultaneously launched advertising campaigns that bombarded the airwaves with information about the new prescription-drug benefit. One could not turn the pages of the newspaper or drive on a highway without encountering multiple Medicare Advantage advertisements. Newspapers in Puerto Rico ran stories of Medicare beneficiaries being harassed by companies trying to get them to enroll. For example, in an article entitled "Avalanche of Calls Confuse Beneficiaries," a reporter from *El Nuevo Día* claimed:

> In October, Doña Hermes Rivera's telephone became her worst enemy. It rang nonstop with offers of "villas and castles" to try and woo her to sign up for one of the Medicare Advantage alternatives. . . . The same thing happened to Doña Mary Montaner, to Doña Carmen Morales and to the mother of Brenda Cabrera. (Millán Pabón 2005)

The press in Puerto Rico and in the mainland United States ran multiple stories of the elderly and disabled being taken advantage of by unscrupulous sales staff.[8] As a countermeasure, the local government and the AARP took out full-page newspaper advertisements detailing patients' rights. In an interview with a local government health official in 2005, I was told that the office received 100 complaints a day from beneficiaries who thought that they were going to lose their government health plan benefits (for low-income beneficiaries in Puerto Rico) according to what they had been told by a family member or sales representative.

Plans and government agencies received many complaints from beneficiaries who alleged that they were enrolled in a plan without their knowledge. Sales representatives at all plans were paid a commission for enrolling members (some plans also paid a bonus for retention). A common story was that the sales representative would ask a beneficiary to sign a visit form and did not disclose that it was an enrollment application. Plans also fanned rumors that some companies were bankrupt and hence if beneficiaries did not switch plans, they would be left without Medicare coverage. Some plans also allegedly threatened doctors to sign up with their network because if they did not, they would have no patients left, and other plans engaged in marketing practices, like door-to-door sales, that were illegal.

Part of my job at Acme was to track and compile the complaints of former Acme beneficiaries who called to complain that they had been unintentionally enrolled in a competitor's plan. Eventually, Acme presented dozens of these claims to CMS and asked that action be taken to enforce the marketing regulations. When CMS finally intervened during the fall of 2005 to deal with marketing violations, its approach was decidedly nonpunitive in nature; it conducted an educational campaign in which it trained the new Medicare Advantage plans on the regulations that must be followed. Despite the obvious benefits of regulatory capture, Acme's strategy at this point was to try and get CMS to behave like a more traditional regulator by enforcing rules and imposing fines. At a conference sponsored by CMS, agency representatives stated that the way they most often became aware of marketing violations was when one plan reported the violations of another. Their position was that the industry would start to self-regulate.

An Unintentional Choice

Even when beneficiaries were not intentionally deceived, the "choice" to enroll in a plan may not have been fully understood. I came to appreciate some of the complexities of explaining plan benefits and rules when I conducted life history interviews with beneficiaries.[9] Many of the beneficiaries whom I interviewed were unsure about what was happening to their Medicare benefits, and a portion of almost every life history interview I conducted was spent explaining plan rules or what options were available for the new prescription-drug coverage. In many interviews, beneficiaries would produce a stack of unopened mail and explain that their children had not been by lately to read it for them or that their eyesight had gotten worse; one man said that he did not know how to read. I would help them sort through the correspondence and indicate which letters needed some kind of follow-up. The following example from an interview in a town on the northwest coast of the island demonstrates some of the problems with interpreting the rise in enrollment in Medicare Advantage plans as a sign of consumers freely exercising their choice to receive benefits through a private-plan option.

As usual, I got slightly lost on the way to Doña Fátima's house. The hospital name she gave me as a landmark had changed and the house had no number. I stopped and asked a neighbor who happened to be a relative and he directed me to the right place. A metal gate and fence surrounded the property. Inside the compound were two modest con-crete houses—the one on the right was where Doña Fátima lived and the one on the left belonged to her daughter. I called up to the house from the road and Doña Fátima came down and opened the gate. I pulled my car in and she clanked the gate shut behind me. She led the way to the covered front porch where we sat on cushioned chairs and started talking.

Doña Fátima's daughter was inside the house on a long-distance phone call. Doña Fátima suggested we wait until she finished because her daughter might be better qualified to answer the questions. I explained that the interview was about her life so she would prob-ably be the one who could answer the questions best. She agreed and began to describe herself as having a positive attitude and being *bien tranquila* (very laid-back). She told me that she had spent many years living in New York where she worked at various factories. Though she moved to New York with her first husband, he was an alcoholic and left her to raise her two daughters by herself. While working, she saved money that she eventually used to construct this house on land that had belonged to her family. Eventually she moved back to Puerto Rico and married again. Her second husband had since passed away, but he had worked at the electric company and Doña Fátima now received health benefits from his former employer.

When we got to the point in the interview where I started asking about how she enrolled in Acme and what she thought of the services, we reached an impasse. It turned out that Doña Fátima did not know that she had ever enrolled in Acme. She recalled attending a seminar with her niece but did not know that she had changed her insurance. At this point, Doña Fátima brought out some letters and said that she didn't understand what they meant. The letters were Medicare denial notices, which are supposed to explain in clear terms to beneficiaries that Medicare will not pay a claim. The letter states the reason for the denial and informs the beneficiary of his or her appeal rights. In practice, the letters are very confusing. I had seen similar letters previously at Acme where I needed someone to explain them to me. I told Doña Fátima that her claim was denied by Medicare because she had enrolled with a Medicare Advantage plan and so, essentially, the doctor's office was sending the claim to the wrong place. I asked her what insurance card she gave to the secretary at the doctor's office and she reached into her handbag, pulled out her wallet, and emptied its contents onto the chair. There were multiple cards including that of Acme, Blue Cross, Medicare, and other discount cards at pharmacies. She said when she goes to the doctor's office she just hands everything over to the secretary who sorts it out. I picked up the Acme membership card and was surprised to see that Doña Fátima's effective date was 2 years ago. For 2 years, she had belonged to the plan and did not realize it! I asked her if she was still paying the Medicare deductible and she said yes (which, as a member of a Medicare Advantage plan, she was not required to pay). She pointed to the Blue Cross card and said that was the one she used to get her medicine. I explained to her how the different plans worked and why she was getting the denial letters from Medicare. I told her that Acme probably wasn't the best idea for her since she had drug coverage through Blue Cross and she might lose her widow's benefits if she stayed enrolled in a Medicare Advantage plan. I told her she should disenroll from Acme and then just use her Medicare and Blue Cross cards. She agreed and I wrote the disenrollment letter for her, which she signed. After all of this, she called herself *bruta* (stupid).

Unstable Networks; Uncoordinated Benefits

In an interview at Don Victor and Doña Sofia's house, a different problem with "choice" arose. Throughout the interview, Don Victor talked about how mentally sharp he was even though his 89-year-old body was starting to fail him. He insisted that he chose to join Acme and understood all of the implications of that choice. His son-in-law, who was present during the interview, questioned the wisdom of that decision.

Don Victor and Doña Sofia's wedding photo rested above the television set. It was taken outside a church. The groom wore a gray suit, the bride a white dress; the couple was surrounded by their already elderly children. The newlyweds had met after their former spouses passed away and now in one another had found companionship. These two Acme members had been married for 4 years.

During the interview at their home, located across the way from a church off a rural road in Vega Alta, we sat on a sofa and stuffed chairs in a narrow living room. The walls were made of painted concrete blocks and the floor was well-scrubbed terrazzo. When I asked this couple what had changed most in Puerto Rico (besides health care) during their lives, they marveled at the state of their home. Doña Sofia talked about the shack where she had grown up with 11 brothers and sisters, when her father worked in the cane. In that wetness and mud, she never would have thought that she could have something as nice as this house, a four-room concrete house with fruit trees in the backyard. Much better than the houses *allá* [over there, in the United States] that cannot even withstand a tropical storm, much less a hurricane.

Toward the end of the interview Don Victor produced a letter from Acme and asked for help in making sense of it. The letter stated that his primary care physician, Dr. Delgado, no longer accepted La Reforma, so he was assigned to a new physician, Dr. Novo, in order to continue to receive his Acme and Reforma benefits. The letter explained that if Don Victor did not agree with this change, he was free to choose another doctor from Acme's provider directory.

Don Victor proposed going to the Medicaid (La Reforma) office in Vega Alta to clear things up. He knew where the office was and could just tell them that Dr. Delgado is his primary care physician. Don Victor's son-in-law, Don Teodoro, and I tried to explain why this simple solution would not work.

> JM: The problem is that the doctor who you had, Dr. Delgado, is no longer working with La Reforma.
>
> DV: Look, I called the doctor [Delgado], the one in Manatí. And he told me that he was working with Acme. The one he left was Triple-S [his Reforma insurance plan].
>
> JM: Exactly.
>
> DV: He left Triple-S. Now he is working for this plan [Acme] and no one else. It is the same doctor.

JM: The problem is since he isn't working with La Reforma anymore, he
    cannot give you prescriptions for your medications.
DT: Okay, I think I'm understanding something to do. You can change to
    [Dr.] Ferrer, to a doctor that takes La Reforma and takes Acme.
JM: Exactly.

The conversation went in circles for several minutes with Don Teodoro
trying to explain the situation to his father-in-law, who grew increasingly frustrated. Don Victor insisted he was willing to pay for his medications to stay with Dr. Delgado.

DV: What do I have to do?
DT: It's that La Reforma no longer covers him [Dr. Delgado]. His prescrip-
    tions don't count for anything in La Reforma.
DV: How is it possible that his prescriptions don't count?
DT: Now I understand what happened with the prescription that he gave
    me. When my wife who is his daughter went to the pharmacy, they
    told her, "No, this man is no longer with La Reforma." That's what
    happened.
DV: What I am saying is that I have to buy the medicine without showing
    the card. That's the point. Our plan is the basic plan and we have to
    buy our medicine. The doctor is the same doctor. What happened is
    that with the prescription that he gives us, you can't use the card at
    the pharmacy. Is that it or not?

Don Victor was correct; he could pay for his own medicine. The problem was that he had a right to have his medication covered because he
was eligible for La Reforma.

The letter informing Don Victor that his doctor had been changed
was nowhere near adequate in explaining what was happening and giving him the tools that he needed in order to coordinate his Medicare
and Reforma benefits. He continued to insist that Dr. Delgado, not Dr.
Novo, was his primary care physician. Don Victor's solution was to pay
for his own medication, which was not a very satisfactory resolution
for his son-in-law. Don Victor said that he knew that he had to have
the same doctor under Acme and La Reforma, but he was told by the
salesperson who signed him up for Acme that since he already paid his

Medicare deductible that year, he should just sign up for Acme and buy his own medicine. This advice from the salesperson was not in Don Victor's best financial interest because it increased his out-of-pocket costs for medication.

The conditions under which beneficiaries like Don Victor "choose" to join a managed care plan are extremely complex. For beneficiaries who are eligible for both Medicare and La Reforma, there were considerable barriers to coordinating care and benefits under the two programs. Managed competition assumes that beneficiaries can select a plan based on its provider network and benefits. However, Don Victor made his selection based on some inaccurate information (regarding his Medicare deductible) and based on a network that itself was constantly changing. In the end, he "chose" to receive fewer benefits. In the process, Don Victor insisted that he had made an informed decision to join Acme and grew frustrated with his son-in-law who tried to offer him advice.

Undecidable

These examples raise important questions about the role of choice in market-based health policy. What does it mean to claim that consumers want more health plan choices? Who benefits and who loses when beneficiaries are increasingly responsible for making choices? The market provided a dizzying array of choices that were sold by some less-than-scrupulous agents working on commission. For Doña Fátima, this resulted in her carrying multiple insurance cards in her wallet without necessarily understanding which one she was enrolled in.[10] For Don Victor, it meant buying his own prescription drugs.

Ironically, even the sales agents charged with enrolling beneficiaries in Acme understood that "choice" was far more complicated than objectively weighing the options in the marketplace. Sales agents at Acme developed their own profile of beneficiaries that in turn informed their sales strategies. First, the sales agents claimed that beneficiaries tended to stay with a known entity—they developed a preference for the plan they already belonged to, that a friend recommended, or that an employer had provided as a benefit. The second tendency was to change plans every few months according to offers in the press or

Figure 6.2. Medicare prescription torture. Jeff Parker, *Florida Today*.

direct marketing from the competition. Neither profile is based on a consumer making cost-benefit analyses based on perfect information. Instead, the sales team was convinced that beneficiaries decided based on their social networks, work histories, and personal encounters with plan representatives. The sales strategy then entailed getting to the beneficiary first and calling people back more frequently than the competition.

When we contextualize the conditions under which consumers make decisions, there is a disjuncture between neoliberal ideas of personhood that assume an informed consumer will make rational choices in the marketplace and the differentiated reality of varying literacy rates, social networks, confusing plan structures, changing provider networks, incomplete information, and outright lies. The newspaper reports and government officials paint this as victimization and coercion. But there may be a more fundamental problem at work; the dilemma choice poses is akin to what the sociologist Ulrich Beck terms the "risk society":

> The ultimate deadlock of risk society, however, resides in the gap between knowledge and decision . . . the situation is radically "undecidable"—but we none the less *have to decide.* The risk epoch imposes on each of us the burden of making crucial decisions which may affect our very survival without any proper foundation in knowledge. (1999, 78)

The problem posed by the centrality of consumer choice in the MMA is, as Beck states, that the situation is often undecidable. The onus of making a choice, however, has been shifted from state planners and the public health system to individual beneficiaries who are entrusted with managing their own health conditions and choosing their health plans.

Shifting more choice onto consumers has implications on notions of personal responsibility. Market health policies equate moral behavior with rational, economic decision making (Lemke 2001, 201). Consumers who are unable to make decisions or who make them without full knowledge of the implications are considered irresponsible, unsophisticated, and inefficient. It was this moral obligation to choose correctly that compelled Doña Fátima to call herself *bruta* and Don Victor to insist that he was not tricked. In so doing, they both took responsibility for their choices. Beck suggests that they are misplacing the blame; market-based health care may very well create choices that are *undecidable.*

Public Policy Choices: Colonial Constraints

Choice in the Medicare Advantage program refers primarily to the rather narrow domain of consumer choice in picking a plan, but focusing exclusively on consumer choice masks the absence of choice in other domains. Public-policy choices, for example, are quite limited. The federal government's emphasis on the market value of choice is complicated in Puerto Rico by colonial relations of power that hamper the Puerto Rican state from either developing fully autonomous programs or enjoying the funding levels and voice in policy making afforded to the states of the union. In Puerto Rico, the health care system moved away from a universal model in the 1990s by privatizing the provision of care, which left many former beneficiaries without coverage. When a new governor who was interested in rolling back some of these market-oriented reforms was voted into office in 2004, he encountered substantial resistance on the part of federal officials. I describe here how the federal government's focus on consumer choice in picking a plan constrained the public-policy choices available in Puerto Rico in the wake of the passage of the MMA.

One way in which policy makers' choices are constrained in Puerto Rico has to do with the concept of "preemption." The Medicare Advantage program mandates that federal law preempt state law for Medicare Advantage organizations except in the domains of licensing and financial reserves. The federal legislation attempts to make it easier for Medicare Advantage programs to carry out their activities without interference from states. Because of this, Medicare Advantage plans in Puerto Rico bypass the Puerto Rican state and report to a CMS regional office in New York. "Preemption" in Puerto Rico is a powerful term. It essentially means that Medicare Advantage HMOs can operate on the island with virtually no local regulatory oversight. For example, other health plans in Puerto Rico are required to abide by Puerto Rico Law 194, the Patient's Bill of Rights and Responsibilities, and to report encounter data to the Puerto Rico Department of Health. Medicare Advantage plans can respond to these requests for information from the Commonwealth by claiming that federal law preempts local law on this matter and therefore the information will not be produced. Other aspects of Commonwealth law that Medicare Advantage HMOs do not have to follow are claims payment rules and appeals and grievances. Both of these areas are covered by federal law.[11] Preemption creates tension between the Medicare Advantage organizations and the local government. In interviews with personnel from local health agencies, there was a sense of distrust and skepticism toward Medicare Advantage that is directly related to the problem of oversight and regulation as well as the influx of complaints surrounding the implementation of the MMA and the opening of many new plans in the Puerto Rico market. The upshot is that a sector of the insurance market that could potentially cover 600,000 people is not subject to local law except for in the realms of licensing and financial reserves. Given Puerto Rico's colonial status, this represents a significant constraint on local autonomy in developing a public health system.[12]

Medicare Platino and the Mandatory Market

When Governor Aníbal Acevedo Vilá was elected in 2004, his administration was immediately faced with developing a proposal for how to administer the block grant awarded to Puerto Rico for beneficiaries who were eligible for both Medicare and Medicaid under the MMA.[13] The Acevedo Vilá government sent a proposal to CMS regarding how it would like to administer the block grant. CMS rejected the administration's proposals several times until a program called Medicare Platino was developed.

In the 2004 elections, Medicare Platino was part of Acevedo Vilá's campaign platform regarding health care. However, the Medicare Platino of 2004 does not resemble the program that was eventually implemented with CMS approval. Documents from the campaign describe Medicare Platino as a government-run health program that does not include an HMO as the middle man. The proposed program sought to eliminate insurance companies as intermediaries in the delivery of health care, it emphasized the importance of basing health care in the doctor/patient relationship, and sought to roll back utilization control mechanisms that rationed care. The Acevedo Vilá campaign also explicitly stated that it was against privatization. As such, the campaign platform evoked the public health goals of the regional health care system that was replaced by La Reforma in 1993 (Aníbal Gobernador 2004 Campaign 2004). This proposed program was in conflict, however, with the policy platform of the MMA, which required that the prescription-drug benefit be delivered by private plans, not by a government-run program as Acevedo Vilá had proposed.

The final Medicare Platino program, which was made public in October 2005, created a new category of Medicare Advantage plans for dual eligible beneficiaries in Puerto Rico where they would receive a reduction in their Medicare premiums and comparatively low copayments for prescription drugs (ASES 2005). In other words, the Medicare Platino program that was approved by CMS was based on contracting with private plans to offer an enriched benefit package to dual eligible beneficiaries. Of course, that a newly elected governor could not implement the health plan that was promised in the campaign is not in itself terribly remarkable. What is interesting is that the opposition to the governor's plans came from a federal agency. CMS clearly preferred that private health plans, rather than a government-run complementary plan, administer the benefit. Here, Puerto Rico was free to choose how to administer the block grant as long as that choice corresponded with the market-based health care model coming out of Washington.

In sum, choice was an important market value in several ways. The need for choice was one of the fundamental policy justifications for managed care in Medicare. When Medicare is contracted with several plans in a beneficiary's area, consumer choice is thought to bring about a cycle of innovation as competition drives down prices and spurs improvements to the system. Consumers are also imagined as demanding choices in their health care, as refusing a public system where an endless array of providers, procedures, and pharmaceuticals might be closed off to them. But despite the rhetorical concern with choice in health policy and the focus on consumer choice in the marketplace, the kinds of choices that were available were actually quite narrow in scope. In practice, the intense proliferation of consumer choice in selecting a plan created a marketplace where consumers were confused by their options. In the discussion of negotiations over how to implement pieces of the MMA in Puerto Rico, it became clear that choice was in fact compulsory—though insular policy makers had a different vision for how the public health system in Puerto Rico should be run, the federal government insisted upon competition among private plans (rather than a government-run system). There was then a hierarchy of choice—most people could make choices *in* the marketplace, but others made choices *about* the marketplace. Legislators, lobbyists, and the regulators at CMS made a number of choices that shaped the contours of the Medicare program by opening it up to further marketization. Those same kinds of political choices were not available to policy makers in Puerto Rico.

Conclusions: The Failure of Market Values?

This chapter began with the assertion that market values matter because they naturalize and legitimize market-based reforms to public programs by uniting market reforms with what is considered good, right, and important in society. Major transformations in "common sense" have certainly taken place over the last 30 years in both the United States and Puerto Rico concerning beliefs about the proper role of government. Neoliberal ways of thought that advocate downsizing government, increasing choice, decreasing taxes, and minimizing regulation are commonplace in the media and in political discourse. If voting trends are any indication, citizens at least partially share these neoliberal orthodoxies because they keep electing public officials who run on and pursue market-based reform projects.

But when examined ethnographically, market values do not always succeed at compelling us to behave in a certain way or even transforming themselves into common sense. Upon ethnographic examination, they are shot through with contradictions. Partnering can be hierarchical and lead to regulatory capture. Government partners, furthermore, may not be interested in becoming more efficient and businesslike. The kinds of partnering recognized by government agencies favor professionals and the highly educated or those with political clout. Choice, on the other hand, can be overwhelming, particularly when there is not a big difference between the products, other kinds of choices are off-limits, and beneficiaries are deceived in the marketplace.

Looking at the shortcomings of market values helps bring us back to the question of why market reforms go wrong. How is it that they fail to achieve utopian aims while all the while relentlessly achieving the aim of restructuring public-service provision? The social theorist David Harvey argues that this contradiction exists because the primary purpose of neoliberal reforms has been to consolidate class power and accumulate capital:

> The theoretical utopianism of neoliberal argument has, I conclude, primarily worked as a system of justification and legitimation for whatever needed to be done to achieve this goal. . . . This in no way denies the power of ideas to act as a force for historical-geographical change. But it does point to a creative tension between the power of neoliberal ideas and the actual practices of neoliberalization that have transformed how global capitalism has been working over the last three decades. (2005, 19)

Throughout this book, I have tried to take seriously the promises of market reform and interrogate them ethnographically. As such, I find

Harvey's analysis compelling but also unsatisfying. Why do market reforms continue to enjoy popular support among elected officials and some segments of the public if they have so persistently failed to achieve their aims? How powerful are market values for shoring up market-reform projects irrespective of the performance of these reforms? Is the growing inequality that has been brought about by privatizing health care likely to intensify (some left uninsured, partnering only for the educated and affluent; those who make good choices are celebrated while others are vilified)? In the next chapter, I analyze the failures of market reform in health care and account for why, despite its shortcomings, market reform continues to be the only item on the menu when it comes to public-service reform.

Conclusion

Ungovernability as Market Rule

> Governmentality may be eternally optimistic, but government is a congenitally failing operation. (Rose, O'Malley, and Valverde 2006, 98)

The privatization of the Medicare and Medicaid programs in Puerto Rico radically transformed the health system on the island. Currently, almost half of the island's population receives government-sponsored health benefits through private managed care health plans. In less than 10 years, managed care went from nonexistent on the island to the dominant form of receiving health care.

Proponents of privatization promised more rational and efficient care management, expanded access to pharmaceuticals and specialists, and a new emphasis on self-care practices that would ultimately make the population healthier. Few of these promises were realized. Instead, privatization was accompanied by a number of failures. Rather than producing a health system that was rational and easy to navigate, privatized managed care created new barriers to accessing care through eligibility requirements, enrollment processes, and administrative procedures for securing authorization. Other failures include escalating costs and care rationing by physicians and health plans, especially in La Reforma. Whether it was obtaining durable medical equipment (DME), securing a mental health appointment, or being able to purchase prescription drugs, care coordination never quite worked for the most vulnerable people whom I interviewed. Little evidence exists that efforts to alter patients' behavior through care management has produced improved health outcomes.

This book argues that privatized managed care failed to deliver on many of its promises. But why? Where did managed care go wrong? There are four interconnected answers to that question. First, privatized for-profit managed care is far better at making and managing money than managing health (or people). Second, neoliberal health programs are based on asocial and ahistorical understandings of human subjects and behavior. Third, these programs are undermined by their own hubris. Fourth, in Puerto Rico, colonial relations of rule have contributed to the failures of managed care and the creation of a health system that is largely unmanageable. Before explicating each of these answers, a final ethnographic example illustrates what I mean by unmanageable.

Managing Costs, Monetizing Care

Gina logs in to the case management program. Thirty new prior authorization requests appear in her queue. She clicks on the patient number with the oldest receipt date. The physician requested an Accu-Chek blood glucose monitor with preloaded testing strips and an extra-large display. Gina checks the patient diagnosis. The patient meets the criteria for a blood glucose monitor due to a diabetes diagnosis, but there is no diagnosis of visual impairment or limited dexterity that would support the more expensive version of the machine. Following the health plan's criteria, she will recommend a denial.

Gina asks, why did the doctor request this monitor? He has been with the plan for 2 years and should know better. First, she calls the doctor's secretary to see if there are any other diagnoses that were not entered on the request form. The secretary says she is very busy but will check the record when she gets a moment. Gina will not speak to the physician, who does not attend to such minutiae, but she hopes to hear back from the secretary. She documents the call in the system. It was a standard request, so she has 14 days to approve or deny. She hits the back button to the first screen and under "case status," she pulls down a menu of terms. She selects "pending more information from MD." If a denial is issued, it may take a month for the patient to receive his or her supplies. Often, the physician will resubmit the request upon learning of the denial and ask for the standard blood glucose monitor.

Acme had negotiated down the price on standard blood glucose monitors in exchange for agreeing to supply one brand exclusively. For other brands and models, Acme pays the retail price. Members though, and the new ones especially, do not like switching brands. They tend to like their old machines. Gina does not speak with patients often; instead, she reads the notes in the electronic system that are recorded by customer service representatives.

Gina looks through the patient's prior claims history for evidence of treatments or diagnoses that support the current request. She likes to find a way to be able to issue an approval.[1] After unsuccessfully scouring the claims and customer service electronic records, looking for additional health information for the member, Gina clicks the "submit" button and returns to her queue. She selects the patient with the next-oldest receipt date and begins again.

Gina is a prior authorization nurse and performs some of the actual work that goes into "managing care." Managed care purports to eliminate inefficiencies in patient care by denying unnecessary treatment, monitoring under- and overutilization, enrolling the chronically ill in disease-management programs, shortening or eliminating hospital stays, and promoting preventive care. In the case just discussed, the company will save money on the cost of the blood glucose monitor. However, other costs are incurred, such as salaries for staff like Gina, the transfer of administrative functions onto the physician's secretary, and the time delay in getting the patient the machine, which may result in additional diabetic complications. Beyond this cost-benefit calculus, the patient will likely experience duress and frustration when the blood glucose monitor is denied (the patient may in fact have no idea that the doctor requested the more expensive version of the machine).

In the time that I worked at Acme, DME was a perpetual problem for the organization. Items that were supposed to be approved were not, the company that had been subcontracted to deliver the equipment failed to get it to beneficiaries' homes, and grievance logs grew precipitously. Rather than see these failures as an exception or an aberration, the inability to manage patients' care was actually the rule. This is because efficiency and cost-control mechanisms created new layers of bureaucratic procedures and more opportunities to deny care. In the end, these utilization control mechanisms can make it more difficult for patients to manage chronic health conditions like diabetes. Managing costs at Acme with an eye toward maximizing profits trumped care management in the form of getting members the medical equipment they wanted in the most timely way possible. It is important to keep in mind that these savings did not return to the Medicare program but contributed to the company's bottom line. Therefore, when considering efficiency and cost savings, we must ask: savings to whom? Efficiency to what end?

Clearly, there are instances when monitoring overutilization can both benefit an insurance company economically and contribute to better (or at least equivalent) health outcomes: examples include eliminating unnecessary surgeries such as elective cesarean sections, promoting the use of generic instead of brand-name drugs, and denying truly unnecessary medical equipment. The problem is that, in practice, the focus is more on managing costs than care. Certain care setbacks are tolerated if they translate into cost savings. Overutilization tends to be targeted more than underutilization (which could potentially cost the company far more). In sum, many of the promises of managed care seem intuitive or good, but when examined ethnographically and in their for-profit form, they do not achieve all of their aims and often create barriers to accessing care.

These findings reinforce and extend earlier qualitative and ethnographic research on the role of utilization review in managed care. This research has consistently uncovered a considerable gap between managed care's purported rationale of ensuring that care is medically appropriate and reducing waste, and its actual effect of creating access barriers and elevating financial considerations over health outcomes (Abadía and Oviedo 2009; Maskovsky 2000; Wagner 2005; Willging 2005). As has been found in other reforms, privatization disproportionately impacted those who were most vulnerable, including those with the most complex medical needs (Maskovsky 2000), those in need of mental health services (Willging 2005), rural beneficiaries, developmentally disabled patients, and those without reliable access to a phone, much less, a computer (L. López 2005). Of the Medicare beneficiaries whom I interviewed, it was the poorer patients, those with complex medical needs, and those who did not have family members advocating for them, who struggled to access adequate care, pay for their medications, secure transportation to medical appointments, and obtain all of the home care and equipment that they needed. Managed care worked fairly well for people who had access to insurance in their working lives, who could rely on family members to help them navigate the system, whose Medicaid eligibility status did not change frequently, who did not need multiple specialists, and who did not have mental health care needs. One of the primary reasons that market-based health reforms have disproportionately negative impacts on the poor and disabled is because these reforms are based in culturally specific and classed ideas about how people behave. Market reformers assume that health care "consumers" want to act as rational, economic subjects, constantly weighing the costs and benefits of various health options. The problem is that too little attention is paid to the information asymmetries, economic struggles, and lack of social capital that constrain choice and create barriers to accessing care.

Managed Care and Optimistic Neoliberalism in Puerto Rico

Why did reformers and their constituents support market-based reforms to the health system in the United States and Puerto Rico? David Harvey's (2005) account of the construction of consent for neoliberalism in the United States details how economic elites promoted the importance of individual freedom over government intervention, partnered with religious conservatives, and took over cultural institutions (like think tanks, universities, media outlets, and political parties) in order to broadcast and advance a neoliberal worldview. These cultural initiatives were combined with more coercive measures such as hard-line law enforcement that particularly targeted the poor and communities of color, dismantling unions, and forcing democratically elected governments to implement austerity measures in the face of budget crises. For Harvey, the combination of efforts to construct consent with more hard-line coercive measures explains the hegemony of neoliberal policies. This account, however, underappreciates the role of optimism, hope, and progress as harnessed by neoliberal reformers. These more positive and inspirational elements of neoliberal discourse accounted for its ability to garner support for quite radical reforms to the health care system in Puerto Rico.

Though in hindsight privatization projects may look cynical, many people, including physicians and government health workers, supported La Reforma in the hopes that the health system would actually improve and would equalize the disparities that existed between the public and private systems.[2] Privatizing the health system tapped into frustration with the status quo and promised to bring greater efficiency, advanced technology, more equity, and progress to the health system. Failure to achieve these objectives makes disappointment with La Reforma particularly acute even as many of its promises still hold appeal.

On the eve of the implementation of La Reforma the health system was widely described as being in chaos and crisis, with 69% of the population reporting that health services suffered from serious deficiencies on the island (Ferré 1992). Pedro Rosselló, the pro-statehood governor under whose administration La Reforma was implemented, claimed that privatizing public hospitals would end "economic discrimination" in the health system by allowing the poor to use the private system. He went on to promote the efficiency of the private sector in comparison to the government: "What we're saying is take government out of those areas where it's been shown to be inefficient" (Hemlock 1991). Public health employees were assured by the Secretary of Health that privatization would represent an opportunity for training, advancement, and better pay in the private sector (*San Juan Star* 1993). The legislation that created La Reforma stated its goals in this same optimistic language; the reform sought to eliminate the unequal, two-tiered system already in place, control costs, downsize the health care bureaucracy, and deliver high-quality care to the medically indigent (Commonwealth of Puerto Rico 1993, 1–2). These goals assume that the market is the best mechanism for the delivery of care and that private companies will ensure higher quality, decrease bureaucracy, and increase equality.

Similarly, changes to the Medicare program issued from this exuberant optimism and faith in private enterprise as an engine of better and more efficient health care. The Medicare Modernization Act (MMA) of 2003 shaped the care available to Medicare beneficiaries in Puerto Rico by extending the role of private managed care organizations and private prescription-drug plans within the Medicare program. As we saw, in the speech he gave while signing the MMA into law, former President

George W. Bush described the purpose of the new legislation as "giving our seniors more health care choices," enhancing freedom, and allowing seniors to be in charge so that "health care plans within Medicare will have to compete for their business by offering higher quality service. For the seniors of America, more choices and more control will mean better health care" (Bush 2003). This is an extraordinarily optimistic vision of human behavior and the market. Choices necessarily lead to progress (it does not even seem possible here to make bad choices). These two market-based health reforms issue from a deep skepticism about the role of government in providing public services, yet they contain an exuberant faith in private businesses to effectively manage and improve the population's health (while simultaneously making a profit and becoming more efficient).

This book has shown that market-based health programs were promoted and implemented in the name of efficiency, economization, transparency, quality care, consumer rights, and choice. It has discussed these neoliberal keywords both as *management strategies* that apply business logics and methods to maximize health and profit and *market values* that seek to naturalize market solutions to social problems. Market-based health reforms harnessed patients' aspirations for health and for many health professionals they represented a step forward, a way to create a more efficient and modern health care infrastructure on the island. This persistent optimism is difficult to reconcile with health reform's track record. And therein lies the central paradox of health reform on the island: its optimistic promises were promoted to great effect, but rarely realized. As the quote that opens this chapter intimates, market-based health reform was a thoroughly optimistic, yet perpetually failing, undertaking.

The Case for Failure

Clearly, managed care *has* succeeded in radically reorganizing the health system. It has created new alliances and relationships among citizens, corporations, the federal government, and the insular government. Central among these new relationships is transforming government into a contractor who pays private managed care firms to deliver health care services to eligible beneficiaries. In the process, citizens are called on to behave as consumers and take charge of their own health care. Market-based reforms have also won a symbolic victory by crafting a commonsense understanding that a private system is more modern and efficient than a system where the government directly provides care. La Reforma built new forms of political belonging through the government health insurance card by offering new benefits such as access to private physician offices and dental care to low-income beneficiaries. Privatized managed care has created jobs and generated profit (though the profit often leaves the island). Finally, it has reorganized the practice of medicine and the experience of seeking treatment, particularly for the poor. Care management, quality measurement, obtaining prior authorization, presenting an insurance card (or admitting a lack thereof) at the doctor's office, and having claims denied are all now commonplace features of the insurance-based health system.

So when I say that privatized, for-profit managed care is unmanageable or has failed, I do not mean that it has *only or exclusively* failed. I certainly recognize that it has also radically remade the health system. Though it has had many effects in the world, it has stubbornly fallen short of some of its central aspirations and promises.

A summary of the major gaps between (1) market-based health reforms as an optimistic, neoliberal project for making health care more efficient, cost-effective, and accessible and (2) the track record of these programs in practice includes the following:

- La Reforma was initially intended to be available to *all* Puerto Ricans on the island. However, when the public health system was converted to a managed care model in the 1990s, this created a category of uninsured people in Puerto Rico for the first time. This group is made up of people who are not eligible for La Reforma (usually because they do not meet the income or assets requirement) and those who are eligible but do not complete the enrollment process. According to data from the U.S. Census (2009), the total civilian noninstitutionalized population was 3,938,846, and out of this 330,299 individuals were uninsured (8.3%). So privatized managed care excluded some people from the health system and thereby created new forms of inequality.
- Care rationing by primary care physicians and health plans became common. Though access to care was extended to some segments of the

population, this was done with certain limitations. The press featured widespread documentation of care rationing by health plans particularly for mental health care (Hernández Cabiya 2005; Sosa Pascual 2005a, 2005c; see also chapter 5) and for referrals from primary care physicians to see specialists and obtain prescriptions for pharmaceuticals (Comisión Para Evaluar el Sistema de Salud 2005; PAHO 2007; Parés Arroyo 2008b; see also chapter 1). Increased access to insurance coverage was accompanied by the implementation of utilization control measures that limited the population's access to covered services. Through capitation, La Reforma in particular introduced financial considerations into the relationship between primary care physicians and their patients in what was widely described as an ethics violation and a conflict of interest.

- Bureaucracy was not downsized or eliminated. Introducing insurance companies as middlemen actually duplicated many bureaucratic structures. Each insurance company had its own administrative organization, highly paid executives, information technology system, care-management programs, and so on. These multiple insurance company bureaucracies in turn created additional work and expense for health care providers who must follow different plan rules, authorization procedures, and claims submissions guidelines for each insurance company with whom they contract. Furthermore, the government continued to exercise an oversight and auditing function that required extensive personnel and administrative infrastructure. Finally, administrative costs at insurance companies are much higher than in government-run programs like Medicare, which spends around 3–5% of its premiums on costs related to administration while private Medicare Advantage plans spend around 16% (AMA 2005; GAO 2008; Sullivan 2001; Woolhandler, Campbell, and Himmelstein 2003).

- Medical education suffered. When hospitals were privatized, many residency programs disappeared and opportunities for research diminished (Parés Arroyo 2008a; see also chapter 1). According to reports in the major daily newspaper *El Nuevo Día*, the number of interns and residents decreased by 68% between the implementation of La Reforma and 2005 (Sosa Pascual 2005g).

- Safety-net institutions were negatively impacted by La Reforma, particularly Centro Medico and federally qualified community health centers (Hayashi et al. 2009) who had to serve more patients (including the uninsured) with less government funding.

- Ethnographic evidence from participant observation at Acme and interviews I conducted with beneficiaries showed a disconnect between the
health promotion and prevention goals of privatized managed care and
how beneficiaries actually experienced the health system. Beneficiaries
continued to look to the government to provide care, did not religiously
engage in the self-care practices promoted by insurance companies, and
were often overwhelmed and confused by choice in the health care marketplace. They also experienced barriers to accessing care, including
delays in receiving medical equipment, difficulty obtaining referrals to
specialists, confusion regarding plan rules, and problems completing the
application and recertification process for eligibility under La Reforma.
- Auditing and oversight have either been largely absent (La Reforma) or
characterized by significant shortcomings (Medicare Advantage). Ethnographic research of federal audits at Acme revealed an audit culture that
values internal oversight mechanisms, easily quantifiable data points, and
maintaining good social relations over evaluating the quality of the care
provided by contracted health plans (see chapter 2). Auditors seemed
uninterested in enforcing some rules (such as marketing rules that were
clearly being violated on the island) and instead took a much more cooperative approach to oversight that focused on the development of corrective action plans.
- Privatized managed care is more costly and less efficient than both traditional fee-for-service Medicare and the regional health system. The
2003 Medicare legislation that extended the use of managed care plans
and added a prescription-drug benefit vastly increased the cost of the
Medicare program and in turn resulted in a larger federal bureaucracy to
oversee the new plans. Furthermore, nationally managed care in Medicare costs 13% more to provide than traditional fee-for-service Medicare
(Zarabozo and Harrison 2009, W55) with "no apparent quality gains"
(Gold 2009). In Puerto Rico, managed care organizations have been
paid at 180% of fee-for-service rates on the island (MedPac 2009, 179).[3]
The value received in exchange for these high payments is questionable
because the strongest quality rating for Medicare Advantage plans on
the island is 2.5 stars (out of a possible 5), with some plans receiving this
rating: "Caution—This plan got low ratings from Medicare 3 years in a
row" (CMS 2012a). Likewise, the cost of health care has increased under
La Reforma (C. López 2005). The proportion of the government budget

Table C.1. Proportion of the Puerto Rican Government Budget That Is Dedicated to Health Care

1990	1992	1994	1996	1998	2000	2002	2004
3.62%	2.76%	3.20%	3.12%	6.56%	9.65%	12.98%	14.34%

Source: Alm (2006), 342.

dedicated to health expenditures vastly increased after the implementation of La Reforma (Alm 2006).

- Health reform has failed to improve many basic health indicators. As we have seen, the following are among the most important health problems that either stayed the same or got worse under La Reforma:
  - Infant mortality rates were higher in La Reforma than in the private sector. Between 1981 and 2003 there were dramatic increases in the rates of cesarean sections, low birth weights, and premature deliveries (Comisión Para Evaluar el Sistema de Salud 2005, 75). Almost half (49%) of pregnant woman on Mi Salud (the new name for La Reforma) began their prenatal care in the second or third trimester in 2010–2011 (Parés Arroyo 2012b).
  - A broad-based team of public health officials and academic researchers concluded that "the evidence does not show an improvement in the quality of services offered to hypertensive, asthmatic, and diabetic patients" (Comisión Para Evaluar el Sistema de Salud 2005, 75). The health system on the island was found to be ineffective in bringing about improvements in health for the leading causes of mortality: "heart disease, cancer, diabetes, chronic pulmonary disease, hypertension, strokes, kidney and liver diseases, and HIV" (Comisión Para Evaluar el Sistema de Salud 2005, 77).
  - Access to specialized care and treatment were particularly challenging for cancer patients who "continue being diagnosed in advanced stages of their cancer, they do not receive timely treatment following their diagnosis, and they do not accept or do not complete the proscribed treatment regimen" (Comisión Para Evaluar el Sistema de Salud 2005, 75).
  - Access to mental health was a problem in Puerto Rico as a whole where "almost three quarters of adults and children who need mental health services do not receive them" (Comisión Para Evaluar el Sistema de Salud 2005, 75).

- The impact of La Reforma on access to emergency services was also drastic: "in 2001 only 58 of the 78 municipalities had emergency facilities operating 24 hours a day, 7 days a week" (PAHO 2007, 34). Previously, these services had been provided by government-run treatment and diagnostic centers.
- Finally, the shift to managed care put the focus of the health care system on curative (acute) care, rather than prevention. A recent study found that only 12% of beneficiaries of the government health plan in Puerto Rico (formerly La Reforma, now renamed Mi Salud) attended a preventive-care visit during the year 2010–2011 (Parés Arroyo 2012c). A study conducted by the Health Insurance Administration (ASES) in 2010 found that in Puerto Rico, patients use the emergency room 40% more than in the United States, which indicates that they are not accessing appropriate preventative and outpatient care (Parés Arroyo 2012a).
- The influence of Medicare Advantage on health outcomes is more difficult to assess. I am not aware of any population-based quantitative studies that have taken up the question of whether health outcomes have significantly improved for Medicare beneficiaries in Puerto Rico after the upsurge in Medicare Advantage enrollment that began in 2005. This is an important area for future research. National studies show no significant difference in quality of care when Medicare Advantage is compared to Original Medicare (Gold 2009). Most Medicare Advantage plans on the island offer benefit packages that reduce patient cost sharing in comparison with Original Medicare. So they have offered access to care at lower prices from the beneficiary's perspective. However, this comes with a significant price tag; Medicare Advantage rates in 2009 equaled 180% of Original Medicare (MedPac 2009). It is concerning that so much of the Medicare Advantage payments went to profit and administrative overhead, rather than to improvements in care.[4]
- There is, finally, a widespread problem with the lack of public data about managed care's effectiveness (Comisión Para Evaluar el Sistema de Salud 2005). When the health system was privatized, so, too, were much of the data; this lack of public data makes the task of health planning and prevention more difficult. Furthermore, quality and performance data on the managed care plans contracted with La Reforma are virtually nonexistent.

Interpreting Failure

This book has laid out the evidence that privatized managed care is a perpetually failing—or unmanageable—undertaking. But how can we make sense of and begin to understand these failures? How is it that reform programs, whose purpose is to economize and optimize health care delivery, so persistently fail to achieve their aims yet continue to be the only policy option available in Washington, San Juan, and beyond? The following are four interrelated arguments about how and why the effort to manage care went awry in Puerto Rico.

1. Managing Money, Not Health

The first explanation to account for the failures of market reform in health care is that *privatized for-profit managed care is far better at making and managing money than managing health (or people)*. Private insurance is a financial instrument for profiting from risk. From the perspective of insurers, the primary objective of private health insurance is to hedge its bets that the premiums received will be higher than the medical and administrative expenditures, thereby resulting in profit. Health insurance companies have been remarkably successful in this regard.[5] Recent record profits in the insurance industry amid a deep and prolonged recession have been attributed to shrinking demand for health services, particularly as more costs have been shifted onto consumers in the form of deductibles, higher premiums, and copays (Abelson 2011). In other words, insurance companies benefit (at least in the short run) when patients receive less care. Though considerable health-management functions have been added to insurance companies' product lines, many of these health-management programs are primarily aimed at controlling costs by limiting utilization rather than maximizing health. Those health-management functions that are directed at improving health outcomes have shown limited cost savings (Bott et al. 2009; Fireman, Bartlett, and Selby 2004; Motherall 2011; Russell 2009).[6] When I asked an Acme senior executive directly about the efficacy of disease-management programs, he told me that everyone knows they are not successful at reducing costs and improving outcomes. Their major advantage, he added, was that they are great public relations tools. He thought Acme's decision to create its own disease- and case-management program, rather than pay an established company that specializes in this field, was a particularly smart financial decision.

The utopian promises and market values that accompanied privatization—promises of an efficient, cost-effective, health care marketplace full of choice that benefits everyone—are stubbornly elusive. One way to make sense of this disconnect between the promises of privatized managed care and its accomplishments is to think about these utopian promises and market values as a mask or cover for the underlying economic motivations of reform programs, which are to make money for insurance companies, their shareholders, and other vested interest groups like pharmaceutical and medical technology manufacturers in the health care marketplace. This line of reasoning echoes the argument that David Harvey has made about neoliberalism more generally. We can, he says,

> Interpret neoliberalization either as a *utopian* project to realize a theoretical design for the reorganization of international capitalism or as a *political* project to re-establish the conditions for capital accumulation and to restore the power of economic elites. (2005, 19)

By associating the spread of neoliberal rationalities with a particular class, whom he refers to as the "economic elites," Harvey draws attention to the economic goals of reform programs to generate profit and consolidate wealth for a particular class of individuals. He also points out that market reform programs are characterized by considerable internal contradictions. For example, neoliberal policies are often implemented through coercion (rather than the much slower process of subject formation) and when personal gain potentially conflicts with the free market, many economic elites are likely to pursue personal economic gain. Ultimately, for Harvey, the political and economic project of neoliberalism has dominated the utopian project.

These insights can be applied to the market-based reforms in health care examined in this book. Clearly, financial motives often trump health promotion motives in privatized managed care settings. I encountered many examples during my fieldwork. For instance, Acme contracted with companies like the MBHO (managed behavioral health organization) and the DME provider in order to save money despite evidence that these companies were not delivering high-quality care. Further, a "risk assessment physical" was heavily promoted for new members at Acme in order to game the risk-adjusted payment methodology in use by the Centers for Medicare and Medicaid Services (CMS).[7] Rather than primarily about getting members the services they needed, the purpose of the physical exam was to register as many diagnoses as possible for each member, thereby resulting in a higher risk score for each beneficiary and higher premium payments from the government. The many buyouts and mergers that characterized the Medicare Advantage market on the island were primarily about generating profit for shareholders and owners rather than improving health outcomes or becoming more efficient. Within La Reforma, the ethical conflicts created by capitating primary care physicians are another example of how the financial ends of reform projects conflicted with or undermined the health promotion objectives of the program. On a more macro policy level, the architects of the Medicare Modernization Act of 2003 could be understood as "economic elites" who benefited directly from this piece of neoliberal legislation; "at least 15 congressional staffers, congressmen and federal officials left to go to work for the pharmaceutical industry, whose profits were increased by several billion dollars" (Kroft 2007).[8]

Ultimately, the market-based health reform programs this book has scrutinized are based on a false equivalency: that managing health is the same as managing money. However, health is not easily managed, particularly by an insurance company whose central goal is to turn a profit, not necessarily to improve health outcomes.[9] As outlined above, many conflicts exist between a company's health promotion and profit maximization goals. Furthermore, the evidence shows that managed care plans in Medicare have not been able to increase quality when compared with traditional fee-for-service Medicare and private non-Medicare plans (Berenson and Dowd 2009). Quality gains were also absent under La Reforma (Comisión Para Evaluar el Sistema de Salud 2005).

As these examples illustrate, there is ample evidence to support the claim that privatized managed care is primarily about managing and making money rather than promoting health, but economic explanations alone are not enough.

2. Asocial and Ahistorical Subject Theories

The second reason that market-based health-reform programs have fallen so short of their promises is because they are based on *asocial and ahistorical subject theories*. Market-based health-reform projects are based on a theory of the subject (i.e., people are first and foremost cost-benefit-calculating health care consumers) that does not reflect how actual subjects think about themselves and act in the world. This vision of the health care consumer as an informed choice maker is not a reflection of the world as it is, but a projection of how policy makers would like it to be. In my research, market-based health policy failed to transform patients, family members, workers, and citizens seamlessly into neoliberal health care consumers in Puerto Rico. This is primarily because the model of the decision-making consumer does not account for the moral and social criteria that people actually employ when making decisions about their health care. It is based on able-bodied, individualistic assumptions that are out of place in describing how people react to and experience illness, disability, and dependency. Further, due to multiple economic pressures and the structure of knowledge in medicine (i.e., doctors have more knowledge than patients), choice in the sense of "therapeutic and economic self-determination" (Tomes 2006) is severely constrained in market-based health systems. Instead, beneficiaries of public programs tend either to be overwhelmed by too many choices in the marketplace (as is the case with selecting a Medicare Advantage plan to join) or forced to choose among sameness (Hill, Zimmerman, and Fox 2002; McWilliams et al. 2011).

Though anthropologists, sociologists, and even some economists have repeatedly critiqued the assumptions on which this "economic man" is based, the hyperrational cost-benefit-calculating consumer citizen continues to be the building block on which market-based public-policy schemes are erected. What's more, mere cost-benefit calculations are no longer sufficient. Contemporary health policy enlists the consumer in his or her own self-care—we are surrounded by forms of responsibilization that valorize health-maintaining activities on the one hand (like checking one's blood sugar, maintaining a healthy weight, and exercising) and that punish the sick and noncompliant on the other hand (with very high copays for emergency room visits, disapproval from health care providers, or being refused care). Many ethnographic accounts have analyzed the cultural, power-laden conflicts that arise between biomedical caregivers and patients who are struggling to manage their chronic conditions and adhere to treatment regimens (see, for example, Borovoy and Hine 2008; Ferzacca 2000). Others have demonstrated the devastating results and questioned the ethical basis for casting the noncompliant as irrational or undeserving of medical care (Farmer 2010; Metzl 2010). There is, furthermore, a highly classed component to the type of behavior that is called for by neoliberal health programs where behaving like a middle-class subject—with adequate health insurance coverage, fluency in biomedical culture, and an interest and ability to engage in health-promoting activities like eating diets rich in fruits and vegetables—is cast as morally meritorious. The beneficiaries I interviewed did not fit this middle-class template. Finally, the highly individualized approach of disease-management and care-management programs does not address the social determinants of health or view patients in their larger cultural and economic context, which we know can exercise a large influence on health outcomes and health-related behaviors (CSDH 2008). While designing and engineering health systems that allow individuals to maximize their health through responsible choices has a certain appeal, when the people making the choices turn out to be something other than the *homo economicus*, then the well-laid plans of policy makers are often derailed.

3. Hubris

The third explanation that accounts for the shortcomings of privatized managed care is hubris—the overconfidence that authorizes the belief that medical technology, management strategies, and the market can simultaneously improve health, lower costs, and reap profit. The market-reform programs I studied shared a common aspiration to plan, manage, and remake the health system on an ambitious scale. The legislation that extended the role of managed care in Medicare touted Medicare as the largest medical payer in the world that could therefore "drive changes in the entire health care system" (*Federal Register* 2005, 4589). Similarly, the legislation that created La Reforma described this health program as a radical reform that would bring about modernization. Spurred on by their own hubris, policy makers concocted massive reform programs that promised far more than they were able to deliver.

These market-based reform programs in health care put great faith in rational planning and management as the key to progress. The behavior of providers, patients, and institutions was imagined as highly malleable and ready to be shaped by market forces like competition and choice. According to James Scott, this planning ideology—which has underwritten many development projects in the 20th century from Brasília to the Cultural Revolution—is "uncritical, unskeptical, and thus unscientifically optimistic about the possibilities for the comprehensive planning of human settlement and production" (1998, 4). He describes this ideology as issuing from "an imperial or hegemonic planning mentality that excludes the necessary role of local knowledge and know-how" (6; see also Li 2007).

This uncritical confidence could be found in abundance in the corporation where I worked—it is what undergirded Acme's decision to dissolve its complicated network of Mom and Pop DME providers in favor of a single contract with one DME company to cover the entire island. This Miami-based company arrived in Puerto Rico with no local knowledge. The DME company wanted physicians to change how they wrote up and transmitted their orders, but the providers did not comply and the information technology and e-ordering systems never quite worked. When they attempted to deliver equipment, the drivers couldn't find people's houses and complained that the streets were unmarked and the houses unnumbered. Acme's confidence in its ability to rationalize and simplify the order and delivery process for durable medical equipment quickly confronted innumerable obstacles, but it took more than 3 years for the upper management to change course and recontract with local firms. Hubris also characterized the management training programs at Acme that coached that the workforce could be more productive, happy, and efficient with enough positive thinking and the application of innovative management techniques. When management innovations fell short, workers were simply fired. Management strategies were not themselves questioned, but individual workers were deemed incompatible with the system. Finally, faith in the market and competition seems utterly impervious to evidence that market-based health care does not lower costs or make the overall system more affordable. The health system shared by the United States and Puerto Rico is the most expensive in the world in exchange for mediocre health outcomes. Despite spending more per capita on health care than any other country, globally the United States' health system ranks 37th in performance (OECD 2008; WHO 2008).

In addition to the hubris of policy makers and corporate planners, in medicine, hubris takes on an added dimension. Managed care must be seen as part of scientific and medical endeavors to control and stave off death. Hubris is part of the "culture of biomedicine" and leads to the "astonishing claim that ultimately death itself can be 'treated,' or at least 'medically managed'" (Kleinman 1995, 35). Chronic care-management programs, for example, attempt to monitor and direct every aspect of a consumer's medical care and even to transform his or her eating, sleeping, and physical activity. These programs issue from a belief that biomedical knowledge coupled with rational planning is capable of extending life. While hubris in medicine has certainly spurred innovation, it also tends to make practitioners blind to their own limits and contributes to the widespread use of iatrogenic practices in medicine (from unnecessary cesarean sections to heroic end-of-life interventions to cancer treatments that harm as much as they heal).

When these two forms of hubris—the management and the medical—coalesce, policy makers' grand aspirations to create a more perfect health system fail to take into account their own limitations and steadfastly reject the claims of local knowledge. The result in Puerto Rico was a health system that is more expensive than the model it replaced and is unable to achieve its health promotion and prevention aims.

4. Colonial Relations of Rule

The final explanation for the shortcomings of privatized managed care in Puerto Rico is *the role of colonialism*. Colonial relations of rule have consistently interfered with the ability of Puerto Rican policy makers to design and implement a health system that responds to local conditions. The colonial relationship with the United States has also locked

Puerto Rico into an employer-based system and, subsequently, privatized managed care.

Historically, proponents of public health as well as policy makers in Puerto Rico have advocated for a far more expansive role for government than the one currently imagined in neoliberal reform projects. The government was seen as the rightful steward of public health with a responsibility for ensuring that the poor had access to medical and preventive services. One illustration of how colonial power has limited the autonomy of the Puerto Rican government to set its own health agenda involves the deletion of a section of the Bill of Rights from the Constitution of the Estado Libre Asociado at the behest of the U.S. Congress. In 1952, the Constitution was approved by the people of Puerto Rico in a democratic vote by a margin of 372,649 to 82,923 (Zapata 2003, 242). However, the Constitution also had to be approved by the U.S. Congress, which required that language dealing specifically with public health and social justice be removed from the document. The excised language recognized the following human rights:

> The right of every person to a standard of living adequate for the health and well-being of himself and of his family, and especially to food, clothing, housing and medical care and necessary social services. The right of every person to social protection in the event of unemployment, sickness old age or disability. The right of motherhood and childhood to special care and assistance. The rights set forth in this section are closely connected with the progressive development of the economy of the Commonwealth and require, for their full effectiveness, sufficient resources and an agricultural and industrial development not yet attained by the Puerto Rican community. (Office of the Commonwealth of Puerto Rico 1964, 173)[10]

The deleted section articulates the Commonwealth's commitment to bettering the social and economic status of Puerto Rico. The Puerto Rican framers wanted to include this statement because it symbolically addressed the social goals of the new government.[11] That the U.S. Congress would remove the social justice provisions from the document illustrates how the colonial relationship between the United States and Puerto Rico limits island policy makers from creating an independent public health system that responds to local realities and conceives of health care as a right.[12]

The "failure" of privatized managed care in Puerto Rico must be viewed in its colonial context. Conditions of colonial rule, such as lower reimbursement rates in Medicaid and Medicare, the lack of autonomy for insular health policy makers (such as the need to submit Medicaid and Medicare programs for federal approval), and the use of block grants (which often have unclear administrative requirements), all contribute to a health system that is exceedingly difficult to manage. Federal preemption is another example of a requirement that robs Puerto Rico of control over its own health system. As we have seen, CMS has a history of rejecting proposals by the Puerto Rican government that advocate returning to a government-led health system model and moving away from privatized managed care. Unpredictable and uneven regulation and enforcement by federal authorities ensure that many rules are regularly broken. Together, these colonial characteristics of the relationship between the island and the mainland make it very difficult to imagine how insular policy makers could truly develop a health system of Puerto Rico's own choosing. Ironically, "failures" in the health system are sometimes deployed as a technology of colonial rule that subjects the "disorderly" colony to even more metropolitan oversight. As market-based reforms to health systems become more and more entrenched in the United States, Puerto Rico may have even less room to maneuver.

* * *

La Reforma and Medicare Advantage held out utopian promises of rational medical management, better prevention, increased efficiency, and higher-quality care. However, these promises butted against the desires of health maintenance organizations (HMOs) to make profits, unruly subjects, overconfidence in their own efficacy, colonial relations of rule, and the limits of market medicine as an efficient and cost-saving enterprise.

The most recent round of health reform implemented by the Obama administration relies on many of these same optimistic and utopian premises. In the name of increasing access, improving quality, and reducing costs, the Affordable Care Act created insurance marketplaces and mandated that the uninsured purchase private coverage. I am not optimistic that another dose of health reform that is rooted in increasing access to private insurance through market-based exchanges will be any more manageable. Interestingly, the governor of Puerto Rico also appears skeptical of the insurance exchange concept. He recently opted not to establish an insurance exchange and instead to dedicate the $925 million that the island received in federal funds as part of the Affordable Care Act to expanding Mi Salud, the new version of La Reforma (Belaval Díaz 2013). Governor Alejandro García Padilla has repeatedly characterized health care as a right and called for universal access to coverage. However, his reform proposal entails maintaining an insurance-based and managed care system.

For decades, both Puerto Rico and the United States have experienced a health system constructed around market values and managerial imperatives. It is time that we learn from this experience and question the underlying assumptions about human behavior, values, and the social good that are built into market-based policy programs. Perhaps then we could begin to create policies that are based less in management and more in care.

A METHODOLOGICAL APPENDIX

As I've given professional presentations and talked with anthropology colleagues and friends about this project over the years, questions about my methods and research ethics almost always arise. How did I get access to study Acme? How did the company and Acme employees react to my analysis? Did I conduct covert research at the company? Was it ethical to be on the payroll of an insurance firm? Have I disclosed too much of what I observed? Conversely, have I disclosed too little?

This wide-ranging curiosity about research methods and ethics is symptomatic of a discipline that is changing and trying to adapt to new objects of study (technoscience, corporations, bureaucracies) and new ways of being an anthropologist (such as being an adjunct or performing applied work). One sign of our collective ethical unease is that the American Anthropological Association (AAA) has revised its statement on ethics three times since I began graduate studies (in 1998, 2009, and again in 2012).

In response to these questions from colleagues and reviewers, I take a moment to comment here on the methodological and ethical implications of my research. While aspects of the methodology are described throughout the book, this appendix pulls those discussions together and elaborates in more detail on my research methods, the human subjects review process, and research ethics.

Working (in) the Field

Anthropologists' new objects of study in the technosciences, large bureaucratic organizations, and the financial sector call for reconfiguring and adapting our methodologies: "corporate arenas form one

232 << APPENDIX 1

of the key sites . . . for the development of new anthropologies and ethnographic practices to reflect upon, inform, and reconstruct the changing worlds and emergent forms of life in which we live" (Fischer 2009, 227). Working (i.e., performing labor where one receives compensation) while in the field is one such "new practice" for negotiating access into these domains. Recent books in medical anthropology and the anthropology of finance were written by researchers who were also employees or volunteers: Angela Garcia worked the graveyard shift at a detox center as part of her research for *The Pastoral Clinic* (2010), while Karen Ho[1] worked and was fired as an internal management consultant on Wall Street in *Liquidated* (2009) and Claire Wendland volunteered as an obstetrician in the Malawian hospital that she observed in *A Heart for the Work* (2010). So a combined employee/researcher role is becoming more common. For some, working while in the field is a way to be useful to one's research subjects; for others, it affords access to otherwise privatized domains. Increasingly, it is a solution to the problem of obtaining funding for research projects. As more anthropologists are employed as adjuncts who have less economic security, they are less able to spend time conducting unpaid research.[2] In my case, I adopted this methodological approach primarily as a way to gain access to a field site and to finance the kind of long-term research that defines ethnography.

Within applied anthropology, there has been an increase in "business anthropology," where researchers are commissioned by the company to pursue a research problem such as understanding one's customers better, trying to improve the culture of the firm, or probing human/technology interfaces (Cefkin 2009). My work differs from that in business anthropology because I did not work at Acme *as* an anthropologist. From the company's perspective, I was an employee first and foremost who also happened to be a researcher. Nor did Acme receive any "deliverables" (such as reports or recommendations) as a result of my research. The publication of this book is the first time that my former employers may read my analysis of what I observed while working at the company.

As an employee/anthropologist, I performed a defined role within the organization for which I earned pay. As time went on, I increasingly became a part of what I was researching. I was absorbed into and shaped by the organization and because of this my own experience as an employee became "data." I make no pretense of "fly on the wall" objectivity. Despite—no—*because* of this, I submit that working in the field is an invaluable method for learning about modern bureaucratic and corporate life; it is a situated, engaged, and compromised methodology.

Gaining Access to Acme

Gaining access to elite power circles and private organizations has been a perennial barrier to "studying up" (studying powerful institutions and people) (Nader 1972, 292–293). Unfortunately, I cannot offer a how-to guide for gaining ethnographic access in corporate settings. As mentioned above, I arrived at this project more by accident than design (though knocking on multiple doors, getting comfortable with being turned away, and being open to fortuitous and unplanned research leads all certainly helped).

My interest in studying Acme developed after I was already employed there for some time. I initially sought to study women's reproductive health and high female sterilization rates in Puerto Rico. This is what I wrote my dissertation proposal about and I secured a small grant from Harvard to get started. I went into the field, planned to get adjusted, start some research, and apply for grants.

I learned about the job at Acme through my network of friends; an acquaintance was leaving her position to study for medical school and she thought I might be interested in the job. When I started working at Acme, it was for 20 hours a week. I also taught one class in the anthropology department at the University of Puerto Rico. The insurance company needed someone with English writing skills to proofread policies and procedures in anticipation of an upcoming audit from mainland regulators. I hoped this job would allow me to learn about the health care system in Puerto Rico, but mostly that it would help me to finance my field research on women's reproductive health.

After 6 months on the job at Acme, I was promoted to supervisor. Soon after, my reproductive health project stagnated. Instead of thinking of the insurance company primarily as a means to finance research, I began to see it as a research problem itself. Who were these American executives? Why was Medicare contracting with private insurance firms in Puerto Rico? How was managed care transforming the quality of care on the island? And what was quality anyways?

I decided to approach my boss with my idea to study managed care and quality. She knew I was in the middle of a Ph.D. program, and she encouraged me to approach the CEO for permission. I was nervous to speak with him, because I thought he would balk at my request. Who would allow an anthropologist unfettered access to their company? Instead, he enthusiastically supported my idea. His support stemmed in part from his conviction that Acme was modernizing the health system in Puerto Rico and bringing about improvements in the standard of care.

After our conversation, I drew up a research agreement and the CEO signed it. The research agreement stated that I had permission to conduct research at the organization as well as to interview members, staff, and providers. The statement described the purpose of the research as follows: "this research is for academic purposes only, though I may make policy recommendations based on research findings. My purpose is to collect information on the delivery of Medicare in Puerto Rico. I am particularly interested in how quality care is defined and monitored. If Acme so desires, the researcher agrees to a de-briefing session in which she will share her findings with the company." But, at the end of my time at Acme, the company never requested a debriefing. The statement that the research was for academic purposes was intended to address the company's concern that I would not share proprietary information with competitors.

In addition to agreeing to obey federal regulations regarding privacy and confidentiality as it pertained to members' health information, I agreed to use pseudonyms in all published work for the name of the company, providers, staff, and members. I have consistently used pseudonyms in this and all other work that came from this research.

Shortly after obtaining the CEO's permission to research at Acme, I received human subject approval from the Institutional Review Board (IRB) at Harvard to conduct research at the corporation and to interview members.

Three months later, I was promoted again, this time to manager. I agreed to expand my hours to 35 hours a week. I knew then that I was no longer writing a book about reproductive health.

Studying Through and Interviewing Acme Members

I did not want to write a narrow case study of Acme. I was interested in "studying through," rather than just studying up. In other words, I wanted to understand the interrelationships among regulators, the corporation, and plan members as part of a larger effort to transform the experience and organization of health care on the island. "Studying through" is a methodological approach that tracks "the interactions (and disjunctions) between different sites or levels in policy processes" and utilizes ethnography to "trace policy connections between different organizational and everyday worlds even where actors in different sites do not know each other or share a moral universe" (Shore and Wright 1997, 14; see also Reinhold 1994). Studying through meant examining health policy from at least three distinct "organizational and everyday worlds": (1) the policy world inhabited by the politicians and regulators who create and run the Medicare program; (2) the managerial world of the executives, administrators, and workers at the health maintenance organization (HMO); and (3) the patient world that takes the perspective of health plan members and their families as they attempt to access care. An essential part of my research was to interview plan members and providers about how their experiences with the health system had transformed as a result of the two waves of privatization that hit the island in the 1990s and first decade of the 2000s.

In order to explore member perspectives on managed care, I needed a way to contact them to request interviews. I decided that obtaining a random list from the company would give me a sufficiently varied group of members that ranged in terms of gender, age, disability status, income level, and region of residence. Ultimately, I requested a randomly selected list of members from Acme's IT department that sampled relatively equally from the metro San Juan area and the rest of the island. Given the recent passage of federal privacy rules in health care known as HIPAA, I anticipated problems with the human subjects review process when it came to gaining access to a list of Acme members. To my surprise, my access was actually facilitated by my employee status, because, as an employee, I already had access to member names and health information. For medical anthropologists, it may be important to note that an insurance company is not the same as a clinical setting like a hospital where patients may be going to access care. There was no internal review board at Acme that assessed my research protocols as there would be at a hospital or other facility.

For life history interviews with plan members and providers, I developed my subject recruitment methods, informed consent procedures, and research forms in consultation with the IRB at Harvard. I sent each member on the list a letter explaining the study. The letter stated that I was both an employee of Acme and a researcher; it also explained that I would follow up with a phone call. When I called each member, I restated the purpose of the study and redisclosed my dual role as an employee and researcher. I asked each member if he or she would agree to be interviewed. Many accepted the invitation; if anyone refused, I did not contact them again. All but two interviews took place in the interviewees' homes. At the time of the interview, I again explained the purpose of the interview, once again disclosed my role as an employee and researcher, and went over the informed consent document. Each interviewee was given a copy of the informed consent form but was not required to sign it per guidance received from the IRB. It is a common and widely accepted practice for anthropologists to not ask for a form to be signed when the research subject's literacy level may be low or when a signature could endanger instead of protect the subject (as with interviews with undocumented immigrants in the United States). In these instances, the onus is on the anthropologist to thoroughly explain the purpose and risks of the research and to make sure that the research subject has the opportunity to ask clarifying questions and refuse participation.

Acme members were very hospitable and interested in talking. Some wanted me to explain who I was in more detail, usually not relative to my occupational position, but because I was visibly an outsider. Many interviewees were interested in trying to make sense of why I was in Puerto Rico; they asked questions about my personal life and relationship with Puerto Rico more than about my job. As I mentioned in chapter 3, for many of the interviewees, our conversation probably resembled a social service interview that they might have to go through to qualify for benefits or get recertified for La Reforma. Some took the opportunity to ask clarifying questions about their coverage and especially the new prescription-drug benefit, Medicare Part D. The interviews were open-ended life histories that focused on experiences with the health care system.

Ethical Considerations

My research departs from some classic anthropological conventions for conducting fieldwork: rather than studying only subjects who were less socially, economically, and/or politically privileged than I as a researcher, I studied up and through, meaning that I studied subjects like corporate executives and federal regulators who wielded considerable social, economic, and political capital. I was also employed by the entity that I was studying and could be fired at any time (remember, one executive characterized Acme as a runaway train that could run workers over). Part of the difficulty of doing this kind of fieldwork is that I was absorbed by the company, remade by its ideologies, and had to behave in a way that comported with company policy. It was only after leaving the company and reflecting with some time and distance from the job that I was able to analyze my role more fully and critically. The ethical orientation that my coworkers and I brought to our jobs became an explicit object of analysis and a theme that recurs throughout the book.

Though I have endeavored to comply with the professional research ethics expressed in AAA policy documents, I am nonetheless troubled by what I see as a misfit between these policy statements and my research. This is because our professional statements about what constitutes ethical research are largely designed to protect "vulnerable" populations. For example, the AAA Code of Ethics calls on anthropologists to recognize that we incur obligations to those we study. But what happens when we study multiple social actors, of whom some may be economically or politically vulnerable and some who may be extraordinarily powerful or privileged? What are our obligations to powerful corporations and government regulators? In my view, my primary obligation as a researcher is to the elderly and disabled Puerto Ricans who invited me into their homes and who shared their stories of struggling to raise their families, navigate the health care system, and cope with aging. The corporation is protected by our research agreement and its ample legal and financial resources.

238   <<   APPENDIX 1

The primary dictate of the AAA statement on research ethics is to do no harm. In the most direct sense, I have done no harm. No one was injured and no care was denied as a result of this study. If anything, I helped a few people navigate the company bureaucracy better in order to get their needs met.

Indirect forms of harm, such as damage to a research subject's reputation, are more difficult to assess. I am critical of many aspects of managed care and those criticisms stem from my concerns about the social and political effects of neoliberal ideologies and what I directly observed while working at Acme. As such, my former employers may not be pleased by or agree with my interpretations.

I have struggled to craft descriptions in this book that are true to what was told to me by the people I interviewed, whether they were plan members or executives. I have tried to understand the ethical commitments that Acme employees brought to their work and to place my interpretations in cultural, historical, and economic contexts. This, I think, is the purpose of anthropology. I have opted not to discuss gossip or employees' personal lives as this seems unnecessarily salacious and falls outside of the scope of this study. Though I have tried to represent my colleagues fairly, I anticipate that not everyone will agree with the portraits of them that I have created here. That is to be expected. As anthropologists, I do not believe that we are obligated to produce only flattering portraits of those we study; that would make critical work impossible.

The second major directive in the 2012 version of the AAA Code of Ethics calls on anthropologists to be "open and honest regarding your work." This directive stems from a longer history of anthropologists collaborating with military and colonial authorities and conducting covert research on occupied and subject peoples. The concern with openness and honesty was reactivated more recently when anthropologists were covertly employed by the Department of Defense to study local communities as part of the Human Terrain System (HTS) in the U.S. wars in Afghanistan and Iraq. Essentially engaged in military reconnaissance, HTS researchers were charged with studying local communities in an effort to make U.S. military interventions more culturally appropriate and effective (Rylko-Bauer 2008). Reactions to the HTS program mobilized the 2012 revision of the AAA Code of Ethics, which places issues of covert research in a much more prominent position than previous versions of the Code of Ethics (such as the 1998 revision, which was the one that was in effect when I conducted my fieldwork).

Though I agree that covert research with the military clearly violates anthropological ethics, I wonder how appropriate the no deception dictum is for research that seeks to study powerful social actors such as corporations whose "cultural invisibility . . . is as much a part of their privilege as their wealth and power, and a democratic anthropology should be working to reverse this invisibility" (Gusterson 1997, 115). I remain unconvinced that covert research is always unethical (see Allen [1997] for a treatment of the debates surrounding covert research in sociology).

Nonetheless, in the research conducted for this book, I did follow the AAA Code of Ethics and did not conduct covert research, nor did I deliberately deceive anyone. As discussed above, I obtained permission to study at Acme and the project went through the IRB process at Harvard and at Connecticut College where I held a postdoctoral fellowship. However, with any project that involves participant observation, it is difficult to know where to draw the line in terms of disclosing one's role as a researcher. Did I try to hide my research? Certainly not. But nor did I wear a placard proclaiming that I was an anthropologist. When you live for 2 and a half years as a participant observer, it gets difficult to determine what exactly constitutes "covert." While acting in my capacity as a manager at Acme, I came into contact with colleagues in regulatory agencies, medical care providers, administrative staff, and Acme employees (there were hundreds) who probably were not aware that I was also a researcher. The CEO, my boss, my immediate colleagues, and anyone I interviewed were aware that I was also a researcher. They also knew I was interviewing members, observing the organization, and teaching in the anthropology department at the University of Puerto Rico. One of the ways I address the ethical ambiguity of being a researcher in a large corporation was that I limit my detailed descriptions of Acme employees in this book to those individuals who knew that I was a researcher. I also protect the identity of all Acme employees by not revealing identifying information or by changing some details in order to disguise the individuals (where appropriate). For company executives, disguising their identities is more difficult.

I bring up these issues in the spirit of openness and honesty. However, some of the questions I have received from fellow anthropologists make me uncomfortable, because I see anthropology treating ethics with the same kind of perfunctory legalism that I observed in auditing at Acme. Ethics are not easily resolved. They are not neat. And no amount of paperwork or precise definitions of ethical behavior can absolve us of our responsibilities. There are larger ethical issues that, within this discipline, I hope we will think about: Should we avoid research projects where ethics are potentially messy or complicated? Do powerful actors and private institutions deserve to be protected from research? Does our profession require us to be silent if we witness abuses of power and the powerful have not consented to be studied? Whose interest does our research serve?

INTERVIEW DESCRIPTIONS

INTERVIEW 1
Don Enrique, 69 years old
Don Ignacio, age unknown
Two brothers, both divorced/separated
Río Grande
May 2004
The brothers grew up in Río Grande and migrated throughout their adult lives between Puerto Rico and the United States. They had worked in factories in New York and Chicago, where their children still lived. Both suffered from diabetes and received La Reforma in addition to Medicare services from Acme.

INTERVIEW 2
Doña Yolanda, 75 years old
Married
Bayamón
June 2004
Doña Yolanda left school in the sixth grade to care for her grandmother. She worked as a cook and housecleaner for an American family in Santurce until she was married. She lived with her elderly husband, daughter, and granddaughters. She had suffered two strokes and was in a wheelchair.

INTERVIEW 3
Don Cristóbal, in his 50s
Married
Vega Baja
June 2004

Don Cristóbal grew up in Brooklyn and moved to Puerto Rico as an adult. He served in the military and went on disability for mental health reasons. His wife, who suffered from scoliosis, was also on disability. He lived on land shared among other members of his extended family and was still in the process of constructing his house.

INTERVIEW 4

Doña Giuliana, 59 years old

Married, daughter of Don Valentín

Don Valentín, 90 years old

Widower

Lajas

June 2004

Doña Giuliana cared both for her incapacitated father and her husband who had recently undergone an amputation as a result of diabetes. A former factory worker, Doña Giuliana received help from a home health agency, but she cooked, cleaned, and shopped for her father and husband. Don Valentín was a veteran and received his Medicare benefits through Acme. He had an eighth-grade education and was a former sugar-cane worker.

INTERVIEW 5

Doña Helena, 67 years old

Married, daughter of Don Eustacio

Don Eustacio, 90 years old

Widower

Cabo Rojo

June 2004

Doña Helena was a homemaker who lived with her husband. They lost their medication coverage when his part-time agricultural earnings and Social Security placed them just above the income cutoff for La Reforma. Doña Helena also cared for her bed-ridden father, Don Eustacio, who had worked cutting sugar cane and as a migrant farm laborer in the United States.

INTERVIEW 6

Don Lucas, 73 years old

Married

Aguadilla

June 2004

Don Lucas left Patillas at age 17 to study. Soon after, he migrated to New York, enlisted in the army, and served in Korea. In New York, he worked in a furniture factory and injured his back. In 1978, he and his wife returned to Puerto Rico, where he qualified for Medicare due to disability. The Veterans' Administration paid for his medication.

INTERVIEW 7

Don Jacinto, 78 years old

Divorced twice, separated from current spouse

Rincón

June 2004

To help his family, Don Jacinto left school after the first year. He worked in sugar cane and later became a truck driver. He had diabetes and a wound on his foot that would not heal. Neighbors told him that the two beat-up cars he drove as *públicos* (informal taxis) disqualified him for La Reforma, so he skipped his recertification appointment.

INTERVIEW 8

Doña Miranda, 83 years old

Widow

Esteban, age unknown

Oldest of Doña Miranda's 12 children

Cupey

July 2004

As a child, Doña Miranda's family was displaced several times when they moved from the countryside to San Juan in search of work. After their house was expropriated, they resettled on family land in Cupey. She was diabetic and fighting with Acme to obtain a blood glucose monitor. She left La Reforma so that she could keep seeing her family physician. She was recently informed that her house would be expropriated to expand the road.

INTERVIEW 9

Doña Caridad, 54 years old

Married

Bayamón

July 2004

Doña Caridad's parents moved to Pennsylvania and opened a grocery when she was 13. There, she struggled with English and left school after the eighth grade. Her husband injured his back and she became the family breadwinner. Back in Puerto Rico, she worked at a garment factory but went on disability at age 39. Though in debt from medical bills, she was removed from La Reforma because she had too high of an income.

INTERVIEW 10

Doña Fátima, 79 years old

Widow

Manatí

July 2004

Doña Fátima was born in Puerto Rico but spent much of her adult life working in factories in New York and saving for the construction of her house in Manatí. She left her first husband, an alcoholic, and married again. Her prescription coverage was a survivor's benefit from her second husband, an electric company employee. She did not know that she was enrolled in Acme.

INTERVIEW 11

Don Martín, 74 years old

Divorced

Guayama

July 2004

Don Martín's family grew crops and raised cattle in the dead time between sugar-cane harvests. At 14, Don Martín hopped a ship for New York where he didn't know a soul and was surprised by the racism he encountered. After serving in Korea, he became a machinist working in factories in the United States and on the island.

INTERVIEW 12

Don Celestino, 72 years old

Married

San Juan

July 2004

Don Celestino left school after the fourth year when his mother passed away. He moved with siblings to New York as a teenager and served in Korea. He returned to Puerto Rico and became a police officer. He tried to eat well and had attended Acme's health education activities. He wished he were stronger, like when he was young.

INTERVIEW 13
Don Luis, 61 years old
Divorced
Caguas
July 2004
Don Luis was raised in a volatile household on a small dairy farm with a jealous mother and unfaithful father. He worked in factories and drove a taxi in New York and Florida. He went on disability for mental health reasons and described himself as nervous and aggressive. Because he felt that he was not respected, he left La Reforma.

INTERVIEW 14
Don Octavio, 75 years old
Widower
Caguas
July 2004
Don Octavio's mother was from Corozal and died when he was a boy. In the army he was stationed in Germany and Panama, but he had always lived in Puerto Rico. He retired from the telephone company after 20 years of steady employment. Despite diabetes and high blood pressure, he felt good for his age.

INTERVIEW 15
Doña Sofia, 93 years old
Married
Don Victor, 89 years old
Married
Don Teodoro, age unknown
Married to Don Victor's daughter
Vega Alta
July 2004

Doña Sofia and Don Victor grew up in the same rural area of Vega Alta where their fathers labored in the sugar cane. The couple married in their 80s after their former spouses had died. Doña Sofia lost her Reforma benefits when she missed her renovation appointment. Don Victor's primary care physician stopped participating in La Reforma, so he, too, was losing his medication benefits.

INTERVIEW 16

Don Silvestre, age unknown (late 50s)

Married

Doña Mercedes, 52 years old

Married

Vega Alta

August 2004

The couple met in the Bronx and ran off to marry when Doña Mercedes was only 16. Don Silvestre retired early from his factory job because of heart troubles and diabetes. His pension kept him from qualifying for La Reforma. Doña Mercedes qualified, but she preferred to pay for a private plan where she did not have to struggle to obtain prescriptions and referrals.

INTERVIEW 17

Doña Socorro, 48 years old

Divorced

Arecibo

August 2004

Doña Socorro married at 15, had a child, and finished the 12th grade during night school. She cared for her youngest daughter, who had Down syndrome. Doña Socorro worked at a food-packing plant for 21 years but went on disability due to a repetitive strain injury. She left La Reforma to join Acme, losing her dental and medication benefits. Her new doctor was a good listener and gave her injections for her pain.

INTERVIEW 18

Don Hugo, 70 years old

Married

Doña Brisa, 70 years old

Married

Aibonito

August 2004

Married for almost 50 years, the couple owned their home outright. Before
he retired, Don Hugo ran a small bar and grocery in Coamo. As a self-
employed entrepreneur, he did not pay into Social Security and the couple only received $157 a month. An in-home daycare brought in much-
needed cash, but they were getting too old to keep it open. Paying for
medication was a constant struggle.

INTERVIEW 19

Doña Claudia, 67 years old

Widow

Salinas

August 2004

Doña Claudia's father worked for the owner of the local sugar-cane plan-
tation who gave him the waterfront land on which her house stood.
Her mother operated a small store in the neighborhood that Doña
Claudia eventually took over. She received widow benefits from the
Veterans' Administration and Social Security and never applied for La
Reforma.

INTERVIEW 20

Doña Marta, 67 years old

Widow

Coamo

September 2004

Her father was a barber in Coamo and she studied through fifth grade.
Doña Marta worked for 24 years in a garment factory but went on disability due to *nervios*. She received $542 a month from Social Security
and was also on Reforma.

INTERVIEW 21

Doña Fortunata, 72 years old

Widow

Peñuelas

August 2004

Doña Fortunata was mourning the recent death of her mother. Doña Fortunata married at 18, but her husband drank too much and was abusive. She was grateful to the town mayor, who gave her a job as a janitor. She received La Reforma but did not plan on attending the recertification appointment because it required too many documents.

INTERVIEW 22

Don Pablo, 62 years old

Divorced

Juana Diaz

September 2004

Don Pablo was from Ponce; his father drove a passenger van from Ponce to San Juan. Don Pablo was a nurse, but he injured his back working in a hospital in New York and went on disability. He was on La Reforma and wanted to quit smoking.

INTERVIEW 23

Don Zacarías, age unknown (est. in his 70s)

Divorced

Guánica

September 2004

Don Zacarías's mother died when he was an infant. He left school in the first grade because there was no money for shoes or books. While growing up, he cut cane and later became a migrant farm worker in the United States. His Social Security check of $200 a month qualified him for La Reforma. He lived alone and hardly ate, but he still drank rum.

INTERVIEW 24

Don Augusto, 84 years old

Married

Bayamón

August 2004

Don Augusto grew up in Coamo where his father owned a small *finca* (farm) that grew plantains and tobacco. Don Augusto finished his second year of high school and went on to work in pharmacies—he started by sweeping the floor and by the time he retired he was filling prescriptions.

He took care of his wife; her emphysema had recently developed into pneumonia.

INTERVIEW 25
Doña Estela, 73 years old
Widow
Manatí
September 2004
Doña Estela's father worked cutting cane. She graduated from high school and studied to be a secretary. She married at 28, but her husband drank and gambled. She could not depend on him to pay the bills, so she always worked. Since her husband's death, Doña Estela has lived with her sister. She also received La Reforma.

INTERVIEW 26
Don Julián, 70 years old
Married
Doña Adoración, 63 years old
Married
Carolina
July 2005
When they were adolescents, Don Julián moved from Orocovis to San Juan, and Doña Adoración moved from Morovis to San Juan. Don Julián continued to work part time in the men's clothing store where he had spent most of his career. Doña Adoración worked as a secretary at a psychiatric hospital and a public health clinic until she retired. Doña Adoración received government retirement benefits.

INTERVIEW 27
Doña Carmen, 66 years old
Divorced
Carolina
August 2005
Doña Carmen's father was a security guard and her mother operated a small sewing business. She graduated from high school and married. When the marriage fell apart, Doña Carmen became the primary caretaker for

her two disabled sons. She suffered from depression and struggled to provide her sons with adequate care on their meager Social Security payments. She also received La Reforma.

INTERVIEW 28

Doña Candelaria, 65 years old

Married

Bayamón

August 2005

Doña Candelaria's father owned a mechanic shop and her mother sold handmade baby clothes. Doña Candelaria met her husband at a night school where she was the secretary. After returning from Korea, her husband went on disability for *nervios* and schizophrenia. She was his caretaker.

INTERVIEW 29

Doña Eduarda, age unknown (est. 67 years old)

Widow

Cupey

August 2005

Doña Eduarda grew up in Vega Alta, finished high school, and began university studies. After serving in the military, her husband became a police officer and was killed in the line of duty. Doña Eduarda worked in various factories and when she retired, she lived on a combination of pension from the police, Social Security, and veterans' benefits.

INTERVIEW 30

Doña Bárbara, 72 years old

Divorced

Río Grande

September 2005

Doña Bárbara was born to a single mother and adopted by her grandparents. She studied through the second year of high school and married at 15. She migrated to New York where she worked in factories and raised her three children. After living in the city for 45 years, Doña Bárbara retired to her hometown where her pension stretches further.

INTERVIEW 31
Teresa Ramírez, 43 years old
Single
Guaynabo
September 2005
Teresa Ramírez was raised by her grandparents in Caguas where she excelled
in public school. After a debilitating bout of depression and anxiety,
she abandoned her university studies. She found work as a newspaper
photographer but went on disability after injuring her ankle. When her
depression returned, she struggled to obtain adequate care and to qualify
for government assistance.

INTERVIEW 32
Don Felix, 69 years old
Divorced
San Juan
September 2005
Don Felix was a college-educated artist living alone in San Juan. He was
originally from Fajardo, where his father was a rancher. He controlled
his Type 2 diabetes with medication and home remedies. After a brief
stint as an Acme member, he switched to another Medicare plan, claim-
ing that Acme was lazy and inefficient.

INTERVIEW 33
Doña Gisela, 62 years old
Married
Carolina
September 2005
Doña Gisela was born in the Dominican Republic and married a Puerto
Rican. She moved with her husband to Puerto Rico at age 17 and worked
as a nanny. Her husband was a mechanic and still drove a taxi for 4 hours
a day. She went on Medicare for disability after an accident in the restau-
rant kitchen where she cooked.

INTERVIEW 34
Doña Paloma, in her 50s
Separated/divorced

San Juan

September 2005

Doña Paloma watched her grandchildren during the day. She was the matriarch of the family and on disability after having formerly worked in factories. She described struggles getting authorizations approved on La Reforma, but she was fine with this situation. It should not be too easy, she said, you have to be patient and work a little bit for it.

INTERVIEW 35

Don Anastasio, 64 years old

Married

Trujillo Alto

September 2005

Don Anastasio grew up in a rural area near Caguas. He planned to go to college, but the tuition money he saved cutting cane was spent by his father. He married and moved to Trujillo Alto, where he held jobs with the electric company, as a mechanic, and as an operator of heavy machinery. He went on disability due to complications from diabetes and received La Reforma.

NOTES

1. In an effort to make *Unmanageable Care* more readable, detailed theoretical
   discussions as well as lengthy references to the scholarly literature are largely
   confined to the endnotes.

   The author and activist Barbara Ehrenreich (2009) argues that self-help manuals like *Fish!* are part of a larger positive-thinking ideology in American culture
   that contributed to the financial crisis of 2008–2011 because they irresponsibly
   promoted the notion that anything is possible if one just has the right attitude.
   Positive thinking serves to eliminate critical thinking from the workplace.

2. The reforms to the health care system in Puerto Rico are part of a larger ideological shift in the purpose and function of government known as neoliberalism
   that took place globally in the last quarter of the 20th century. The term "neoliberalism" appears throughout the book and is used in three distinct but interrelated ways: (1) as a political and economic policy: pro-market policies were
   implemented beginning in the mid- to late 1970s to dismantle Keynesian and/
   or socialist-based economies, including eliminating government price fixing,
   stabilizing inflation, imposing conservative fiscal policy, promoting free trade
   and free markets, relaxing or eliminating government regulation, and privatizing government-run industries and services; (2) as a moral discourse: neoliberalism is not just a package of policies but also a way of understanding what is
   right and what is wrong; government intervention is wrong, personal freedom
   to choose is the ultimate good; and (3) as a theory of how subjects behave: free,
   information-processing consumers are the building blocks of neoliberalism.
   Recall Margaret Thatcher's claim that "there is no such thing as society, only
   individual men and women" (quoted in Harvey 2005, 23). Though the term has
   recently received criticism that it is used indiscriminately or as a substitute for
   sustained political economic analysis (cf. Kingfisher and Maskovsky 2008), I
   continue to think that anthropological engagement with neoliberalism is essential to understanding how the contemporary world is being remade.

3. Privatization in Puerto Rico occurred later than in other countries in Latin
   America that faced the brunt of neoliberal reforms beginning in the 1980s

(Armada and Muntaner 2004, 30). See Franco-Giraldo and colleagues (2006) for an account of the negative impact of structural adjustment programs on basic health indicators in Latin America. The authors link declines in per capita GDP and overall public spending to declines in life expectancy and increases in infant mortality.

4. These new organization and oversight strategies are examples of what Michel Foucault has termed governmentality (Foucault 1991). See also Barry et al. (1996), Burchell et al. (1991), Dean (1999), Ferguson and Gupta (2002), Gordon (1991), Lemke (2001), O'Malley (1996), and Rose, O'Malley, and Valverde (2006). The neologism "governmentality," also rendered as "governmental rationality" (Gordon 1991), creates a language for talking about politics and government that is not limited to analyses of the state. Instead, government is defined more broadly; it takes place through the practices that attempt to manage the conduct of individuals and populations. Governmentality joins the practice of governing with the generation of knowledge: "The semantic linking of governing ('gouverner') and modes of thought (mentalité) indicates that it is not possible to study the technologies of power without an analysis of the political rationality underpinning them" (Lemke 2001, 191). Managed care can be seen as a form of governmentality in which insurance companies employ new technologies aimed at shaping the practices and self-understandings of consumers, providers, and workers in an effort to create calculative, responsible, and profitable subjects.

5. See Li (2007) and Morgen and Gonzales (2008) for exceptions.

6. Though the HMO Act was passed in 1973, there were many precursors to HMOs. Prepaid health plans have a complicated political and social history—some originated in mutual aid societies while others were formed by unions, religious groups, or employers. Some forms of prepaid health care date to the 1800s "when railroads, lumber, mining, and textile firms hired 'company doctors' to treat their injured employees" (Coombs 2005, 3). Prepaid group practices existed at least since the end of the 19th century in the United States (Gray 2006, 317). In Puerto Rico, a prepaid health plan was founded in 1883 by the Christian Sociedad Española de Auxilio Mutuo y Beneficencia (currently known as Auxilio Mutuo [2009], this plan includes hospital and outpatient health services). However, managed care in its contemporary form did not arrive on the island until the 1993 health reform discussed here.

7. Bradford H. Gray argues that managed care organizations transformed significantly from the 1980s to 1990s: "The typical HMO in 1980 was a locally controlled nonprofit plan whose salaried physicians served the plan's enrollees on a full-time basis. By the middle of the decade, the typical HMO was a for-profit plan that was part of a national firm and that contracted with office-based physicians who saw other patients as well as the HMO's patients" (310). The general trend was a movement from local, nonprofit organizations with in-house physicians to for-profit companies that operated with a large network of providers.

8. Paul Starr attributes the declines in medical inflation in the 1990s to one-time savings as HMOs limited in-patient hospital stays, kept premiums low in order to capture larger segments of the insurance market, and negotiated prices down with providers (2010, 144). Others argue that the dip in health care inflation was partially the result of the 1990–1991 recession, rather than the efficiency of HMOs (Sullivan 2001).

9. "By the end of the twentieth century many HMOs and insurance companies were indistinguishable. Both were contracting with loosely organized networks of providers, and their primary administrative focus was the management of costs rather than patient care" (Coombs 2005, xii). In other words the HMO has largely been subsumed into "managed care" and health insurance more generally, thereby losing its distinctiveness (Gray 2006, 328–331).

10. As states face renewed budget pressures and implement the Medicaid expansion that is part of the Affordable Care Act, they are increasing the proportion of beneficiaries enrolled in Medicaid managed care (Iglehart 2011). Under most managed care arrangements, states have predictable Medicaid expenditures because they pay a premium per enrolled beneficiary and the managed care organization assumes the risk for the medical care incurred. States began contracting with managed care organizations to provide Medicaid services in the late 1960s (Engel 2006, 236). But the growth of managed care in Medicaid was slow: "By 1976 approximately 6 percent of all Medicaid care was being provided through prepaid HMOs" (137). In 1997, this figure had jumped to 50% (237).

11. Though studies show that managed care tends to save states money on Medicaid expenditures (Lewin Group 2009; MACPAC 2011; McCue and Bailit 2011), there is less quantitative evidence regarding how managed care impacts access to and quality of care (Iglehart 2011; MACPAC 2011). Cost savings generally come from decreasing in-patient and pharmaceutical utilization (Lewin Group 2009) and also by contracting with providers at extremely low reimbursement rates, restricting benefits, and shrinking access to specialty care. Anthropologists who have studied Medicaid managed care in New Mexico and Pennsylvania have found that managed care in Medicaid creates access problems for specialty care, mental health, and pharmaceuticals (Maskovsky 2000; Wagner 2005). It has also led to "de facto disentitlement" due to bureaucratic enrollment procedures (L. López 2005) and the shifting of both care-giving and administrative work onto already strained safety-net providers (Boehm 2005; Horton et al. 2001; Waitzkin et al. 2002). Other studies show that publicly traded Medicaid managed care plans tend to score lower than their nonpublicly traded counterparts on "quality-of-care measures related to preventive care, treatment of chronic conditions, members' access to care, and customer service" (McCue and Bailit 2011). The publicly traded plans also have higher administrative costs. Nonetheless, the Medicaid expansion that is part of the Affordable Care Act will likely bring significant positive health impacts. It bears mentioning that coverage through a privatized Medicaid plan is still better than no coverage at all. Sommers and

colleagues found that Medicaid expansions have resulted in "reduced mortality as well as improved coverage, access to care, and self-reported health" (2012, 1). Of course, *how* the expansion is carried out matters, as the Puerto Rico example demonstrates.

12. In February 2004, La Reforma covered 1.6 million people and 236,217 of these were also on Medicare. The total population of Puerto Rico was 3,927,776 in 2006 (U.S. Census Bureau 2006). The funding for La Reforma comes from the following sources: 12%, federal; 3%, SCHIP (State Children's Health Insurance Program); 10%, municipalities; and 75%, central administration (Rullán 2004).

13. As mentioned above, the island did not experience a backlash in the same way one had occurred in the United States. These differences are described further in chapter 1.

14. Before the 2003 Medicare Modernization Act (MMA), the managed care component of Medicare was called Medicare + Choice per the Balanced Budget Act of 1997. The name Medicare + Choice replaced the earlier Medicare Risk program. Currently, the program is known as Medicare Advantage.

15. A major issue in the development of the managed care program under Medicare has been calculating the appropriate per member per month (PMPM) capitation rate. This was formerly done per county and was set at 95% of the average spending in fee-for-service Medicare in that county. This payment methodology was known as the "adjusted average per capita cost" (AAPCC). Rates could vary widely for adjacent counties and by region. The rates in 1997 ranged from "a low of $220.92 in Arthur County, Nebraska to a high of $767.35 in Richmond County, New York (Staten Island)" (CMS 2004). The methodology changed in 1997 with the passage of the Balanced Budget Act. This change took away the direct connection between expenditures in the fee-for-service sector and managed care. Instead, a floor amount was established and annual increases were mandated. The result was a significant increase in the rates. In 2003, with the MMA, the methodology changed again by returning to a more direct link with the fee-for-service rates and adding the risk adjustment component. By 2007, the payment was 100% risk adjusted. Risk adjustment takes into account demographic data like age, sex, and Medicaid eligibility as well as clinical factors such as diagnoses as reported on hospital and doctor office claims. Therefore, under the risk system, the plan is paid more for sicker, older, and poorer beneficiaries. With changes in payment methodology, Medicare managed care is more expensive than fee-for-service Medicare. In Puerto Rico, plans are paid far more than the going rates in fee-for-service Medicare, about 180% more (MedPac 2009, 179). In the United States, Medicare managed care rates average 113% of fee-for-service Medicare (Zarabozo and Harrison 2009). However, the plans also typically offer a richer benefit with less out-of-pocket spending than fee-for-service Medicare.

16. Hugh Gusterson (1997) termed Nader's project of studying up a "critical repatriated anthropology." One problem for realizing this goal has been issues of

access: "The cultural invisibility of the rich and powerful is as much a part of their privilege as their wealth and power, and a democratic anthropology should be working to reverse this invisibility" (Gusterson 1997, 115). Lack of access has led to an expansion of the anthropological toolkit to include other methods that are more appropriate to studying up, such as "polymorphous engagement," which means "interacting with informants across a number of dispersed sites, not just in local communities, and sometimes in virtual form; and it means collecting data eclectically from a disparate array of sources in many different ways" (116). Polymorphous engagement entails using many of the same eclectic methods as "studying through," but what I like about studying through is that it shifts the object of study away from the powerful and elites per se and toward understanding policy processes as they take place across domains. In the end, the projects of "studying up," polymorphous engagement, and studying through share a common kinship and critical aim.

17. The interview methodology is described in greater detail in chapter 3 and appendix 1. All translations from the Spanish are the author's.

18. See Pfeiffer and Chapman (2010) for a critical account of how structural adjustment policies, such as privatization, decentralization, the introduction of user fees, and a move toward private insurance markets (as implemented by international development institutions like the World Bank and the International Monetary Fund), have negatively impacted basic health indicators as well as the ability of national health systems to serve their populations.

19. Because ethnographies are in-depth case studies produced through long-term participant observation and open-ended interviews, they do not lead to broadly generalizable conclusions. Despite its uniqueness, however, the managed care model in Puerto Rico must be understood as part of a larger transformation in the form and function of government that relies on downsizing, privatization, and the contracting out of public services to improve "efficiency." There are, furthermore, important similarities between the managed care models in Puerto Rico and those in the United States and elsewhere. The anthropological record suggests that certain common features characterize market-based reform. Such features are access difficulties, increased inequality, disgruntled providers, high administrative costs, work and care shifting, and gaps between aims and performance. An excellent bibliography of the anthropological literature on insurance and health reform is available at http://www.medanthro.net/stand/insurancebibliography.html.

NOTES TO CHAPTER 1

1. The term "La Reforma" is commonly used in the press and the insurance industry as shorthand for the privatized, managed care–based health system implemented in 1993. In 2010, Governor Luis Fortuño from the pro-statehood party embarked on a rebranding campaign to call the program Mi Salud (My Health).

2. A note on periodization: 1954 marks the implementation of the pilot for regionalization known as the Bayamón project. In 1952, the Estado Libre Asociado
was created. By this time, the emphasis on hygiene and sanitation had shifted
to a concern with the need for modern housing and healthy industrial workers
within the framework of modernization and development. A more nuanced
periodization might separate the initial military period from the subsequent
programs that were developed as part of the New Deal. However, even during
the construction of health clinics with New Deal moneys, the model was based
on the old municipal organization and lacked the public health focus of the
later, regional intervention. According to Kelvin Santiago-Valles, "the decade of
the forties can, in retrospect, be seen as a transition period between (a) the first
half of a century which was overwhelmingly agricultural, rural, and practically
monocultural, and (b) the second half of a century which was more industrial,
urban, and Welfare-State based" (1994, 195).

3. This was also true in the Philippines where the United States assumed that a
public health infrastructure was totally lacking. Warwick Anderson (2006,
21–22) argues that the infrastructure was instead overwhelmed by an increase
in the sick and injured and in turn destroyed by the Philippine-American war:
"Thus as Americans assumed control they found little evidence of previous
scientific and medical endeavor and felt justified in representing the Spanish
period as a time of unrelieved apathy, ignorance, and superstition, in contrast to
their own self-proclaimed modernity, progressivism, and scientific zeal" (22).

4. Arana-Soto describes a *practicante* as a type of minor surgeon or physician's
assistant (1974, 602–608). According to the Mountin report, a practicante is
"a male nurse who also may be licensed to do minor surgery such as lancing
abscesses, extracting teeth and dressing wounds" (1937, 36).

5. Recently health and hygiene in the early U.S. colonial period in Puerto Rico
have received renewed scholarly attention. Previous studies were concerned
with either celebrating the U.S. contribution to progress and the demographic
and epidemiological transition on the island or with rewriting the Black Legend
of inept Spanish colonialism (i.e., Arana-Soto). Two dissertations have been
written about this period: "Conquests of Death: Disease, Health and Hygiene in
the Formation of a Social Body (Puerto Rico, 1880–1929)" by Ivette Rodríguez-
Santana (Yale University, Department of Sociology, 2005) and "Health Beyond
Prescription: A Post-Colonial History of Puerto Rican Medicine at the Turn of
the Twentieth Century" by Nicole E. Trujillo-Pagán (University of Michigan,
Department of Sociology, 2003).

6. The assertion that "these latitudes" share a similar disposition also draws on
a much older framework for explaining the origin of diseases—that of medical geography where "pathological agency" derived from climatic conditions
(Anderson 2006, 24).

7. The U.S. Congress also had the authority to annul any legislation passed in
Puerto Rico (Office of Puerto Rico 1948, 74–75).

8. This official report resonates with travel accounts and government reports being produced at this time that reveled in descriptions of filth and dirt. See for example Kelvin Santiago-Valles's (1994) analysis of the writings of Governor Theodore Roosevelt, Jr., Interior Secretary Harold L. Ickes, Brigadier General George W. Davis, and sociologist Fred Fleagle. Similar analyses can be found in Rodríguez-Santana (2005).

9. Puerto Rican physicians at this time were also organizing into a medical association of their own and articulated a critique of the municipal health system, which they said suffered from insufficient funds and undue political interference in medical matters (Trujillo-Pagán 2003, 128–139). The Asociación Médica de Puerto Rico was formed in 1902 and affiliated with the American Medical Association in 1912.

10. The Popular Democratic Party (PPD) was formed in 1938 and led by Luis Muñoz Marín, who was president of the senate from 1941 to 1948 and then governor from 1948 to 1964. The PPD's slogan was "Pan, Tierra, y Libertad" (Bread, Land, and Liberty), and the party was initially part Latin American–style populism and part a New Deal Keynesian economic reform program (Pantojas-García 1990, 38–45).

11. As a result of its new Constitution, Puerto Rico was removed from the list of nonsovereign territories in 1953 at the United Nations. Nonetheless, the relationship between the United States and Puerto Rico remains a colonial one—federal law supersedes Puerto Rican law, Congress can unilaterally change the relationship between Puerto Rico and the United States, the island lacks voting representation in the U.S. Congress, and island residents cannot vote for president. This colonial political framework continues to impose considerable constraints on the ability of Puerto Rican policy makers to design a health system of their own choosing as discussed in chapter 6 and the conclusion.

12. Some scholars argue that the additional autonomy in the Constitution had been operating in practice since the 1940s and the Constitution "changed nothing in the fundamental social, political and economic relations of the island to the United States" (Silver 2004, 150). See Patricia Silver (2004, 149–153) for a summary of this position.

13. In addition to fostering economic development in order to increase employment opportunities for newly urban Puerto Ricans, the PPD-led government actively promoted migration to the mainland in order to remedy the island's population "problem" (Duany 2002, 2004). Island residents are U.S. citizens; therefore they may move freely between the island and the mainland. Though the government relocation programs were short-lived (they began in the late 1940s), voluntary migration continued to be an important personal strategy for financial betterment and a political strategy for development: "Between 1945–1965, Puerto Rico's development strategy expelled a large share of its population, primarily to mainland cities that required cheap labor, such as New York City, Chicago, and Philadelphia. Afterwards, Puerto Ricans tended to move abroad when job

opportunities were more attractive on the mainland and returned when economic conditions improved on the Island" (Duany 2004).

14. Operation Bootstrap is the name given to the development model in Puerto Rico at this time (in Spanish it is known as Manos a la Obra, or Hands to Work). It involved attracting foreign investment in manufacturing through tax incentives and government-sponsored improvements in infrastructure, which "essentially replaced earlier initiatives to expand local employment through public investment" (Rivera-Batiz and Santiago 1996, 8–9; see also Dietz 2003, 42–67).

15. For a discussion of Puerto Rico as a social laboratory, see Lapp (1995). He argues that progressive social planners in the United States in the 1940s were increasingly disappointed with the direction that New Deal policies were taking. They found in Puerto Rico a staging ground to test their theories on state-led growth and economic planning. This activist social science perspective resonated with the aspirations of the emerging PPD leadership. For 20 years, American planners worked with PPD officials to reengineer the political and economic landscape of the island. By the 1960s, this alliance was collapsing due to economic strains, the rise in power of the rival statehood party, and new social science perspectives that were far less optimistic about the potential for social change. An example of the latter was Oscar Lewis's (1966) application of the "culture of poverty" concept on the island. In the context of the Cold War, the achievements of social planners and politicians in Puerto Rico were held up as "a social laboratory, a model for Third World economic development, and a 'showcase of democracy'" (Lapp 1995, 170). Puerto Rico was also used as a laboratory for testing new contraceptive technologies like the pill (Briggs 2003; I. Lopez 2008). Currently, it is the home of burgeoning biotech and pharmaceutical manufacturing industries that continue the legacy of using the island as a laboratory (Dietrich 2013; Duprey 2010).

16. When Nine Curt wrote in 1972, health insurance companies did not play a big role in the delivery system on the island. Nine Curt estimated that, despite growth in the industry during the preceding 10 years, fewer than one-third of Puerto Ricans received coverage through an insurance plan (Nine Curt 1972, 91). Compare this to the United States, where, in 1965, 74% of Americans held a hospital insurance policy (Engel 2006, 3–4). Currently health insurance plans cover the majority of people in Puerto Rico. Nine Curt attributed the low use of insurance companies to the general low income and inability to pay the premium as well as the existence of a free public system.

17. During this period, control of the executive branch alternated between the New Progressive Party (PNP) and the Popular Democratic Party (PDP): in 1969–1973 (PNP, Luis Ferré), 1973–1977 (PDP, Rafael Hernández Colón), 1977–1985 (PNP, Carlos Romero Barceló), and 1985–1993 (PDP, Rafael Hernández Colón).

18. Unless otherwise noted, all interviews were conducted in the mid-2000s in Puerto Rico in Spanish with the author. All translations are the author's. See

appendix 2 for a complete list of the Medicare beneficiaries who were interviewed for this project.

19. This translates to a monthly contribution from the federal government that approximates "$330 per participant per month while the amount in Puerto Rico was about $20 per participant per month" (University of Puerto Rico and the Vanderbilt Center for Better Health 2008, 2).

20. According to the Kaiser Family Foundation, a slightly higher percentage of adults in Puerto Rico (70.7%) versus in the United States (68.5%) had their teeth cleaned in the last year (KFF 2010).

21. Some studies have been conducted, largely by researchers affiliated with the School of Public Health at the University of Puerto Rico. Almost all of the studies focus on particular aspects of mental health care such as how the health reform impacted access to mental health care (Alegría, McGuire, Vera, Canino, Matías, et al. 2001), mental health provider turnover (Albizu-García et al. 2004), reallocation of mental health services according to greater need (Alegría, McGuire, Vera, Canino, Albizu, et al. 2001), and utilization of outpatient mental health services (Alegría, McGuire, Vera, Canino, Freeman, et al. 2001). In November 2005, a final comprehensive report was issued by the Comisión Para Evaluar el Sistema de Salud del Estado Libre Asociado de Puerto Rico. The report was produced at the behest of the PDP governor, Aníbal Acevedo Vilá. The report proposes returning to a regional system and details the lack of data produced on the impact of the health reform.

22. Cesarean rates in Puerto Rico were 49.2% of all live births in 2007 and 48.5% in 2008 (Departamento de Salud n.d.). These rates are among the highest in the world. Studies and guidance from the World Health Organization suggest that "for the health of both the mother and the neonate, and until further research gives new evidence, a frequency of between 5% and 10% seems to achieve the best outcomes, whereas a rate of less than 1%, or of higher than 15%, seems to result in more harm than good" (Althabe and Belizán 2006).

23. I would argue that many insurance companies do know what people are getting sick from and how much it costs to treat those illnesses. At least at the company I worked at, this information was extracted from claims payment databases and closely tracked. In fact, one of the biggest attempts to change how doctors practice medicine was to incentivize more specific coding of diagnoses and treatment and the use of electronic claims submission. The bigger issue is whether or not these data are made public and available for health planning purposes.

NOTES TO CHAPTER 2

1. The equation "Gringos + Boricuas = Results" spins colonial hybridity into a valuable corporate asset. In the "contact zone" that characterizes corporate culture in Puerto Rico, multinational companies often try to appear more local and less like outsiders. The explicit and self-conscious attempt to combine Puerto Rican and U.S. cultures was common in corporate life on the island. A more

detailed analysis of this phenomenon falls outside the scope of this chapter, which focuses on regulation, audit, and the disposability of workers, but see Dávila (1997, 2012) for accounts of how corporations harness cultural nationalism and symbols of Puerto Ricanness as marketing tools.

2. Likewise, David Harvey argues that the neoliberal "wave of creative destruction . . . is unparalleled in the history of capitalism" (2007, 39). Processes including privatization, financialization, crisis management, and state redistributive practices like regressive tax policies have contributed to "accumulation by dispossession" on a global scale (33–39). In economic theory and the popular business literature, the term "creative destruction" is also commonly used, although in a more positive valence.

3. As an example of how federal programs exclude or do not take into account U.S. colonial possessions, the territories were hardly mentioned in the MMA. In the 415-page Medicare Prescription Drug, Improvement, and Modernization Act of 2003, the territories are mentioned 7 times and Puerto Rico is mentioned 14 times. Every mention of Puerto Rico is related to increasing the hospital reimbursement rate from 50% to 75% of the federal level. The territories were not covered directly by the provisions of the legislation and were required to submit separate plans to the Secretary of Health and Human Services for coverage of eligible residents. In other words, a separate process had to be followed by the territories in order to garner prescription-drug coverage under the Medicare program. The legal status of citizens is hence kept ambiguous and ill-defined.

4. *60 Minutes* also reported on the role of pharmaceutical companies and lobbying in the development of the MMA and argued that the high cost of the program was due in part to relationships among industry members, lobbyists, and those in the Bush administration who designed and implemented the bill (Kroft 2007).

5. Puerto Rico's high rates of Medicare Advantage penetration are partially due to the high premiums that Medicare pays insurance contractors. The per-member-per-month (PMPM) Medicare Advantage premium in San Juan in 2005 for a Medicare beneficiary who aged in to Medicare was $501.92 (CMS 2006a). This included hospital and outpatient services but not prescription drugs. This rate was then adjusted according to other risk factors garnered from physical exams and claims records. Before the recession, the interest alone that could be made on these remittances was big business in Puerto Rico. In contrast, the average Reforma beneficiary PMPM for 2005–2006 was $79.34 and included medical and prescription-drug costs (ASES 2006). Beginning in 2012, Medicare Advantage premiums are scheduled to decrease nationwide as a result of the Obama administration's Affordable Care Act, but these decreases are likely to be offset by new initiatives to reward plans that meet the minimum quality scores.

6. Acme was run by a combination of executives from Puerto Rico and the mainland, though the primary decision makers and the ones who reaped the greatest profits were not from Puerto Rico.

7. Many residents of Puerto Rico do not have Part B of Medicare (which covers outpatient services) given the expense of the premium (which in 2009 was $96.40 per month) and lower incomes on the island (MedPac 2009, 179).

8. Polo T-shirts embroidered with the company's name were common at many places of employment in Puerto Rico, including for schoolteachers. It saved employees from having to purchase a separate wardrobe of work clothes. It also seemed to mark out a particular class of worker. It signaled that one worked in a professional capacity but did not do physical labor and was not an executive.

9. As demonstrated by its attitude toward marketing violations, discussed in chapter 6, the federal government in practice did not consistently enforce rules. The perception then that the federal government was more concerned with compliance than the Puerto Rican government did not always correspond to how these respective bureaucracies actually acted.

10. Clearly, elderly beneficiaries relied on their families for help in navigating the health insurance bureaucracy and for accessing medical care. In health research, Latinos more broadly have been described as exhibiting "familism," a characteristic that stresses family unity and respectability and may be health protective, especially for recent immigrants. "Researchers and the media typically portray Latino families with strength, solidarity, and unity derived from their 'familism'—a form of family values in which the needs of the family as a group are more important than the needs of any individual family member" (Zambrana 2011, 39). Though familism is often described in a positive light, the concept relies on essentialist and static understandings of family and cultural traits. It also ignores harmful aspects of familism such as sexism, patriarchy, and homophobia. For a thorough critical assessment of research on Latino families, see Zambrana (2011). In Puerto Rico, writing about the family is even more complicated because of the national myth of La Gran Familia Puertorriquena. This myth has served to erase internal difference: "women, blacks, and more recently, Puerto Rican migrants in the U.S., have all been marginalized and symbolically excluded from the national imaginary as a result of this myth" (Moreno 2010, 76). For these reasons, I do not find familism to be a helpful analytic concept even as I do recognize that family support was very important to the Medicare beneficiaries in Puerto Rico whom I interviewed.

11. Power (1997) also discusses the gap between what audits set out to do and what they achieve in practice. Drawing on Rose and Miller, Power distinguishes between "programmes and technologies": "The auditing field is characterized by a gap between the explosion of programmatic demands and expectations of auditing and the more 'local' stories which are told of its underlying operational capability" (7). By programmatic, he is referring to the normative or policy-related goals of auditing as opposed to the practices through which audits are conducted. The essential point here is that audits often fail to achieve their aims of creating greater transparency and accountability.

12. The claim that individuals within the corporation submit to regulation and exhibit a disposition toward compliance merits clarification. I do not mean to say that individuals *always* responded to government regulators or Compliance staff by internalizing a will to follow the rules. Some employees were likely motivated by a sense of moral obligation; compliance was seen as the right thing to do. Others probably sought to protect the company from alleged wrongdoing or to avoid being fired for committing an infraction. However, compliance can be and was resisted on a number of fronts from executives who did not want to follow federal rules that limited their autonomy to employees who refused to be micromanaged or to have to follow mind-numbingly complex policies. Furthermore, it is impossible to say, based on the research I conducted, whether changes brought about by the inculcation of compliance were in any way permanent or had altered someone's self-understanding. Claims about such things would do well to proceed with modesty. I do not know if people's internal lives were made over by compliance and the kind of work they did at Acme. I suspect that in part they were. I realize from my own experiences (see the fieldnote excerpts from the introduction) that these practices were quite persuasive and insidious. However, my experiences certainly should not be taken to be identical to those of other Acme employees. Nonetheless, what I can show and what I repeatedly observed is how these processes of creating awareness and monitoring levels of compliance filtered into many people's daily work processes at the company. This may not have influenced who they were in any sort of internal sense, but it certainly shaped what they *did*.

13. Another example of the absurdity of the audit's focus on process rather than content is discussed in chapter 4 where the major quality deficiency identified at the plan by a CMS audit was that documents pertaining to the quality program were not properly signed by the Board of Directors.

NOTES TO CHAPTER 3

1. Since the 1980s "the use of the term *health-care consumer* as a synonym for patient (along with its doctor analogue, *health-care provider*) has become commonplace in the United States" (Tomes 2006, 83). Despite the routine association of "consumer" with a market model for distributing medical care, the term initially gained traction within the consumer rights movements of the late 1960s and 1970s. Supplanting the passive "patient" with the more active "consumer" was aimed at challenging medical paternalism. Importantly, the term both predates and signifies more than its contemporary market-oriented connotations.

2. The Centers for Medicare and Medicaid Services (CMS) explicitly prohibits its contractors from using solely the term "seniors" to refer to Medicare beneficiaries because it is inaccurate and discriminatory. Medicare also covers individuals with disabilities and ESRD (end-stage renal disease).

3. Similarly, in their study of neoliberal reforms in Great Britain, Clarke and colleagues argue that we should not assume that consumers exist, but rather the

object of social analysis should be to trace how consumers "are summoned in one field of social practice (the use of public services) and how people experience themselves—and what identifications they deploy—in relation to these practices" (Clarke et al. 2007, 12–13). This chapter undertakes that very project. For an account of how "consumers" have influenced health policy in the United States, see Hoffman and colleagues (2011).

4. I was also appropriated in more mundane ways, such as being asked to explain plan rules, read correspondence from the health plan to beneficiaries, and assist in disenrolling from the plan.

5. For an account of the use of home remedies in Puerto Rico based in life histories with *curanderos* (healers), see Benedetti (2003). See Koss-Chioino (1992) for an ethnographic account of the work of spiritists in mental health care in Puerto Rico and also Hohmann and colleagues (1991) for an epidemiological study of the prevalence of spiritism.

6. In 1950, Don Anastasio would have been about 9 years old. The infant mortality rate (number of deaths of children less than age 1 per 1,000 live births) in Puerto Rico was 68.3 in 1950 (Dietz 2003, 8) compared with 10.2 from 1998 to 2000 (CDC 2003). The average life expectancy at birth in 1950 was 61 (Dietz 2003, 8) compared with 75.5 years in 2000 (CIA 2000). Clearly, the population had an overall better health status in 2000 than in 1950. Nonetheless, Don Anastasio remembered his youth as a much healthier time.

7. Following Kleinman, "retrospective narrativization can readily be shown to distort the actual happenings (the history) of the illness experience, since its raison d'être is not fidelity to historical circumstances but rather significance and validity in the creation of a life story" (1988, 51).

8. These are starchy vegetables such as green plantains, yucca, and sweet potatoes.

9. Zafra is the time of year when sugar cane is cut and milled.

10. In this respect, his life followed a pattern experienced by many Puerto Ricans during this time period. The distribution of the population became more urban than rural: "Between 1960 and 1980, the urban population of the island rose from 44.2 percent to 66.8 percent. By 1990, the percentage of the population in urban areas was 71.2 percent" (Rivera-Batiz and Santiago 1996, 83).

11. This is a common technique for developers who try to build in the rocky, hilly terrain of Puerto Rico. By removing the top of a hill, they have a flat expanse on which to build. However, this practice also causes many environmental problems such as poor drainage and excessive runoff.

12. The employer may have been sending him to receive treatment through the state-sponsored worker's compensation program, but this was not clear in the interview.

13. While in the United States, he worked as a truck driver. He initially traveled to the States to seek medical care for his son who had spinal bifida.

14. Don Anastasio's emphasis on work as health was a common theme with the working-class men whom I interviewed. Don Lucas (interview 6) and Don

Martín (interview 11) similarly associated health and productivity with their working lives and viewed their current physical state and medical needs as a sign of loss.

15. Patricia Alvarez, then a student from the University of Puerto Rico who was studying anthropology, participated in this interview and contributed valuable insights to its analysis.

16. Sue Estroff (2004) would characterize this as a "second-person narrative." Second-person narratives are "produced by family and others intimately involved with the diagnosed person. . . . These stories are often told by relatives in a witnessing mode similar to that of the first-person narratives" (283–284). Estroff urges researchers to attend to the differences between first-, second-, and third-person narrations of schizophrenia because representing what the disease means and how it is experienced is an endeavor marked by dispute and competing representations. I limit my observations here to how market-based health policy influenced the kind of care that Manuel and Enrique received. I do not offer observations on how Manuel and Enrique understood their health care as I did not conduct the kind of research that could effectively speak to their subjective experiences. For examples of ethnographies that do render the experiences of people diagnosed with schizophrenia, see Corin et al. (2004), Desjarlais (1997), Estroff (1981, 2004), and Lucas (2004).

17. Job Corps was created in 1964 and is operated by the U.S. Department of Labor. The program is directed at low-income youth from ages 16–24. While enrolled, participants live at the Job Corps school, take their meals there, and receive a small stipend. It is an educational and vocational program where students can earn a GED and/or career training. There are currently three Job Corps programs in Puerto Rico. The official website boasts 90% job placement either with private companies or the military following successful completion of the program (U.S. Department of Labor 2007).

18. The Clínica Julía was created in 1925 and was the first private institution for mental patients on the island (Torres Pérez 1994, 2).

19. The form of her story shares much with the "problematic year" described by Rogler and Hollingshead in their influential work on schizophrenia in Puerto Rico: *Trapped: Families and Schizophrenia* (1965).

20. Up to this point, I have referred to interviewees with the term of respect "Don" or "Doña" followed by their first name. However, because Teresa Ramírez is much closer in age to me (she is 13 years older than I am), "Doña" is not appropriate. Therefore, I refer to her with her first and last name only.

21. The Industrial Hospital is operated by the Corporación del Fondo del Seguro del Estado (the Corporation for the State Insurance Fund). This is the agency that processes worker's compensation claims.

22. This is an association of small retailers and business owners that offers insurance plans to members.

23. MediMed refers to the discount-drug card program that was part of the Medi-care Modernization Act. It was a stopgap measure to aid low-income beneficia-ries who did not qualify for Medicaid while Part D of Medicare was being rolled out. In Puerto Rico, the program was administered via a block grant given to the local government. Beneficiaries could apply for the card, which provided coverage for prescription drugs at participating pharmacies.

24. For example, in 1982, 25.7% of the labor force was employed in public adminis-tration and public utilities (Dietz 1986, 258).

25. Breckenridge and Vogler also make this point: "Disability studies teaches that an assumed able body is crucial to the smooth operation of traditional theories of democracy, citizenship, subjectivity, beauty, and capital" (2001, 350). See also Kleinman (1988, 47).

26. See chapter 4 for a description of how Doña Carmen qualified for Social Secu-rity benefits.

NOTES TO CHAPTER 4

1. This chapter originally appeared as "It Gets Better If You Do? Measuring Quality Care in Puerto Rico" in *Medical Anthropology* 29(3) (2010):303–329.

2. The policy focus on quality-measurement initiatives can be understood in part as a reaction against more extreme versions of neoliberalism that see little to no value in government regulation. Hence, the contemporary focus on perfor-mance represents an attempt to "realign neo-liberal governance with a revived (if much attenuated) attention to the public realm" (Clarke 2004, 131). In this view, quality measurement satisfies a public regulatory obligation to monitor performance and moves from the premise that more quantified and transparent information will lead to improved care and, overall, a better health system.

3. For example, the National Committee for Quality Assurance reports that it began measuring how many heart attack patients were receiving beta-blocker drugs in order to prevent a second heart attack in 1996. At that time, "fewer than 2 in 3 patients were receiving the right care. But in 2006, more than 97 percent of heart attack patients received beta-blockers" (NCQA 2007, 10). The NCQA report attributes the increase to the act of measurement.

4. HEDIS, which stands for Health Plan Employer Data and Information Set, is a commonly used quality-measurement instrument developed and administered by the NCQA.

5. "*Ataques de Nervios* are an idiom of distress used by Puerto Ricans and other Latinos to express dislocations in the social world of the family" (Guarnaccia et al. 1996, 343). *Ataques de nervios* are sometimes translated as nervous attacks or nervous breakdowns.

NOTES TO CHAPTER 5

1. Several co-occurring processes contribute to these transformations in citizen-ship, including (1) the transnational movement of people, media, and capital;

(2) the preponderance of international organizations carrying out governmental functions; (3) the widespread trend toward downsizing and privatizing formerly state-run services; and (4) the ability of social, ethnic, and religious movements that are not state-bound to inspire allegiance and to orient action.

2. These processes have been described as biological citizenship (Petryna 2002; Rose and Novas 2005) or therapeutic citizenship (Nguyen 2005). Petryna defines biological citizenship "as a massive demand for but selective access to a form of social welfare based on medical, scientific, and legal criteria that both acknowledge biological injury and compensate for it" (2002, 6). Her work describes the process of making demands on the Ukrainian state for access to medical care and social welfare following the Chernobyl disaster. She locates this as a particularly "post-socialist" phenomena in which citizenship claims were being radically transformed in the wake of state-building projects in the former Soviet Union.

3. The legislative framework for appeals and grievances, as amended by the Medicare Modernization Act (MMA), can be found at 42CFR § 422, Subpart M (*Federal Register* 2005). The more detailed manual instructions are available in chapter 13 of the *Medicare Managed Care Manual* (CMS 2006c).

4. Following CMS, I use "complaints" as a broad umbrella term that includes all grievances, appeals, exceptions, and redeterminations. The major distinction that CMS makes is between appeals and grievances. Grievances are expressions of dissatisfaction while appeals are requests for reconsideration of any initial decision regarding payment or provision of a service. Exceptions and redeterminations are types of appeals for receiving coverage for a prescription drug not on the plan's formulary or for a denial of prescription-drug coverage under Part D of Medicare, respectively. Appeals are subject to a more highly regulated review process, because they involve protecting due process rights as explained below.

5. QIOs have come under considerable criticism for keeping the details of their investigations secret from beneficiaries, for disproportionately taking the sides of physicians and care providers rather than beneficiaries, for paying exorbitant salaries to their CEOs and board members, and generally for operating as partners, instead of regulators, of providers (Gaul 2005). The trend toward conceptualizing regulation as a "partnership" is discussed in detail in the next chapter.

6. Marc Rodwin examined class action suits that led to the creation of independent medical review processes at the state level (much like the *Grijalva* lawsuit did at the federal level). Though patients initially came together to form a class and advocate for their rights collectively in these lawsuits, one of the unintended consequences of the new appeals processes is that it individualizes the review. Patients no longer dispute health plan decisions as a class, but as individuals. And since independent medical review panels do not create precedents with their rulings (as happens in the judicial system), individual appeals do

not change policy (Rodwin 2011, 181). Rodwin advocates for collecting appeals and grievance data and making them publicly available so that it is possible to monitor and track trends in appeal reasons and overturn rates.

7. The boilerplate enrollment form was modified by inserting "Acme" for "plan name."

8. This follows a trend that was common throughout the United States in the 2000s. Partially as a response to the managed care backlash of the 1990s, health plans implemented fewer stringent utilization management policies and expanded their provider networks. PPO (preferred-provider organization) plans grew and had more lenient network rules. In Medicare, PFFS (private fee-for service) plans expanded, which allowed members to see any provider who accepted Medicare and employed very few, if any, utilization review and care-management protocols.

9. The tendency to decide an appeal case in the member's favor even when Acme could legitimately have upheld the initial denial was partially made possible by the exorbitant reimbursement rates in Medicare Advantage on the island, which were 180% of Original Medicare in 2009 (MedPac 2009). Rates are currently going down, and Medicare Advantage companies are becoming more stringent in their denial practices, thereby letting off less steam through their safety valves.

10. The investigation report from APS stated that the clinical coordinator was not told that the man was in crisis and he did not request to be hospitalized or see a psychiatrist (Sosa Pascual 2005e).

NOTES TO CHAPTER 6

1. See Schlesinger (2005) for an account of how marketizing health care financing and provision came to be accepted in the United States by both liberals concerned with consumer choice and conservatives who favored reducing the size of government in the 1990s.

2. The *Federal Register* is published daily by the Office of the Federal Register, National Archives and Records Administration. It is "the official daily publication for rules, proposed rules, and notices of Federal agencies and organizations, as well as executive orders and other presidential documents" (GPO Access 2011).

3. The partner metaphor also mischaracterizes the power balance between managed care organizations and state regulators. According to Willging, an irony of the partnership relationship is that the state does not have as much power as it might seem: "At the same time as state officials are entrusted to regulate the activities of MCOs and BHOs, they operate under the threat that these corporations will withdraw from the Medicaid marketplace if state oversight becomes too onerous. . . . This threat of withdrawal complicates, and essentially inverts, the power relationship between the state government and its MMC contractors" (Willging 2005, 88).

4. Managed competition emerged as a way to unite two opposing political groups in the United States behind market-based reforms in health care: liberals wanted to expand consumer choice and challenge the authority of the medical establishment and conservatives wanted to increase efficiency and reduce health spending (Schlesinger 2005, 100–101).

5. Special needs plans were a particularly interesting addition because they were targeted at beneficiaries who were dual eligible (for Medicare and Medicaid) or those with "complex and disabling conditions." In other words, the legislation created health plans whose membership was restricted to beneficiaries with certain diagnoses. Some examples of special needs plans include those whose members share a diagnosis of end-stage renal disease (ESRD) or chronic obstructive pulmonary disease (COPD). These plans in turn received a higher premium payment from the government because their members' health care costs were higher than the average beneficiary. The creation of these specialized plans follows a trend in U.S. medicine to tailor treatment and interventions to individuals' biological specificities and personal, consumer taste (such as genetic medicine, scheduling a C-section, and new forms of "concierge care"). It also follows global trends to focus on specific disease categories (such as drug-resistant tuberculosis or HIV) often at the expense of holistic, primary care (Paluzzi 2004). The justification for these plans was that by focusing on care coordination and the specific needs of certain populations, health plans could offer highly specialized services that would improve the quality of care. However, current evidence does not indicate that quality increases faster in private plans than in traditional Medicare (Berenson and Dowd 2009, W33).

6. I often heard from Acme employees—especially those who had direct contact with beneficiaries like health educators and sales representatives—that literacy rates were low for the island's elderly population. These observations reinforced my own experiences with beneficiaries who asked me to read their mail or had difficulty with the informed consent form I used when interviewing. Examining educational attainment statistics reveals that although formal literacy rates may be high (94% in 2002 according to the CIA Factbook for 2011), years of formal schooling were not (particularly among the elderly). In the year 2000 for men over 65, 53% had less than a ninth-grade education. For women over 65, 61% had less than a ninth-grade education (U.S. Census Bureau 2000). Though they may meet minimal standards of literacy, it is likely that members of this population experienced considerable challenges in navigating the complex bureaucratic documents distributed by Medicare Advantage plans.

7. None of the interviewees had access to the Internet. Population-wide statistics on access to the Internet in Puerto Rico were not available for the time period during which this study was conducted. An AARP survey of 801 randomly selected Puerto Rico residents age 25 and older in 2008 found that 44% "never go online to use the Internet or World Wide Web" (32). Though the data were

not broken down by age, this proportion is likely to be much higher among residents 65 and over.

8. Other examples of critical news pieces in Puerto Rico include González (2005a, 2005b, 2005c). For the mainland United States, see Pear (2005, 2007a, 2007b, 2007c, 2008) and the *New York Times* (2007).

9. The life history interview methods are described in more detail in chapter 3 and appendix 1. I conducted 35 semistructured interviews with Acme beneficiaries.

10. Being enrolled without one's knowledge did not just occur in Puerto Rico. See Pear (2007a, 2007b, 2007c) for examples from the mainland United States. A recent study of national survey data from 2004–2007 also argues that "complex Medicare Advantage choices may overwhelm seniors—especially those with impaired decision making" (McWilliams et al. 2011).

11. On one level, preemption is necessary because local law and federal law regulate the same areas but impose different compliance requirements. For example, the time frame and notification procedures for claims payment differ. The handling of member complaints and appeals is also done through different systems so that a plan could not comply with both federal and Commonwealth requirements simultaneously.

12. The lack of direct oversight of Medicare Advantage plans should not be taken to mean that there is no interaction between the plans and the local government. Medicare Advantage organizations interact regularly with the Puerto Rican government on issues such as obtaining copies of practitioners' licenses, the exchange of Medicaid eligibility information, and health education.

13. Aníbal Acevedo Vilá was a member of the Popular Democratic Party and served as governor from 2005 to 2008. In 2004, he ran against former governor and statehood candidate Pedro Rosselló (New Progressive Party). In some respects, the election was a referendum on Rosselló's tenure from 1993 to 2001. Rosselló's administration implemented La Reforma and was plagued by corruption scandals. Acevedo Vilá, however, won by a narrow margin of 3,566 votes (and the election was not officially decided until several weeks after the vote). Popular party and first female governor Sila María Calderón was in power from 2001 until 2004.

NOTES TO THE CONCLUSION

1. As a recent study of health reforms to Medicaid in New Mexico has shown, "the work of mid-level professionals (nurses, nurse practitioners, and physician assistants) and clerical workers . . . were crucial in 'making the system work'" (Lamphere 2005, 4). These workers develop strategies for ensuring that cases are processed through the company bureaucracy amid changing rules, policies, and computer systems. At Acme, patient processors like Gina often searched for some medical rationale for approving authorization requests. If they could not justify an approval, the case would be referred to a medical director (a physician) for a final determination.

2. Of course, everyone did not support privatizing the health system. In an interview with Sarah Huertas Goldman, a psychiatrist and faculty member at the University of Puerto Rico School of Medicine, she described public hearings held at the medical school leading up to the implementation of La Reforma. Even though only three people presented their views at the hearing, they voiced their concerns that the proposed reforms would have a negative impact on the most disadvantaged. It turned out that we were right, she said.

3. Nonetheless, the average Medicare Advantage Benchmark in Puerto Rico in 2007 was $569 (this is the unadjusted premium amount that Medicare Advantage plans were paid for each enrolled member per month). This was the lowest benchmark in the United States in 2007; the highest was in Louisiana at $947 (CBO 2007).

4. The data on Medicare Advantage in Puerto Rico are inconclusive. In a letter submitted as testimony to the House Ways and Means Committee in June 2009, the Medicaid and Medicare Advantage Programs Association of Puerto Rico claimed that "between 2004 and 2008 we have made demonstrable improvements in health care delivery and health status for our enrollees. Some examples are: colorectal cancer screenings have increased by 70%; breast cancer screenings by 26%. Hypertension control has increased 24%. Our flu vaccination programs have reduced flu hospitalizations by 60% and flu-related deaths by 80%" (MMAPA 2009) I cannot confirm these claims because the MMAPA provides no citation or support for its figures. In published studies of both Original Medicare and Medicare Advantage, Puerto Rico ranks low compared to its mainland counterparts. NCQA health plan rankings for 2012 (this is the first year for which data from Puerto Rico have been made public) place Puerto Rican plans that submitted enough data and have consented to have their scores revealed in positions 176, 179, 337, 346, 347, 363, 378, 379, and 382 out of 395 plans (with 1 being the highest-ranked plan). Plans in Puerto Rico tend to score well in consumer satisfaction categories and poorly in prevention and treatment (NCQA 2012). As described in chapter 5, satisfaction surveys may suffer from serious validity concerns in Puerto Rico; the tendency to report satisfaction when surveyed may hide significant quality-of-care and access concerns that emerge when other methods like qualitative interviews are employed. In national comparative studies of Original Medicare, Puerto Rico ranked 52 out of 52 for the baseline (Jencks et al. 2000) and follow-up study (Jencks et al. 2003). A more recent study that looked at all of the territories found "compared with hospitals in the US states, hospitals in the US territories have significantly higher 30-day mortality rates and lower performance on every core process measure for patients discharged after AMI [acute myocardial infarction], HF [heart failure], and PNE [pneumonia]" (Nunez-Smith et al. 2011, 1528). Another recent study found "Medicare beneficiaries in Puerto Rico report generally worse healthcare experiences than beneficiaries in the U.S. mainland for several

Consumer Assessment of Healthcare Providers and Systems outcomes and lower immunization rates" (Elliott et al. 2012).

5. Since passage of the Medicare Modernization Act, Medicare Advantage plans have earned profits that often exceeded their own predictions. A report by the Government Accountability Office found that "[o]n average, MA organizations reported earning profits of 6.6 percent of total revenue in 2006—which was higher than their projected profits of 4.1 percent. MA organizations reported spending an average of 83.3 percent of total revenue on medical expenses, but had projected spending an average of 86.9 percent of total revenue on those expenses" (GAO 2008). In other words, Medicare Advantage organizations spent 16.7% of the premiums that it received from the federal government and Medicare beneficiaries on administrative costs, including salaries, marketing, and profit. Traditional Medicare by contrast operates with administrative costs of 3.1% (AMA 2005).

6. One example of the tension between controlling costs and enhancing health outcomes involves disease-management programs. The evidence suggests that chronic care disease-management programs are not successful at saving money and improving health outcomes simultaneously, though many in the health care industry remain optimistic that better-designed programs will be more effective (Bott et al. 2009; Motherall 2011; Russell 2009). The most effective programs for improving health outcomes are both labor- and cost-intensive (Fireman, Bartlett, and Selby 2004). One recent study found that "[t]he great hopes engendered by disease management—that more consistent intervention in chronic illnesses and better treatment using clinical guidelines from evidence-based medicine would lower costs—have yet to be realized. Health care, like many other institutions and agencies, has found that 'better' and 'cheaper' do not always partner well" (Fireman, Bartlett, and Selby 2004, 63). Many of the articles I have come across that extoll the virtues of disease- and case-management programs are authored by individuals with financial relationships with case management providers or managed care firms.

7. The Department of Justice has investigated Medicare plans on the island for gaming the risk-adjustment system and presenting their beneficiaries as being sicker than they actually are (González 2011). Risk-adjusted payments in Medicare have also received criticism because they have increased overpayments to Medicare Advantage plans. Some estimates put the price tag on this overpayment at US$ 282.6 billion in the period 1985–2012 (Hellander, Himmelstein, and Woolhandler. 2013, see also NBER 2011).

8. The exodus of government officials into lobbying and corporate positions following the passage of the MMA is discussed in chapter 2. The high cost of the prescription-drug program in Medicare has been linked to connections between industry, lobbyists, and members of the Bush administration who designed and implemented the bill.

9. Ethnography alone does not provide the tools that could definitively assess whether or not care-management programs are successful in reducing costs and improving health outcomes. Population-based studies are necessary to demonstrate whether or not the care-management program at Acme successfully improved health outcomes, saved money in medical costs for the plan, or was able to produce outcomes that were better than Original Medicare. However, these studies have not been done. One major problem with the care-management literature that has been published is that much of it is produced by parties who have financial and professional interests in demonstrating that care management is effective. Based on my research in Puerto Rico and that of other anthropologists on self-management initiatives for diabetics (Borovoy and Hine 2008; Ferzacca 2000), I have doubts that care-management programs will be very effective with an elderly, largely poor population that is habituated to certain ways of eating and living that are not easily changed. Also, this focus totally elides the social determinants of health—it is individualistic and asocial when we know that health outcomes are responsive to all kinds of environmental and social variables that are ignored in care management. In highly controlled, intensive, or short-term demonstrations, care management could indeed be effective. But as a strategy for enhancing population health—it is fundamentally misguided.

10. The section was removed from the approved version of the Constitution, and we are left with a footnote in the second edition of *Documents on the Constitutional History of Puerto Rico* that reads: "By Resolution number 34, approved by the Constitutional Convention and ratified in the Referendum held on November 4, 1952, section 20 of article II was eliminated" (Office of the Commonwealth of Puerto Rico 1964, 172). For a detailed discussion of the elimination of Section 20, see Zapata (2003). Zapata argues that the battles in the U.S. House and Senate over the Constitution were instigated by the developer Leonard Darlington Long over disputes regarding his taxes in Puerto Rico and disagreements with Luis Muñoz Marín. Long then used his political influence in Washington and fanned rumors that Muñoz Marín was a Communist and dictator. See also Rivera Ramos (2001, 213–215) for a discussion of the motivations of the framers of the Puerto Rican Constitution and their efforts to extend the notion of rights beyond a purely individualist conception to include social rights.

11. When I first read the Constitution in its entirety, I was surprised that the section on health care was gone. From talking with health policy officials on the island, I had repeatedly been told that Puerto Rico was different than other places because the right to health care is written into the Constitution. Deleted or not, the passage survives in Puerto Rico. The constitutional right to health care is mentioned in many accounts of the public health system on the island, including Román de Jesús (2002, 47), Puerto Rico Legislative Assembly (1974, 73–74), and Luis Izquierdo Mora (personal interview).

12. Likewise, as Arbona and Ramírez de Arellano (1978, 72–76) argue, federal programs like Medicare and Medicaid contributed to the development of a parallel private system that made the public, regional system less efficient.

NOTES TO APPENDIX 1

1. Karen Ho classifies the time when she was employed at Bankers Trust New York as "pre-field work" (2009, 14). She says that she abided by anthropology's ethical norms and did not conduct covert fieldwork. Instead, she kept a journal that recorded her personal observations and experiences in which she "took care not to describe in detail the thoughts and actions of my coworkers and friends who—although they knew of my research interests—were 'on the job.'" She says that her fieldwork from this period was not based on "any information that was considered private or proprietary." Unlike Ho, I did negotiate formal research access with the company and was granted access to propriety information.

2. Up to 70% of college-level teaching occurs off the tenure track. See Kendzior (2012) for a reflection on what the increase in itinerant labor means for anthropology (see also the anthropology blog Savageminds.org, especially the posts from May 5 and 12, 2013).

WORKS CITED

AARP (Association for the Advancement of Retired Persons). 2009. *Achieving Afford-able, Quality Health Care in Puerto Rico: A Survey of Residents Age 25+*. www.aarp.org/health/health-care-reform/info-02 . . . /pr_hcr_09.html (accessed August 18, 2011).

Abadía, César Ernesto, and Diana G. Oviedo. 2009. Bureaucratic Itineraries in Colombia: A Theoretical and Methodological Tool to Assess Managed-Care Health Care Systems. *Social Science and Medicine* 68(6):1153–1160.

Abelson, Reed. 2011. Health Insurers Making Record Profits as Many Postpone Care. *New York Times*, May 13.

Abelson, Reed, Julie Creswell, and Griff Palmer. 2012. Medicare Bills Rise as Records Turn Electronic. *New York Times*, September 21.

Acevedo-Vilá, Anibal. 2005. Hearing on the Future of Medicaid. http://aspe.hhs.gov/medicaid/oct/Puerto_Rico_081705.pdf (accessed March 12, 2008).

AHRQ (Agency for Healthcare Research and Quality). 1999. Agency for Healthcare Research and Quality: Reauthorization Fact Sheet. AHRQ Publication No. 00-P002, December 1999, Rockville, MD. http://www.ahrq.gov/about/ahrqfact.htm (accessed May 23, 2011).

Albizu-García, Ruth Ríos, Deborah Juarbe, and Margarita Alegría. 2004. Provider Turnover in Public Sector Managed Mental Health Care. *Journal of Behavioral Health Services and Research* 31(3):255–265.

Alegría, Margarita, Thomas McGuire, Mildred Vera, Glorisa Canino, Carmen Albizu, Heriberto Marín, and Leida Matías. 2001. Does Managed Mental Health Care Real-locate Resources to Those with Greater Need for Services? *Journal of Behavioral Health Services and Research* 28(4):439–455.

Alegría, Margarita, Thomas McGuire, Mildred Vera, Glorisa Canino, Leida Matías, and José Calderón. 2001. Changes in Access to Mental Health Care among the Poor and Nonpoor: Results from the Health Care Reform in Puerto Rico. *American Journal of Public Health* 91(9):1431–1434.

Alegría, Margarita, Thomas McGuire, Mildred Vera, Glorisa Canino, Daniel Freeman, Leida Matías, Carmen Albizu, Heriberto Marín, and José Calderón. 2001. The Impact of Managed Care on the Use of Outpatient Mental Health and Substance Abuse Services in Puerto Rico. *Inquiry* 38:381–395.

Allen, Charles H. 1901. First Annual Report of Charles H. Allen, Governor of Porto Rico Covering the Period from May 1, 1900 to May 1, 1901. Washington, DC: Government Printing Office.

Allen, Charlotte. 1997. Spies Like Us: When Sociologists Deceive Their Subjects. *Lingua Franca* 7:31–39.

Alm, James. 2006. Assessing Puerto Rico's Fiscal Policies. In *The Economy of Puerto Rico: Restoring Growth*, edited by Susan M. Collins, Barry P. Bosworth, and Miguel A. Soto-Class, 319–398. Washington, DC: Brookings Institution Press.

Althabe F., and J. F. Belizan. 2006. Caesarean Section: The Paradox. *The Lancet* 368(9546):1472–1473.

AMA (American Medical Association). 2005. Administrative Costs of Health Care Coverage. http://healthcarereform.procon.org/sourcefiles/administrative_costs_of_health_care_coverage_ama.pdf (accessed October 14, 2011).

Aníbal Gobernador 2004 Campaign. 2004. *Acceso total salud de primera*. Pamphlet distributed in *El Nuevo Día*, date unknown.

Anderson, Warwick. 2006. *Colonial Pathologies: American Tropical Medicine, Race, and Hygiene in the Philippines*. Durham, NC: Duke University Press.

Arana-Soto, Salvador. 1974. *Historia de la medicina Puertorriqueña hasta el 1898*. San Juan, PR.

Arbona, Guillermo, and Annette B. Ramírez de Arellano. 1978. *Regionalization of Health Services: The Puerto Rican Experience*. Oxford: Oxford University Press.

Armada, Francisco, and Carles Muntaner. 2004. The Visible Fist of the Market: Health Reforms in Latin America. In *Unhealthy Health Policy: A Critical Anthropological Examination*, edited by Arachu Castro and Merrill Singer, 29–42. Walnut Creek, CA: AltaMira.

ASES (Administración de Seguros de Salud). 2005. *Request for Proposal for Access to MA Coverage for Government Health Insurance Plan Population*, October 5.

———. 2006. Primas Contratadas para Salud Física 2005–2006. http://www.gobierno.pr/ASES/Primas/PrimasContratadas.htm (accessed January 24, 2007).

———. 2007. Distribución por Aseguradora. http://www.gobierno.pr/ASES/SaludFisica/MapasDistribucionRegiones/MapaDistribucionRegionesAseguradoras/ (accessed March 7, 2007).

Ashford, Bailey K. 1934. *A Soldier in Science: The Autobiography of Bailey K. Ashford*. New York: William Morrow.

Atkinson, Sarah J. 1993. Anthropology in Research on the Quality of Health Services. *Cadernos de Saúde Pública* 9(3):283–299.

Auxilio Mutuo. 2009. Manual de Socios. http://www.auxiliomutuo.com/Plan_de_Socios.aspx (accessed September 16, 2009).

Barry, Andrew, Thomas Osborne, and Nikolas Rose, eds. 1996. *Foucault and Political Reason*. Chicago: University of Chicago Press.

Beck, Ulrich. 1999. *World Risk Society*. Malden, MA: Blackwell.

Behar, Ruth. 1993. *Translated Woman: Crossing the Border with Esperanza's Story*. Boston: Beacon.

Belaval Díaz, Mario. 2013. Obamacare Takes Center Stage in Healthcare During 2013. *Caribbean Business*, December 26.

Benedetti, Maria. 2003. *Sembrando y sanando en Puerto Rico: Tradiciones y visiones para un futuro verde.* Cayey, PR: Verde Luz.

Berenson, Robert A., and Bryan E. Dowd. 2009. Medicare Advantage Plans at a Cross-roads—Yet Again. *Health Affairs* 28(1):W29–W40.

Berman, Marshall. 1999. *Adventures in Marxism.* New York: Verso.

Biehl, João, with Torben Eskerod. 2007. *Will to Live: AIDS Therapies and the Politics of Survival.* Princeton: Princeton University Press.

Bodenheimer, Thomas. 1996. The HMO Backlash—Righteous or Reactionary? *New England Journal of Medicine* 335(21):1601–1605.

Boehm, Deborah A. 2005. The Safety Net of the Safety Net: How Federally Qualified Health Centers "Subsidize" Medicaid Managed Care. *Medical Anthropology Quarterly* 19(1):47–63.

Borovoy, Amy, and Janet Hine. 2008. Managing the Unmanageable: Elderly Russian Jewish Émigrés and the Biomedical Culture of Diabetes Care. *Medical Anthropology Quarterly* 22(1):1–26.

Bott, David M., Mary C. Kapp, Lorraine B. Johnson, and Linda M. Magno. 2009. Disease Management for Chronically Ill Beneficiaries in Traditional Medicare. *Health Affairs* 28(1):86–98.

Breckenridge, Carol A., and Candace Vogler. 2001. The Critical Limits of Embodiment: Disability's Criticism. *Public Culture* 13(3):349–357.

Briggs, Laura. 2003. *Reproducing Empire: Race, Sex, Science, and U.S. Imperialism in Puerto Rico.* Berkeley: University of California Press.

Brown, Michael F. 2010. A Tale of Three Buildings: Certifying Virtue in the New Moral Economy. *American Ethnologist* 37(4):741–752.

Burchell, Graham, Colin Gordon, and Peter Miller, eds. 1991. *The Foucault Effect: Studies in Governmentality.* Chicago: University of Chicago Press.

Burhans, Linda. 2007. What Is Quality? Do We Agree, and Does It Matter? *Journal for Healthcare Quality* 29(1):39–44.

Bush, George W. 2003. President Signs Medicare Legislation. Text of speech given at DAR Constitution Hall, Washington, DC, on December 8. http://georgewbush-whitehouse.archives.gov/news/releases/2003/12/20031208-2.html (accessed September 17, 2009).

CBO (Congressional Budget Office). 2007. Medicare Advantage Statistics by State, April 2007. http://www.cbo.gov/sites/default/files/cbofiles/ftpdocs/80xx/doc8009/04-17-medicarebystate.pdf (accessed October 2, 2012).

CDC (Centers for Disease Control). 2003. Infant Health among Puerto Ricans—Puerto Rico and U.S. Mainland, 1989—2000. *MMWR* October 24, 2003/52(42):1012–1016. http://www.cdc.gov/mmwr/preview/mmwrhtml/mm5242a2.htm (accessed June 21, 2010).

Cefkin, Melissa. 2009. Introduction: Business, Anthropology, and the Growth of Corporate Ethnography. In *Ethnography and the Corporate Encounter*, edited by Melissa Cefkin, 1–37. New York: Berghahn.

Chassin, Mark R., Jerod M. Loeb, Stephen P. Schmaltz, and Robert M. Wachter. 2010. Accountability Measures—Using Measurement to Promote Quality Improvement. *New England Journal of Medicine* 363(7):683–688.

CIA (Central Intelligence Agency). 2000. *The World Factbook 2000*. "Puerto Rico" entry. http://www.umsl.edu/services/govdocs/wofact2000/geos/rq.html (accessed June 24, 2010).

———. 2011. *The World Factbook*. "Literacy" entry. https://www.cia.gov/library/publications/the-world-factbook/fields/2103.html (accessed August 17, 2011).

Clarke, John. 2004. *Changing Welfare, Changing States: New Directions in Social Policy.* Thousand Oaks, CA: Sage.

Clarke, John, Janet Newman, Nick Smith, Elizabeth Vidler, and Louise Westmarland. 2007. *Creating Citizen-Consumers: Changing Publics and Changing Public Services.* London: Sage.

CMS (Centers for Medicare and Medicaid Services). 2004. Fact Sheet on Federal Payment Methodology to Medicare Health Plans. March 15, 2004.

———. 2005. Partner with CMS. Electronic document. http://www.cms.hhs.gov/partnerships/ (accessed November 19).

———. 2006a. Medicare Advantage Monthly Capitation Rates and Rescaling Factors for 2005. http://www.cms.hhs.gov/MedicareAdvtgSpecRateStats/RSD/itemdetail.asp?filterType=none&filterByDID=-99&sortByDID=1&sortOrder=ascending&itemID=CMS023378, (accessed February 4, 2007).

———. 2006b. Medicare Compare. http://www.medicare.gov/MPPF/Include/DataSection/ComparePlans/ComparePlans.asp (accessed January 26).

———. 2006c. *Medicare Managed Care Manual*. Chapter 13—Medicare Managed Care Beneficiary Grievances, Organization Determinations, and Appeals Applicable to Medicare Advantage Plans, Cost Plans, and Health Care Prepayment Plans (HCPPs) (collectively referred to as Medicare Health Plans). http://www.cms.hhs.gov/manuals/downloads/mc86c13.pdf (accessed March 8, 2007).

———. 2006d. PDP Landscape. http://www.medicare.gov/medicarereform/mapdp-docs/PDPLandscapepr.pdf (accessed February 8).

———. 2008a. Glossary. Electronic document. http://www.cms.hhs.gov/apps/glossary/default.asp?Letter=Q&Language=English (accessed March 7, 2008).

———. 2008b. Health Plans, Reports, Files and Data. http://www.cms.hhs.gov/HealthPlanRepFileData/02_SC.asp#TopOfPage (accessed January 15, 2008).

———. 2009. *Your Medicare Rights and Protections*, rev. 2009. www.medicare.gov/publications/pubs/pdf/10112.pdf (accessed July 12, 2011).

———. 2010. *Medicare Managed Care Manual*. Chapter 2—Medicare Advantage Enrollment and Disenrollment (updated August 17, 2010). https://www.cms.gov/Medicare/Eligibility-and-Enrollment/MedicareMangCareEligEnrol/downloads/FINALMAEnrollmentandDisenrollmentGuidanceUpdateforCY2011.pdf (accessed June 29, 2012).

———. 2011. *Medicare Managed Care Manual*. Chapter 4—Benefits and Beneficiary Protections (Rev. 97, 05–20–11). https://www.cms.gov/Regulations-and-Guidance/ Guidance/Manuals/downloads/mc86c04.pdf (accessed June 27, 2012).

———. 2012a. Find a Plan. Medicare.gov. http://www.medicare.gov/find-a-plan/results/ planresults/plan-list.aspx# (accessed October 2, 2012).

———. 2012b. Medicare Part B (Medical Insurance). http://www.medicare.gov/naviga- tion/medicare-basics/medicare-benefits/part-b.aspx (accessed June 27, 2012).

Collins, John. 2003. Puerto Rico Fights for Equal Medicare Treatment. *Caribbean Business*, October 16. http://www.puertorico-herald.org/issues/2003/vol7n42/ CBPRFightsMedicare-en.html (accessed September 24, 2011).

Colón Reyes, Linda. 2002. Neoliberalismo, globalización y pobreza en Puerto Rico. In *Ensayos sobre la pobreza en Puerto Rico*, edited by Francisco E. Martínez and Francisco A. Catalá, 19–61. Hato Rey, PR: Publicaciones Puertorriqueñas.

———. 2005. *Pobreza en Puerto Rico: Radiografía del Proyecto Americano*. San Juan: Editorial Luna Nueva.

Comisión Para Evaluar el Sistema de Salud del Estado Libre Asociado de Puerto Rico. 2005. *Informe Final*. San Juan, PR.

Commonwealth of Puerto Rico. 1993. *Ley 72*. Salud y Sanidad Parte IX. Seguros de Salud 24 L.P.R.A.§7001. Aprobada el 7 de Septiembre de 1993.

Coombs, Jan Gregoire. 2005. *The Rise and Fall of HMOs: An American Health Care Revolution*. Madison: University of Wisconsin Press.

Corin, Ellen, Rangaswami Thara, and Ramachandran Padmavati. 2004. Living through a Staggering World: The Play of Signifiers in Early Psychosis in South India. In *Schizophrenia, Culture, and Subjectivity*, edited by Janis Hunter Jenkins and Robert John Barrett, 110–145. New York: Cambridge University Press.

Crapanzano, Vincent. 1980. *Tuhami: Portrait of a Moroccan*. Chicago: University of Chicago Press.

CSDH (Commission on Social Determinants of Health). 2008. Closing the Gap in a Generation: Health Equity through Action on the Social Determinants of Health. Final Report of the Commission on Social Determinants of Health. Geneva: World Health Organization.

Dalzell, Michael D. 1998. Helping Hands for HEDIS. *Managed Care* 7(6):34A–34H.

Dávila, Arlene. 1997. *Sponsored Identities: Cultural Politics in Puerto Rico*. Philadelphia: Temple University Press.

———. 2012. *Culture Works: Space, Value, and Mobility across the Neoliberal Americas*. New York: NYU Press.

Dean, Mitchell. 1999. *Governmentality: Power and Rule in Modern Society*. Thousand Oaks, CA: Sage.

Delgado, José A. 2005a. Gobernadores apoyan pareo en fondos Medicaid. *El Nuevo Día*, June 17.

———. 2005b. Sin impacto el recorte de Medicaid. *El Nuevo Día*, October 25.

Departamento de Salud. n.d. Nacimientos por cesáreas por municipio de residencia de la madre: Puerto Rico, Años 2007–2008. http://www.salud.gov.pr/Datos/Esta-disticasVitales/Estadsticas%20Nacimientos/Nacimientos%20por%20Cesareas.pdf (accessed October 11, 2011).

Desjarlais, Robert. 1997. *Shelter Blues: Sanity and Selfhood among the Homeless.* Philadelphia: University of Pennsylvania Press.

Dietrich, Alexa. 2013. *The Drug Company Next Door: Pollution, Jobs and Community Health in Puerto Rico.* New York: NYU Press.

Dietz, James L. 2003. *Puerto Rico: Negotiating Development and Change.* Boulder, CO: Lynne Rienner.

Dietz, James, and Emilio Pantojas-Garcia. 1993. Puerto Rico's New Role in the Caribbean: The High-Finance/Maquiladora Strategy. In *Colonial Dilemma: Critical Perspectives on Contemporary Puerto Rico,* edited by Edwin Meléndez and Edgardo Meléndez, 103–115. Boston: South End.

Donald, Alasdair. 2001. The Wal-Marting of American Psychiatry. *Culture, Medicine and Psychiatry* 25:427–439.

Dranove, David. 2000. *The Economic Evolution of American Health Care: From Marcus Welby to Managed Care.* Princeton: Princeton University Press.

Duany, Jorge. 2000. Nation on the Move: The Construction of Cultural Identities in Puerto Rico and the Diaspora. *American Ethnologist* 27(1):5–30.

———. 2002. *The Puerto Rican Nation on the Move: Identities on the Island and in the United States.* Chapel Hill: University of North Carolina Press.

———. 2004. Puerto Rico—Between the Nation and the Diaspora: Migration to and from Puerto Rico. In *Migration and Immigration: A Global View,* edited by M. I. Toro-Morn and M. Alicea, 177–195. Westport, CT: Greenwood.

Duprey, Marlene. 2010. *Bioislas: Ensayos sobre biopolítica y gubernamentalidad en Puerto Rico.* San Juan, PR: Ediciones Callejón.

Ehrenreich, Barbara. 2009. *Bright-Sided: How the Relentless Promotion of Positive Thinking Has Undermined America.* New York: Metropolitan.

Elliott, Marc N., Amelia M. Haviland, Jacob Dembosky, Katrin Hambarsoomian, and Robert Weech-Maldonado. 2012. Are There Differences in the Medicare Experiences of Beneficiaries in Puerto Rico Compared with Those in the U.S. Mainland? *Medical Care* 50(3):243–248.

Engel, Jonathan. 2006. *Poor People's Medicine: Medicaid and American Charity Care since 1965.* Durham, NC: Duke University Press.

Estroff, Sue E. 1981. *Making It Crazy: An Ethnography of Psychiatric Clients in an American Community.* Berkeley: University of California Press.

———. 2004. Subject/Subjectivities in Dispute: The Poetics, Politics and Performance of First-Person Narratives of People with Schizophrenia. In *Schizophrenia, Culture, and Subjectivity,* edited by Janis Hunter Jenkins and Robert John Barrett, 282–302. New York: Cambridge University Press.

Farmer, Paul. 2010. The Consumption of the Poor: Tuberculosis in the Twenty-First Century. In *Partner to the Poor: A Paul Farmer Reader*, edited by Haun Saussy, 222–247. Berkeley: University of California Press.

Federal Register. 2005. Medicare Modernization Act Final Rule. *Federal Register* 70(18):4588–4741.

Ferguson, James, and Akhil Gupta. 2002. Spatializing States: Toward an Ethnography of Neoliberal Governmentality. *American Ethnologist* 29(4):981–1002.

Ferré, Luis. 1992. El caos en el Departamento de Salud. *El Nuevo Día*, July 8.

Ferzacca, Steve. 2000. "Actually, I Don't Feel That Bad": Managing Diabetes and the Clinical Encounter. *Medical Anthropology Quarterly* 14(1):28–50.

Fischer, Michael M. J. 2009. Emergent Forms of Life in Corporate Arenas. In *Ethnography and the Corporate Encounter*, edited by Melissa Cefkin, 227–238. New York: Berghahn.

Fireman, Bruce, Joan Bartlett, and Joe Selby. 2004. Can Disease Management Reduce Health Care Costs by Improving Quality? *Health Affairs* 23(6):63–75.

Flores Ramos, José. 1998. Virgins, Whores, and Martyrs: Prostitution in the Colony, 1898–1919. In *Puerto Rican Women's History*, edited by Félix V. Matos Rodríguez and Linda C. Delgado, 83–105. Armonk, NY: M. E. Sharpe.

Fortun, Kim. 2001. *Advocacy after Bhopal: Environmentalism, Disaster, New Global Orders*. Chicago: University of Chicago Press.

Foucault, Michel. 1991. Governmentality. In *The Foucault Effect: Studies in Governmentality*, edited by Graham Burchell, Colin Gordon, and Peter Miller, 87–104. Chicago: University of Chicago Press.

Fourcade, Marion, and Kieran Healy. 2007. Moral Views of Market Society. *Annual Review of Sociology* 33:285–311.

Franco-Giraldo, Álvaro, Marco Palma, and Carlos Álvarez-Dardet. 2006. Efecto del ajuste estructural sobre la situación de salud en América Latina y el Caribe, 1980–2000. *Revista Panamericana de Salud Pública* 19(5):291–299.

Friedman, Robert. 2005. Islanders Get Small Return on Taxes for Medicare. *San Juan Star*, October 24.

Gabel, Jon. 1997. Ten Ways HMOs Have Changed during the 1990s. *Health Affairs* 16(3):134–145.

Gabriel, Yiannis, and Tim Lang. 2006. *The Unmanageable Consumer*. Thousand Oaks, CA: Sage.

GAO (United States Government Accountability Office). 2008. Medicare Advantage Organizations: Actual Expenses and Profits Compared to Projections for 2006. http://www.gao.gov/new.items/d09132r.pdf (accessed October 14, 2011).

Garcia, Angela. 2010. *The Pastoral Clinic: Addiction and Dispossession along the Rio Grande*. Berkeley: University of California Press.

Garrett, Laurie. 2007. The Challenge of Global Health. *Foreign Affairs* 86(1):14–38.

Gaul, Gilbert M. 2005. Once Health Regulators, Now Partners. *Washington Post*, July 26.

Giri, Ananta. 2000. Audited Accountability and the Imperative of Responsibility. In *Audit Cultures: Anthropological Studies in Accountability, Ethics and the Academy*, edited by Marilyn Strathern, 173–195. New York: Routledge.

Giroux, Henry A. 2008. *Against the Terror of Neoliberalism*. Boulder, CO: Paradigm.

Gledhill, John. 2005. Citizenship and the Social Geography of Deep Neo-liberalization. *Anthropologica* 47(1):81–100.

Gold, Marsha. 2009. Medicare's Private Plans: A Report Card on Medicare Advantage. *Health Affairs* 28(1):W41–W54.

González, Joanisabel. 2005a. Abandono al beneficiario de Medicare. *El Nuevo Día,* December 19.

———. 2005b. Auditoría a las aseguradoras de Advantage. *El Nuevo Día,* December 21.

———. 2005c. Supervisión federal a aseguradoras. *El Nuevo Día,* December 20.

———. 2011. Ojo federal a planes médicos. *El Nuevo Día,* November 24.

Gordon, Colin. 1991. Governmental Rationality: An Introduction. In *The Foucault Effect: Studies in Governmentality*, edited by Graham Burchell, Colin Gordon, and Peter Miller, 1–52. Chicago: University of Chicago Press.

GPO Access (U.S. Government Printing Office). 2011. *The Federal Register.* http://www.gpoaccess.gov/fr/ (accessed August 25, 2011).

Gray, Bradford H. 2006. The Rise and Decline of the HMO: A Chapter in U.S. Health-Policy History. In *History and Health Policy in the United States*, edited by Rosemary A. Stevens, Charles E. Rosenberg, and Lawton R. Burns, 309–339. New Brunswick, NJ: Rutgers University Press.

Grijalva v. Shalala 152 F.3d 1115 (U.S. Court of Appeals, 9th Cir., 1998).

Grijalva v. Shalala 526 U.S. 1096 (1999).

Grijalva v. Shalala 185 F.3d 1075, C.A. 9 (1999).

Grosfoguel, Ramón. 2003. *Colonial Subjects: Puerto Ricans in a Global Perspective*. Berkeley: University of California Press.

Guarnaccia, Peter J., Melissa Rivera, Felipe Franco, and Charlie Neighbors. 1996. The Experiences of Ataques de Nervios: Towards an Anthropology of Emotions in Puerto Rico. *Culture, Medicine and Psychiatry* 20(3):343–367.

Gusterson, Hugh. 1997. Studying Up Revisited. *PoLAR: Political and Legal Anthropology Review* 20(1):114–119.

Harper, Richard. 2000. The Social Organization of the IMF's Mission Work: An Examination of International Auditing. In *Audit Cultures: Anthropological Studies in Accountability, Ethics and the Academy*, edited by Marilyn Strathern, 21–53. New York: Routledge.

Harvey, David. 2005. *A Brief History of Neoliberalism*. New York: Oxford University Press.

———. 2007. Neoliberalism as Creative Destruction. *Annals of the American Academy of Political and Social Science* 610:22–44.

Hayashi, A. Seiji, Brad Finnegan, Peter Shin, Emily Jones, and Sara Rosenbaum. 2009. Examining the Experiences of Puerto Rico's Community Health Centers under the Government Health Insurance Plan. Geiger Gibson/RCHN Community Health

Foundation Research Collaborative Policy Research Brief No. 8. George Washington University School of Public Health. www.gwumc.edu/sphhs/departments/
healthpolicy/ . . . /PRStudy.pdf (accessed October 20, 2011).

Hellander, Ida, David U. Himmelstein, and Steffie Woolhandler. 2013. Medicare Overpayments to Private Plans, 1985-2012: Shifting Seniors to Private Plans Has Already Cost
Medicare US$282.6 Billion. *International Journal of Health Services* 43(2):305-319.

Hemlock, Doreen. 1991. Rosselló Health Plan Would Privatize Public Hospitals. *San
Juan Star*, October 31.

Hernández Cabiya, Yanira. 2005. Desbanca ASSMCA a las privatizadoras. *El Nuevo
Día*, August 24.

Hill, Shirley A., Mary K. Zimmerman, and Michael Fox. 2002. Rational Choice in
Medicaid Managed Care: A Critique. *Journal of Poverty* 6(2):37–59.

Ho, Karen. 2009. *Liquidated: An Ethnography of Wall Street*. Durham, NC: Duke University Press.

Hoffman, Beatrix, Nancy Tomes, Rachel Grob, and Mark Schlesinger, eds. 2011.
Patients as Policy Actors. New Brunswick, NJ: Rutgers University Press.

Hohmann, Ann A., Madeleine Richeport, Bernadette M. Marriott, Glorisa J. Canino,
Maritza Rubio-Stipec, and Hector Bird. 1990. Spiritism in Puerto Rico. Results of an
Island-Wide Community Study. *British Journal of Psychiatry* 156:328–335.

Holland, Dorothy, Marla Frederick-McGlathery, Donald M. Nonini, Thaddeus C.
Guldbrandsen, Catherine Lutz, Enrique G. Murillo, Jr., and Lesley Bartlett. 2007.
Local Democracy under Siege: Activism, Public Interests, and Private Politics. New
York: NYU Press.

Hopper, Kim. 1991. Some Old Questions for the New Cross-Cultural Psychiatry. *Medical Anthropology Quarterly* 5(4):299–330.

Horton, Sarah. 2004. Land and Rural New Mexicans' Mistrust of Federal Programs:
The Unintended Consequences of Medicaid Eligibility Rules. In *Unhealthy Health
Policy: A Critical Anthropological Exploration*, edited by Arachu Castro and Merrill
Singer, 235–246. Walnut Creek, CA: AltaMira.

———. 2006. The Double Burden on Safety Net Providers: Placing Health Disparities
in the Context of the Privatization of Health Care in the US. *Social Science and
Medicine* 63(2006):2702–2714.

Horton, Sarah, and Louise Lamphere. 2006. A Call to an Anthropology of Health
Policy. *Anthropology News* (January):33, 36.

Horton, Sarah, Joanne McCloskey, Caroline Todd, and Marta Henriksen. 2001. Transforming the Safety Net: Responses to Medicaid Managed Care in Rural and Urban
New Mexico. *American Anthropologist* 103(3):733–746.

Horton, Sarah, César Abadía, Jessica Mulligan, and Jennifer Jo Thompson. 2012. Health
Insurance Reform: Society for Medical Anthropology "Take a Stand" Statement.
http://www.medanthro.net/stand/index.html (accessed August 1, 2012).

———. 2014. Critical Anthropology of Global Health "Takes a Stand" Statement: A
Critical Medical Anthropological Approach to the U.S.'s Affordable Care Act. *Medical Anthropology Quarterly* 28(1): 1-22.

Iglehart, John K. 2011. Desperately Seeking Savings: States Shift More Medicaid Enrollees to Managed Care. *Health Affairs* 30(9):1627–1629.

Ignagni, Karen. 2005. The Health Care Debate. *New York Times*, May 6.

Institute of Medicine. 2001. *Crossing the Quality Chasm: A New Health System for the
21st Century. Committee on Quality of Health Care in America.* Washington, DC:
National Academy Press.

Izquierdo Mora, Luis. 2005. *Declaración de principios:¡¡Basta Ya!!* San Juan, PR.

Jencks, Stephen, Timothy Cuerdon, Dale R. Burwen, Barbara Fleming, Peter M.
Houck, Annette E. Kussmaul, David S. Nilasena, Diana L. Ordin, and David R.
Arday. 2000. Quality of Medical Care Delivered to Medicare Beneficiaries. *Journal
of the American Medical Association* 284:1670–1676.

Jencks, Stephen F., Edwin D. Huff, and Timothy Cuerdon. 2003. Change in the Quality
of Care Delivered to Medicare Beneficiaries, 1998–1999 to 2000–2001. *Journal of the
American Medical Association* 289(3):305–312.

Johnson, Lyndon B. 1966. Statement by the President on the Inauguration of the
Medicare Program, June 30, 1966. http://www.cms.hhs.gov/History/Downloads/
CMSPresidentsSpeeches.pdf (accessed November 12, 2008).

Katz, Michael B. 2008. *The Price of Citizenship: Redefining the American Welfare State.*
Philadelphia: University of Pennsylvania Press.

Kendzior, Sarah. 2012. The Closing of American Academia. Al Jazeera. http://www.
aljazeera.com/indepth/opinion/2012/08/2012820102749246453.html (accessed May
1, 2013).

KFF (Kaiser Family Foundation). 2005. Total Medicare Beneficiaries. http://www.
statehealthfacts.org/comparemaptable.jsp?yr=16&typ=1&ind=290&cat=6&sub=74
(accessed August 15, 2011).

———. 2010. State Health Facts. Percentage of Adults (Ages 18 and Above) Who Report
Having Had Their Teeth Cleaned Within the Past Year. http://www.statehealthfacts.
org/profileind.jsp?ind=109&cat=2&rgn=55 (accessed December 29, 2013).

———. 2011a. Health Insurance Coverage in the U.S., 2010. http://facts.kff.org/chart.
aspx?ch=477 (accessed July 24, 2012).

———. 2011b. Total Medicare Advantage (MA) Enrollment 2011. *State Health Facts.*
http://www.statehealthfacts.org/comparetable.jsp?ind=327&cat=6 (accessed August
30, 2011).

Kim, Jim Yong, ed. 2000. *Dying for Growth: Global Inequality and the Health of the
Poor.* Monroe, ME: Common Courage.

Kingfisher, Catherine, and Jeff Maskovsky. 2008. Introduction: The Limits of Neoliberalism. *Critique of Anthropology* 28(2):115–126.

Kleinman, Arthur. 1988. *The Illness Narratives: Suffering, Healing and the Human Condition.* New York: Basic Books.

———. 1995. *Writing at the Margin: Discourse between Anthropology and Medicine.*
Berkeley: University of California Press.

Koss-Chioino, Joan D. 1992. *Women as Healers, Women as Patients: Mental Health Care
and Traditional Healing in Puerto Rico.* Boulder, CO: Westview.

Kroft, Steve. 2007. Under the Influence. *60 Minutes*. CBS, July 23. http://www.cbsnews. com/stories/2007/03/29/60minutes/main2625305.shtml (accessed March 1, 2009).

Lambie, Laura, and Soeren Mattke. 2004. Selecting Indicators for the Quality of Cardiac Care at the Health Systems Level in OECD Countries. http://www.oecd.org/dataoecd/28/35/33865450.pdf (accessed September 24, 2008).

Lamphere, Louise. 2005. Providers and Staff Respond to Medicaid Managed Care: The Unintended Consequences of Reform in New Mexico. *Medical Anthropology Quarterly* 19(1):3–25.

Lapp, Michael. 1995. The Rise and Fall of Puerto Rico as a Social Laboratory, 1945–1965. *Social Science History* 19(2):169–199.

Lemke, Thomas. 2001. The Birth of Bio-politics: Michel Foucault's Lecture at the Collège de France on Neo-liberal Governmentality. *Economy and Society* 30(2):190–207.

Lewin Group. 2009. Medicaid Managed Care Cost Savings—A Synthesis of 24 Studies, March 2009. Prepared for AHIP. http://www.lewin.com/publications/publication/395/ (accessed July 29, 2012).

Lewis, Oscar. 1966. *La Vida, a Puerto Rican Family in the Culture of Poverty—San Juan and New York*. New York: Random House.

Li, Tania Murray. 2007. *The Will to Improve: Governmentality, Development, and the Practice of Politics*. Durham, NC: Duke University Press.

Lockhart, Chris, and Angela Durey. 2004. Economic Efficiency Versus Community Participation in the Reform of Rural and Remote Health Care. *Anthropological Forum* 14(3):253–267.

López, Cynthia. 2005. Aumenta el costo de la salud tras La Reforma. *El Nuevo Día*, June 17.

Lopez, Iris. 2008. *Matters of Choice: Puerto Rican Women's Struggle for Reproductive Freedom*. New Brunswick, NJ: Rutgers University Press.

López, Leslie. 2005. De Facto Disentitlement in an Information Economy: Enrollment Issues in Medicaid Managed Care. *Medical Anthropology Quarterly* 19(1):26–46.

Lucas, Rod. 2004. In and Out of Culture: Ethnographic Means to Interpreting Schizophrenia. In *Schizophrenia, Culture, and Subjectivity*, edited by Janis Hunter Jenkins and Robert John Barrett, 146–163. New York: Cambridge University Press.

Lundin, Stephen C. Harry Paul, and John Christensen. 2000. *Fish! A Remarkable Way to Boost Morale and Improve Results*. New York: Hyperion.

MACPAC (Medicaid and CHIP Payment and Access Commission). 2011. *Report to the Congress: The Evolution of Managed Care in Medicaid, June 2011*. Washington, DC: MACPAC.

Maskovsky, Jeff. 2000. "Managing" the Poor: Neoliberalism, Medicaid HMOs and the Triumph of Consumerism among the Poor. *Medical Anthropology* 19:121–146.

McCue, Michael J., and Michael H. Bailit. 2011. Assessing the Financial Health of Medicaid Managed Care Plans and the Quality of Patient Care They Provide. http://www.commonwealthfund.org/~/media/Files/Publications/Issue%20Brief/2011/Jun/1511_McCue_assessing_financial_hlt_Medicaid_managed_care_plans_ib_FINAL.pdf (accessed July 29, 2012).

McIntyre, Dennis, Lisa Rogers, and Ellen Jo Heier. 2001. Overview, History, and Objectives of Performance Measurement. *Health Care Financing Review* 22(3):7–21.

McWilliams, J. Michael, Christopher C. Afendulis, Thomas G. McGuire, and Bruce E. Landon. 2011. Complex Medicare Advantage Choices May Overwhelm Seniors— Especially Those with Impaired Decision Making. *Health Affairs* 30(8). doi: 10.1377/hlthaff.2011.0132.

MedPac (The Medicare Payment Advisory Commission). 2009. Report to the Congress: Improving Incentives in the Medicare Program, June 2009. http://www.medpac.gov/chapters/Jun09_Ch07.pdf (accessed June 19, 2012).

Metzl, Jonathan. 2010. Introduction: Why "Against Health?" In *Against Health: How Health Became the New Morality*, edited by Jonathan Metzl and Anna Kirkland, 1–13. New York: NYU Press.

Millán Pabón, Carmen. 2005. Avalancha de llamadas confunde a beneficiarios. *El Nuevo Día*, December 20.

Miller, Peter, and Nikolas Rose. 1990. Governing Economic Life. *Economy and Society* 19(1):1–31.

Mintz, Sidney. 1974. *Worker in the Cane: A Puerto Rican Life History.* New York: W. W. Norton.

MMAPA (Medicaid and Medicare Advantage Programs Association of Puerto Rico. 2009. Letter by Medicaid and Medicare Advantage Programs Association of Puerto Rico. Witness Testimony before the House Ways and Means Committee, Hearing on Health Reform in the 21st Century: Proposals to Reform the Health System, June 24, 2009. http://democrats.waysandmeans.house.gov/Hearings/Testimony.aspx?TID=8160 (accessed October 2, 2012).

Moreno, Marisel. 2010. Family Matters: Revisiting *La Gran Familia Puertorriqueña* in the Works of Rosario Ferré and Judith Ortíz Cofer. *Centro Journal* 22(2):75-105.

Morgen, Sandra and Lisa Gonzales. 2008. The Neoliberal American Dream as Daydream: Counter-Hegemonic Perspectives on Welfare Restructuring in the United States. *Critique of Anthropology* 28(2):219–236.

Morrissey, Marietta. 2006. The Making of a Colonial Welfare State: U.S. Social Insurance and Public Assistance in Puerto Rico. *Latin American Perspectives* 33(1):23–41.

Motheral, Brenda R. 2011. Telephone-Based Disease Management: Why It Does Not Save Money. *American Journal of Managed Care* 17(1):E10–E16.

Mountin, Joseph, Elliot Pennell, and Evelyn Flook. 1937. *Illness and Medical Care in Puerto Rico.* Public Health Bulletin No. 237. Washington, DC: Government Printing Office.

Mulligan, Jessica. 2010. It Gets Better If You Do? Measuring Quality Care in Puerto Rico. *Medical Anthropology* 29(3):303–329.

Nader, Laura. 1972. Up the Anthropologist—Perspectives Gained from Studying Up. In *Reinventing Anthropology*, edited by Dell Hymes, 284-311. New York: Pantheon.

NBER (National Bureau of Economic Research). 2011. The Consequences of Risk Adjustment in the Medicare Advantage Program. NBER Digest OnLine. http://nber.org/digest/sep11/w16977.html (accessed December 29, 2013).

NCQA (National Committee for Quality Assurance). 2006. NCQA: An Overview. http://www.ncqa.org/Communications/Publications/overviewncqa.pdf (accessed November 1, 2006).

———. 2007. The State of Health Care Quality 2007. www.ncqa.org (accessed July 1, 2008).

———. 2008a. HEDIS Measure Development. http://www.ncqa.org/tabid/414/Default.aspx (accessed September 10, 2008).

———. 2008b. Report Cards. http://www.ncqa.org/tabid/60/Default.aspx (accessed September 10, 2008).

———. 2012. NCQA's Health Insurance Plan Rankings 2012–2013. http://www.ncqa.org/ReportCards/HealthPlans/HealthInsurancePlanRankings/PrivateHealthPlanRankings20122013.aspx (accessed October 2, 2012).

Nelson, Nancy. 2005. Ideologies of Aid, Practices of Power: Lessons for Medicaid Managed Care. *Medical Anthropology Quarterly* 19(1):103–122.

New York Times. 2007. Editorial. Medicare Privatization Abuses. May 8.

Nguyen, Vinh-Kim. 2005. Antiretroviral Globalism, Biopolitics, and Therapeutic Citizenship. In *Global Assemblages*, edited by Aihwa Ong and Stephen J. Collier, 124–144. Malden, MA: Blackwell.

Nine Curt, José. 1972. *La salud en Puerto Rico.* San Juan, PR.

Nunez-Smith, Marcella, Elizabeth H. Bradley, Jeph Herrin, Calie Santana, Leslie A. Curry, Sharon-Lise T. Normand, and Harlan M. Krumholz. 2011. Quality of Care in the US Territories. *Archives of Internal Medicine* 171(17):1528–1540.

OECD (Organisation for Economic Co-operation and Development). 2008. *OECD Health Data 2008: How Does the United States Compare?* http://www.oecd.org/dataoecd/46/2/38980580.pdf (accessed March 6, 2009).

Office of Puerto Rico. 1948. *Documents on the Constitutional History of Puerto Rico.* Washington, DC: Office of Puerto Rico.

Office of the Commonwealth of Puerto Rico. 1964. *Documents on the Constitutional History of Puerto Rico.* 2nd edition. Washington, DC: Office of Puerto Rico.

O'Malley, Pat. 1996. Risk and Responsibility. In *Foucault and Political Reason*, edited by Andrew Barry, Thomas Osborne, and Nikolas Rose, 189–207. Chicago: University of Chicago Press.

Ong, Aihwa. 2005. Ecologies of Expertise: Assembling Flows, Managing Citizenship. In *Global Assemblages*, edited by Aihwa Ong and Stephen J. Collier, 337–353. Malden, MA: Blackwell.

Pabón Batlle, Luis H. 2003. *El retorno de polifemo: La medicina de Estado en Puerto Rico al umbral del siglo XX.* Bayamón, PR: Editorial Pluriverso.

Padín, José Antonio. 1997. NAFTA's Future?—The Logic of Puerto Rico's Export-Led Development. *International Journal of Sociology and Social Policy* 17(11–12):8–47.

PAHO (Pan American Health Organization). 2007. *Health Systems Profile of Puerto Rico.* Washington, DC: PAHO.

Paluzzi, Joan E. 2004. Primary Health Care since Alma Ata: Lost in the Bretton Woods? In *Unhealthy Health Policy*, edited by Arachu Castro and Merrill Singer, 63–77. Walnut Creek, CA: AltaMira.

Pantojas-García, Emilio. 1990. *Development Strategies as Ideology: Puerto Rico's Export-Led Industrialization Experience*. Boulder: Lynne Rienner.

Parés Arroyo, Marga. 2008a. A fortalecer la zapata de la salud pública. *El Nuevo Día*, September 10.

———. 2008b. Un riesgo enfermarse en la Isla. *El Nuevo Día*, September 10.

———. 2012a. Abusivo el use de la sala de emergencia. *El Nuevo Día*, January 29.

———. 2012b. Llegan tarde al cuidado prenatal. *El Nuevo Día*, January 30.

———. 2012c. Rezagada la Isla en prevención. *El Nuevo Día*, January 29.

Pear, Robert. 2004. Inquiry Confirms Top Medicare Official Threatened Actuary over Cost of Drug Benefits. *New York Times*, July 7.

———. 2005. Insurers' Tactics in Marketing Drug Plan Draw Complaints. *New York Times*, November 27.

———. 2007a. For Recipients of Medicare, the Hard Sell. *New York Times*, December 17.

———. 2007b. Medicare Audits Show Problems in Private Plans. *New York Times*, October 7.

———. 2007c. Methods Used by Insurers Are Questioned. *New York Times*, May 7.

———. 2008. States Look to Rein in Private Medicare Plans. *New York Times*, May 5.

Pear, Robert, and Robin Toner. 2004. Partisan Arguing and Fine Print Seen as Hindering Medicare Law. *New York Times*, October 11.

Pérez, Gina M. 2004. *Near Northwest Side Story: Migration, Displacement, and Puerto Rican Families*. Berkeley: University of California Press.

Petryna, Adriana. 2002. *Life Exposed: Biological Citizens after Chernobyl*. Princeton: Princeton University Press.

Pfeiffer, James, and Rachel Chapman. 2010. Anthropological Perspectives on Structural Adjustment and Public Health. *Annual Review of Anthropology* 39:149–165.

Porter, Theodore M. 1995. *Trust in Numbers: The Pursuit of Objectivity in Science and Public Life*. Princeton: Princeton University Press.

Power, Michael. 1997. *The Audit Society: Rituals of Verification*. New York: Oxford University Press.

Pratt, Mary Louise. 1992. *Imperial Eyes: Travel Writing and Transculturation*. New York: Routledge.

Puerto Rico Legislative Assembly. 1974. *Informe de la Comisión Sobre el Seguro de Salud Universal*. San Juan, PR.

Rapp, Rayna, and Faye Ginsburg. 2001. Enabling Disability: Rewriting Kinship, Reimagining Citizenship. *Public Culture* 13(3):533–556.

Reinhardt, Uwe E. 2003. The Medicare World from Both Sides: A Conversation with Tom Scully. *Health Affairs* 22(6):167–174.

Reinhold, Susan. 1994. Local Conflict and Ideological Struggle: "Positive Images" and Section 28. Ph.D. dissertation, University of Sussex.

Rivera-Batiz, Francisco L., and Carlos E. Santiago. 1996. *Island Paradox: Puerto Rico in the 1990s.* New York: Russell Sage Foundation.

Rivera Mass, Enrique, Nicolás Fernández Cornier, Andrés Torres Rivera, and Carmen E. Parrilla Cruz. 2004. Análisis de la salud de Puerto Rico, salud mental. Unpublished research paper given to author in 2007.

Rivera Ramos, Efrén. 2001. *The Legal Construction of Identity: The Judicial and Social Legacy of American Colonialism in Puerto Rico.* Washington, DC: American Psychological Association.

Rochefort, David A. 2001. The Backlash against Managed Care. In *The New Politics of State Health Policy,* edited by Robert B. Hackey and David A. Rochefort, 113–141. Lawrence: University Press of Kansas.

Rodríguez-Santana, Ivette. 2005. Conquests of Death: Disease, Health and Hygiene in the Formation of a Social Body (Puerto Rico, 1880–1929). Ph.D. dissertation, Department of Sociology, Yale University.

Rodwin, Marc A. 2011. Patient Appeals as Policy Disputes: Individual and Collective Action in Managed Care. In *Patients as Policy Actors,* edited by Beatrix Hoffman, Nancy Tomes, Rachel Grob, and Mark Schlesinger, 177–191. New Brunswick, NJ: Rutgers University Press.

Rogler, Lloyd H., and August B. Hollingshead. 1965. *Trapped: Families and Schizophrenia.* New York: John Wiley and Sons.

Román de Jesús, José. 2002. *Del bohique a la reforma de salud: De la magia al mito.* San Juan, PR.

Rose, Nikolas. 1996. Governing "Advanced" Liberal Democracies. In *Foucault and Political Reason: Liberalism, Neo-liberalism and Rationalities of Government,* edited by Andrew Barry, Thomas Osborne, and Nikolas Rose, 37–64. Chicago: University of Chicago Press.

———. 2007. *The Politics of Life Itself: Biomedicine, Power, and Subjectivity in the Twenty-First Century.* Princeton, NJ: Princeton University Press.

Rose, Nikolas, and Carlos Novas. 2005. Biological Citizenship. In *Global Assemblages,* edited by Aihwa Ong and Stephen Collier, 439–463. Malden, MA: Blackwell.

Rose, Nikolas, Pat O'Malley, and Mariana Valverde. 2006. Governmentality. *Annual Review of Law and Social Science* 2:83–104.

Rullán, Johnny. 2004. Presentation at the Third Annual Symposium of the Healthcare Sector of Puerto Rico. San Juan, PR, February 18, 2004.

Russell, Louise B. 2009. Preventing Chronic Disease: An Important Investment, But Don't Count on Cost Savings. *Health Affairs* 28(1):42–45.

Rylko-Bauer, Barbara. 2008. Applied Anthropology and Counterinsurgency. *Society for Applied Anthropology Newsletter* 19(1):1–4.

Rylko-Bauer, Barbara, and Paul Farmer. 2002. Managed Care or Managed Inequality? A Call for Critiques of Market-Based Medicine. *Medical Anthropology Quarterly* 16(4):476–502.

San Juan Star. 1993. Health Chief Backs Hospital Program. May 16.

Santiago-Valles, Kelvin. 1994. *"Subject People" and Colonial Discourses: Economic Transformation and Social Disorder in Puerto Rico, 1898–1947.* Albany: State University of New York Press.

Scherz, China. 2011. Protecting Children, Preserving Families: Moral Conflict and Actuarial Science in a Problem of Contemporary Governance. *PoLAR: Political and Legal Anthropology Review* 34(1):33–50.

Schlesinger, Mark. 2005. The Dangers of the Market Panacea. In *Healthy, Wealthy and Fair,* edited by James A. Morone and Lawrence R. Jacobs, 91–134. New York: Oxford University Press.

Schumann, William R. 2007. Transparency, Governmentality, and Negation: Democratic Practice and Open Government Policy in the National Assembly for Wales. *Anthropological Quarterly* 80(3):837–862.

Scott, James. 1998. *Seeing Like a State.* New Haven, CT: Yale University Press.

Scully, Thomas A. 2002. Statement by Thomas A. Scully, Administrator, Centers for Medicare and Medicaid Services on Responding to the Needs of Small Business Health Care Providers before the House Committee on Small Business, May 16. http://www.hhs.gov/asl/testify/t020616.html (accessed August 5, 2011).

Shore, Cris, and Susan Wright. 1997. *Anthropology of Policy: Critical Perspectives on Governance and Power.* New York: Routledge.

———. 2000. Coercive Accountability: The Rise of Audit Culture in Higher Education. In *Audit Cultures: Anthropological Studies in Accountability, Ethics and the Academy,* edited by Marilyn Strathern, 57–89. New York: Routledge.

Silver, Patricia L. 2004. Autonomy "Entre Comillas": Teachers, State and Empire in Neoliberal Education Reform in Puerto Rico. Ph.D. dissertation, Department of Anthropology, American University.

———. 2007. 'Then I do what I want': Teachers, State, and Empire in 2000. *American Ethnologist* 34(2):268–284.

Silvestrini, Blanca G. 1983. La política de salud pública de los Estados Unidos en Puerto Rico 1898–1913: Consecuencias en el proceso de americanización. In *Politics, Society and Culture in the Caribbean,* edited by Blanca G. Silvestrini, 69–83. San Juan: University of Puerto Rico Association of Caribbean Historians.

Smith-Nonini, Sandy. 2006. Conceiving the Health Commons: Operationalizing a "Right" to Health. *Social Analysis* 50(3):233–245.

Sommers, Benjamin D., Katherine Baicker, and Arnold M. Epstein. 2012. Mortality and Access to Care among Adults after State Medicaid Expansions. *New England Journal of Medicine.* doi: 10.1056/NEJMsa1202099

Sosa Pascual, Omaya. 2005a. Bloqueo institucional al trato efectivo. *El Nuevo Día,* October 27.

———. 2005b. Coalición pide salud "sin parches." *El Nuevo Día,* March 3.

———. 2005c. De mal en peor la salud. *El Nuevo Día,* October 27.

———. 2005d. Llega tarde una oferta de ayuda. *El Nuevo Día,* February 26.

———. 2005e. Pesquisas con hallazgos incongruentes. *El Nuevo Día,* March 8.

———. 2005f. Reclamo al gobierno por fallas en APS Healthcare. *El Nuevo Día,* May 19.

———. 2005g. Se reducen en un 68% los internos y residentes. *El Nuevo Día*, March 17.

———. 2005h. Señalamiento contra APS Healthcare. *El Nuevo Día*, March 11.

Stan, Sabina. 2007. Transparency: Seeing, Counting and Experiencing the System. *Anthropologica* 49(2):257–273.

Starr, Paul. 1982. *The Social Transformation of American Medicine*. New York: Basic Books.

———. 2010. *Remedy and Reaction: The Peculiar American Struggle over Health Care Reform*. New Haven, CT: Yale University Press.

Strathern, Marilyn. 2000. Introduction: New Accountabilities. In *Audit Cultures: Anthropological Studies in Accountability, Ethics and the Academy*, edited by Marilyn Strathern, 1–18. New York: Routledge.

Suárez Findlay, Eileen. 1999. *Imposing Decency: The Politics of Sexuality and Race in Puerto Rico, 1870–1920*. Durham, NC: Duke University Press.

Sullivan, Kip. 2001. On the "Efficiency" of Managed Care Plans. *International Journal of Health Services* 31(1):55–65.

Tomes, Nancy. 2006. Patients or Health-Care Consumers? In *History and Health Policy in the United States*, edited by Rosemary A. Stevens, Charles E. Rosenberg, and Lawton R. Burns, 83–110. New Brunswick, NJ: Rutgers University Press.

Tomes, Nancy, and Beatrix Hoffman. 2011. Introduction: Patients as Policy Actors. In *Patients as Policy Actors*, edited by Beatrix Hoffman, Nancy Tomes, Rachel Grob, and Mark Schlesinger, 1–16. New Brunswick, NJ: Rutgers University Press.

Torres Pérez, Orlando. 1994. Utilización de una sala de emergencia por pacientes psiquiátricos. Ph.D. Dissertation, Centro Caribeño de Estudios Postgraduados, San Juan, PR.

Trujillo-Pagán, Nicole. 2003. Health beyond Prescription: A Post-Colonial History of Puerto Rican Medicine at the Turn of the Twentieth Century. Ph.D. dissertation, Department of Sociology, University of Michigan.

University of Puerto Rico and the Vanderbilt Center for Better Health. 2008. Planning for Health Care Improvement for the People of Puerto Rico. www.md.rcm.upr.edu/ehsrc/pdf/report.pdf (accessed September 24, 2011).

U.S. Census Bureau. 2000. Sex by Age by Educational Attainment for the Population 18 Years and Over, Puerto Rico. http://factfinder.census.gov/servlet/DTTable?_bm=y&-geo_id=04000US72&-ds_name=DEC_2000_SF3_U&-mt_name=DEC_2000_SF3_U_PCT025 (accessed August 17, 2011).

———. 2006. Puerto Rico Fact Sheet—American Community Survey Data Profile Highlights. http://factfinder.census.gov/servlet/ACSSAFFFacts?_event=Search&geo_id=&_geoContext=&_street=&_county=&_cityTown=&_state=04000US72&_zip=&_lang=en&_sse=on&pctxt=fph&pgsl=010 (accessed March 11, 2008).

———. 2009. Selected Characteristics of the Uninsured in Puerto Rico. http://factfinder.census.gov/servlet/STTable?_bm=y&-state=st&-context=st&-qr_name=ACS_2009_1YR_G00_S2702PR&-ds_name=ACS_2009_1YR_G00_&-tree_id=309&-redoLog=true&-_caller=geoselect&-geo_id=04000US72&-format=&-_lang=en (accessed September 24, 2011).

U.S. Department of Labor. 2007. What Is Job Corps? http://jobcorps.dol.gov/about.htm (accessed March 2, 2007).

Vannier, Christian N. 2010. Audit Culture and Grassroots Participation in Rural Haitian Development. *PoLAR: Political and Legal Anthropology Review* 33(2):282–305.

Velázquez Vicente, Marissel. 2005. Ponencia del Colegio de Médicos-Cirujanos ante la Comisión Evaluadora del Sistema de Salud. May 12. Centro Médico de San Juan, PR.

Wagner, William G. 2005. Confronting Utilization Review in New Mexico's Medicaid Mental Health System: The Critical Role of "Medical Necessity." *Medical Anthropology Quarterly* 19(1):64–83.

Waitzkin, Howard, Robert L. Williams, John A. Bock, Joanne McCloskey, Cathleen Willging, and William Wagner. 2002. Safety-Net Institutions Buffer the Impact of Medicaid Managed Care: A Multi-Method Assessment in a Rural State. *American Journal of Public Health* 92(4):598–610.

Wendland, Claire L. 2007. The Vanishing Mother: Cesarean Section and "Evidence-Based Obstetrics." *Medical Anthropology Quarterly* 21(2):218–233.

———. 2010. *A Heart for the Work: Journeys through an African Medical School.* Chicago: University of Chicago Press.

West, Harry G., and Todd Sanders, eds. 2003. *Transparency and Conspiracy: Ethnographies of Suspicion in the New World Order.* Durham, NC: Duke University Press.

WHO (World Health Organization). 2008. *The World Health Report: Health Systems: Improving Performance.* Geneva: World Health Organization. http://www.who.int/whr/2008/en/index.html (accessed July 18, 2011).

Willging, Cathleen E. 2005. Power, Blame, and Accountability: Medicaid Managed Care for Mental Health Services in New Mexico. *Medical Anthropology Quarterly* 19(1):84–102.

Woolhandler, Steffie, Terry Campbell, and David U. Himmelstein. 2003. Costs of Health Care Administration in the United States and Canada. *New England Journal of Medicine* 349:768–75.

Zambrana, Ruth Enid. 2011. *Latinos in American Society: Families and Communities in Transition.* Ithaca, NY: Cornell University Press.

Zapata, Carlos R. 2003. El contratista y la constitución: Leonard Darlington Long y la conspiración contra la constitución del Estado Libre Asociado (1951–1952). In *Luis Muñoz Marín: Perfiles de su gobernación,* edited by Fernando Picó, 228–275. San Juan: Fundación Luis Muñoz Marín.

Zarabozo, Carlos. 2000. Milestones in Medicare Managed Care. *Healthcare Financing Review* 22(1):61–67.

Zarabozo, Carlos, and Scott Harrison. 2009. Payment Policy and the Growth of Medicare Advantage. *Health Affairs* 28(1): W55–W67 (published online November 24, 2008; 10.1377/hlthaff.28.1.w55).

Medicare Advantage, 10–11, 62, 65, 76, 79, 87, 153, 165–166, 184, 188, 202–204, 220, 223, 229, 256n14, 270n6, 271n10, 271n12; market share (penetration); 10–11, 66–67, 192–197, 203, 262n5; and preemption, 203, 229, 271n11; premiums in, 11, 19, 66–67, 86, 192, 217–218, 221, 223, 256n15, 262n5, 269n9, 270n5, 272n3, 273n5, 273n7. *See also* Medicare Modernization Act
Medicare Modernization Act (MMA), 4, 17, 65- 67, 90, 108, 120, 141, 182, 188, 190–193, 202–205, 214, 223, 256nn14–15, 262nn3–4, 267n23, 268n3, 273n5, 273n8. *See also* Medicare Advantage
Medicare Part D, 65, 77, 193, 236, 267n23, 268n4
Mental Health and Substance Abuse Administration (ASSMCA), 45, 171
mental health care: access problems, 20, 50, 95–96, 131, 169–175, 209, 212–213, 217, 219, 255n11, 261n21; and advocacy, 109–118, 186–187; and disability, 102–108, 109–118, 242, 245; fifteen minute med checks, 64, 103, 144, 172–174; hospitals, 102–108, 109–118, 266n8; in the regional system, 9, 45; MBHOs, 48, 114, 169; quality complaints, 102–108, 109–118, 143, 169–175; and spiritism, 265n5. *See also nervios, ataques de*
migration: rural to urban, 38, 98, 265 n.10; to the U.S. mainland, 155, 259n13
Mi Salud (new name for La Reforma), 220, 230, 257n1. *See also* La Reforma
Mountin, Joseph, 36–37, 258n4
Muñoz Marín, Luis, 37, 259n10

Nader, Laura, 12–13, 233, 256n16
NCQA (National Committee for Quality Assurance), 130, 133–135, 140, 147–150, 267nn3–4, 272n4. *See also* quality
neoliberalism, 4, 10, 18, 23, 27–28, 41, 46–47, 55, 72, 129, 132, 149–150, 154, 206, 228, 238, 267n2; and consumerism, 28, 53, 89, 91, 102, 108, 118–121, 264n3; and creative destruction, 62–63, 262n2; definition of, 253n2; and flexibility, 2, 61, 64, 83–88, 117, 121; ideas about personhood and subjectivity (or homo economicus), 28, 69–71, 89–90, 121–122, 141, 149, 201, 210, 224–225, 253n2, 264n12; and implementation, 6, 31, 47, 58; and optimism, 213–215, 222
nervios, ataques de, 267n5; symptoms, 111, 146, 158, 247, 250

New Deal, 36, 155, 258n2, 259n10, 260n15
New Progressive Party (statehood party), 9, 10, 22, 25, 46–47, 118, 175, 214, 257n1, 260n15, 271n13
Nine Curt, José, 37, 40–42, 260n16

oral health, 50, 261n10
Operation Bootstrap, 39, 260n14

Pérez, Gina, 94
Popular Democratic Party (PPD), 25, 39, 40, 46, 259n10, 259n13, 260n15, 260n17, 271n13
Puerto Rican Medical Association, 40, 259n9

quality: of care, 22, 159, 186, 234, 270n5; concerns in privatized programs, 50, 55–56, 111, 130–132, 172, 175, 193, 218–220, 223, 255n11, 264n13, 272n4; defined, 133–136; gaming quality measurement, 139–141, 262n6; as a market value, 19, 24, 52, 90, 127–130, 135–138, 141–142, 149–150; measurement of, 4–6, 12, 27, 82, 125–130, 136–141, 216, 267nn1–4, 272n4; from the perspective of beneficiaries, 52, 53, 93, 108, 122, 141–149; as a rationale for privatization 17, 46–47, 170, 190, 214–215, 229. *See also* CMS: and quality; NCQA; QIO
QIO (Quality Improvement Organization), 159, 161–162, 268n5

regional health system, Puerto Rico, 4, 9, 32, 37, 38–47, 48, 52, 54–55, 57–58, 96, 116, 218, 261n21, 275n12
remedios caseros (home remedies), 97, 102, 251, 265n5
research methods, 11–13, 22–24, 89, 92–96, 142–144, 195–196, 231–240
risk adjusted premiums, 223, 256n15, 273n7
Rose, Nikolas, 5, 18, 28, 128, 154, 209, 254n4, 263n11, 268n2
Rosselló, Pedro, 9, 47, 51, 118, 214, 271n13
Rylko-Bauer, Barbara, 21, 28, 238

Santiago-Valles, Kelvin, 35–36, 38, 258n1, 259n8
schizophrenia, 103, 105, 107, 108, 113, 147, 250, 266n16, 266n18
Scully, Thomas A., 66, 180–181, 188
Silvestrini, Blanca, 35
studying through, 12–13, 149, 235, 257n16

ABOUT THE AUTHOR

Jessica M. Mulligan is Assistant Professor of Health Policy and Management at Providence College where she teaches courses in public health, medical anthropology, and gender studies. Trained as an anthropologist, she conducted ethnographic research for this book by working as a compliance manager at an HMO in Puerto Rico. Her new project explores the implementation of "Obamacare" in Florida and Rhode Island.

Lightning Source UK Ltd.
Milton Keynes UK
UKOW02n1130240515

252170UK00007B/439/P